NEWBERY AND CALDECOTT MEDAL AND HONOR BOOKS IN OTHER MEDIA

PAULETTE BOCHNIG SHARKEY

Edited by Jim Roginski

NEAL-SCHUMAN PUBLISHERS, INC.
New York, London

Published by Neal-Schuman Publishers, Inc.
100 Varick Street
New York, NY 10013

Printed and bound in the United States of America

Library of Congress Cataloging-in-Publication Data

Sharkey, Paulette Bochnig.
    Newbery and Caldecott medal and honor books in other media /
Paulette Bochnig Sharkey.
        p.   cm.
    Includes bibliographical references and index
    ISBN 1-55570-119-1
    1. Newbery medal books—Study and teaching—Audio-visual aids—
Catalogs. 2. Caldecott medal books—Study and teaching—Audio-
visual aids—Catalogs. 3. Children's books, Illustrated—Study and
teaching—Audio-visual aids—Catalogs. 4. Children's literature—
Study and teaching—Audio-visual aids—Catalogs. 5. Nonbook
materials—Catalogs. I. Title.
Z1037.A2S4   1992
[PN1009.A1]
028.1'62—dc20   92-15391
                                                              CIP

To J.S.B.S.

CONTENTS

ACKNOWLEDGMENTS

I'd like to thank the staff of the Madison (WI) Public Library interlibrary loan department for their help in obtaining the reference materials necessary to put this book together. Once again, they capably found everything I asked for. Thanks also to Jim Roginski for offering me the project, and to my husband, Tom Sharkey, for his support at home after I agreed to it.

INTRODUCTION

The annual Newbery and Caldecott Medals are the most internationally prestigious awards in the field of children's literature. The Newbery honors the author of the year's most distinguished children's book; the Caldecott is awarded to the illustrator of the year's outstanding children's picture book. Because of the awards' wide recognition and the familiarity of the titles, the medal and honor books inspire many nonbook or media adaptations. The books are usually immediately converted to large print, braille, and talking book formats, which are available free of charge through governmental agencies, with the more commercial adaptations of films, filmstrips, and other formats following.

This volume provides a comprehensive list of commercial and public print and nonprint media adapted from the medal and honor books, beginning with the 1991 award year and going back to the inception of the Newbery (1922) and Caldecott (1938) awards. Media materials about the Newbery

and Caldecott authors and illustrators follow the title listings. This section also includes interviews and other background material on the authors of Caldecott-winning titles, even though they did not directly win Caldecott honors themselves. Thus, information about Donald Hall, Else Holmelund Minarik, James Thurber, Jane Yolen, and Charlotte Zolotow is included.

For librarians, teachers, and parents, this is the place to find the answer to the question, "What filmstrips, posters, videos, etc., have been made from this Newbery/Caldecott book, or about its author or illustrator?"

If you have any comments or information that would be useful for possible future revisions of this book or its companion volume, *Newbery and Caldecott Medalists and Honor Book Winners,* please write to the editor in care of Neal-Schuman Publishers, 100 Varick Street, New York, NY 10013.

HOW TO USE THIS BOOK

The text of this book is arranged by award year, with the Newbery or Caldecott Medal book listed first, followed by the Honor Books in alphabetical order. In those years in which Honor Books were not named, "no record" is indicated.

An alphabetical arrangement of media by type (filmstrip, video, etc.) is used within each book or author/illustrator listing. Within a given media type, the most recent materials are listed first, followed by earlier ones, then those for which no dates were determined. A separate "About the Book" section lists analytical treatments of the titles.

The information presented in this volume was compiled from current publisher and distributor catalogs and a variety of current and retrospective library reference materials. A comprehensive, rather than evaluative, approach was used; selective reviews, major awards, and recommendations are also noted where appropriate.

KEY TO ENTRY FORMAT

Entries are presented in this form:

1. Newbery or Caldecott book citation and notation of Newbery/Caldecott Medal/Honor Book
2. media format
3. "title of program if different from book title"
4. [description as available information allowed]
5. producer/distributor
6. date
7. selected reviews, major awards and recommendations

8. "none located," if no media materials were found.

A sample title entry looks like:

Hatchet by Gary Paulsen. Bradbury, 1987. Newbery Honor Book.

> *Audio:* [cassette] McGraw-Hill, 1989. BKL 9/15/90, SLJ 12/90
> *Filmstrip/sound:* [2 filmstrips/2 cassettes, 280 fr/53 min] McGraw-Hill, 1989. BKL 9/15/90, BKL/E, SLJ 12/90
> *Large print:* Cornerstone, 198?.
> *Talking book:* [RC30535] NLSBPH.
> *Video:* [filmstrip-on-video, 49 min] McGraw-Hill, 1989. BKL 9/15/90, SLJ 12/90

> *About the Book:*

> *Filmstrip/sound:* "New Endings" includes discussion of *Hatchet* [Literature to enjoy and write about series 1, filmstrip/cassette, about 20 min] Pied Piper, 1989. SLJ 5/90
> *Video:* "New Endings" includes discussion of *Hatchet* [Literature to enjoy and write about series 1, about 20 min] Pied Piper, 1989. SLJ 5/90

A sample author/illustrator entry looks like:

Van Allsburg, Chris

> *Audio:* "Caldecott Medal Acceptance Speech 1986" [cassette] Weston Woods, 1986. op

Audio: "Caldecott Medal Acceptance Speech 1982" [cassette] Weston Woods, 1982. op

Filmstrip/sound: "Book Review/Fantasy" discusses work of Chris Van Allsburg [Literature to enjoy and write about series 2, filmstrip/cassette, about 20 min] Pied Piper, 1989. SLJ 5/90

Video: "Book Review/Fantasy" discusses work of Chris Van Allsburg [Literature to enjoy and write about series 2, about 20 min] Pied Piper, 1989. SLJ 5/90

1. Newbery or Caldecott book citation

The bibliographic reference to the first trade book edition of the award-winning title is given. (In the "Media about Newbery/Caldecott Authors and Illustrators" section, this element is replaced with the name of the author or illustrator.)

2. Media format

The following formats are included in this volume:

Audio: CD, cassette (1-7/8 ips tape speed unless otherwise indicated), or record.

Bookmark

Braille: Books transferred to braille format are word-for-word versions of the original text, available through the National Library for the Blind and Physically Handicapped (NLSBPH).

Braille/print: Same as above for braille, with a copy of the print book included.

Calendar

Doll

Film: 16 mm, color, unless otherwise indicated.

Filmstrip: No sound, may be accompanied by a script (also called a picture-cued text booklet).

Filmstrip/sound: Includes separate cassette(s) or record(s).

Kit: A combination of teaching materials.

Large print

Postcards

Poster

Read-along: A book/audio combination.

Read-along/large print: A large print book/audio combination.

Software

Talking book: An unabridged sound recording of a book on cassette, disc, or sound tape reels for the visually impaired.

Talking book/print: Same as above, with copy of print book included.

Television

Video

All media are in color unless otherwise noted.

3. Title of program if different from book title

A media adaptation from a book often appears with a title different from that of the original work, or the media version of a short book may be issued within a larger program (e.g., "Five Stories for the Very Young" includes Drummer Hoff). In this volume, media titles that differ from the original Newbery or Caldecott title are indicated in quotation marks.

4. Description

Descriptions were taken from publisher/distributor catalogs and reference sources listed in Appendix C and are as complete as available information allowed.

The lack of bibliographic detail, along with discrepancies in the information provided by reference books and producer/distributor catalogs, proved the most difficult and frustrating aspects of compiling this volume. Producer/distributor catalogs often offer only scanty descriptions of materials, rarely including production dates or other important information. Physical inspection of the media, though not a practical solution in all cases, was sometimes used to obtain descriptive details not found elsewhere.

Where appropriate, descriptions of media listed in this volume include:

—series, if any.
—descriptors such as "dramatized" or "unabridged" for audio items.
—specifics of format (e.g., "2 cassettes" or "filmstrip/cassette").
—running time in minutes.
—availability of media in languages other than English (e.g., "also Spanish").

Films and videos may be described as either live-action, animated, iconographic (movement of the camera over still illustrations to create a feeling of animation), or, in the case of videos, filmstrip-on-video (filmstrip transferred to videotape). 8 mm films and records are mentioned if the material was originally issued in those formats, though these are now scarce. Check with the producer/distributor for current availability. (See Appendix D.)

For more information, see "Additional Notes about NLSBPH Items" and "Additional Notes about Videos" below.

5. Producer/Distributor

Wherever possible, media are listed with the name of the producer who also distributes the material, rather than with the name of a company acting only as distributor for someone else's product. This distinction was not always clear from sources used to compile these entries. In a few uncertain cases, similar entries that appear here may actually refer to the same item with different distributors; all are included for the sake of thoroughness.

A complete producer/distributor directory of addresses and phone numbers can be found in Appendix D.

6. Date

Dates refer to the year of production in most cases. Again, sources often offered conflicting information. If the release date was found, and varied significantly from the production date, that is also listed. When no date could be determined, "nd" appears in the date space; partial dates appear with a question mark (e.g., "198?"). No dates are given in this volume for braille or talking books.

7. Reviews, Major Awards, and Recommendations

Reviews of media are noted in some cases, as well as major awards and recommendations. All are abbreviated as follows.

8. Abbreviations

Media Abbreviations

b&w: black-and-white
BR: press braille
BRA: handcopied braille
cc: closed-captioned version available
FD: flexible disc (for the visually impaired)
fr: frames (for filmstrips)
in: inches (for poster dimensions)
ips: inches per second (tape speed)
min: minutes
nd: no production or release date located
NLSBPH: National Library Service for the Blind and Physically Handicapped
op: out of print; current distributor could not be identified
RC: recorded cassette (for the visually impaired)
RD: recorded disc (for the visually impaired)
RM: recorded master of a talking book
TB: talking book

Review, Major Awards and Recommendations Abbreviations

AFVF: American Film & Video Association Festival Award; Blue Ribbon and Red Ribbon awarded annually to educational 16mm films and videos in various categories, including children's entertainment
ALSC: Appears on the annual list of *Notable Children's Films and Videos, Filmstrips, and Recordings* of the Association for Library Service to Children, American Library Association; materials of commendable quality for young people through age 14, selected by librarians
BKL: *Booklist* review/recommendation; lists nonprint materials worthy of consideration for purchase by libraries
BKL/E: *Booklist* Editor's Choice; year's best films and videos selected by the editors of *Booklist*
BVC: *Best Videos for Children and Young Adults* recommendation; selective list for basic library video collections
CINE: Council of International Nontheatrical Events Golden Eagle Award; highest award presented each year for excellence in film and video by CINE, the official U.S. organization for accrediting American entries in foreign film festivals
CMCE: *Core Media Collection for Elementary Schools* recommendation; qualitative selection guide for school librarians

CMCS: Core Media Collection for Secondary Schools recommendation; qualitative selection guide for school librarians

ESLC: Elementary School Library Collection recommmendation; primary resource for collection development, selection, and maintenance of library collections for children from preschool through grade 6

JOYS: Journal of Youth Services in Libraries review

L: Learning magazine Best of the Year award; materials judged to be of special interest to classroom teachers of children in kindergarten through grade 8

MMA: A Multimedia Approach to Children's Literature recommendation; guide to quality book-related, nonprint materials for children in preschool through grade 6

PC: Parents' Choice award; the best in children's media, selected annually by parents, teachers, librarians, and children

PCGV: Parents' Choice Guide to Videocassettes for Children recommendation; consumer guide to quality children's video

SLJ: School Library Journal review

VM: Video Movies: A Core Collection for Libraries recommendation; selective guide for librarians

VRG: Video Rating Guide for Libraries review

YASD: appears on annual list of *Selected Films for Young Adults,* Young Adult Services Division, American Library Association; films recommended by librarians for use in programs of interest to young adults

ADDITIONAL NOTES ABOUT NLSBPH ITEMS

For National Library for the Blind and Physically Handicapped (NLSBPH) items, complete identification numbers are shown, except for "works in process" to which numbers had not been assigned in time for this book's publication. According to NLSBPH, press braille volumes (those with "BR" identification numbers) are more readily available than handcopied braille ("BRA" identification numbers). TB ("talking book") numbers indicate older materials that NLSBPH warns may no longer be available or are difficult to obtain. A TB number has been included in this volume only for Newbery or Caldecott titles never issued in an updated NLSBPH format.

ADDITIONAL NOTES ABOUT VIDEOS

Specific video formats (Beta, VHS, 3/4-inch U-Matic) were not included because reliable, consistent information could not be located. In many cases, a producer/distributor can supply a video according to your needs, usually with a higher price tag for 3/4" U-Matic. Check individual producer/distributor catalogs (see Appendix D for addresses and phone numbers) for details. Similarly, obtain information about public performance rights (sometimes requiring additional payment, other times included in the price) directly from the producer/distributor.

MEDIA RELATED TO NEWBERY AND CALDECOTT BOOKS IN GENERAL

Calendar	"Caldecott Calendar" ALA, annual.
Filmstrip/sound	"Reading the Best: Introducing the Newbery Winners" [4 filmstrips/4 cassettes, about 60 min] Cheshire, 1991. SLJ 12/91
Filmstrip/sound	"Randolph Caldecott: The Man Behind the Medal" [filmstrip/cassette, 57 fr/15 min] Weston Woods, 1983. ESLC
Postcards	"Caldecott Banner Postcards" ALA Graphics, 198?.
Video	"Reading the Best: Introducing the Newbery Winners" [about 60 min] Cheshire, 1991. SLJ 12/91
Video	"Choosing the Best in Children's Video: A Guide for Parents and Everyone Who Cares about Kids" [36 min] ALA, 1990. JOYS, Winter 1991
Video	"Caldecott at Fifty: Highlights of the 1987 ALSC Charlemae Rollins Program" [45 min] ALA, 1987.
Video	"Randolph Caldecott: The Man Behind the Medal" [iconographic] Weston Woods, 198?.
Video	"Book Week" [Quest for the Best series, b&w, 20 min] GPN, nd. op

NEWBERY MEDIA: MEDAL AND HONOR BOOKS
1992-1922

1992 NEWBERY AWARDS

Shiloh by Phyllis Reynolds Naylor. Atheneum, 1991. Newbery Medal Book.

  none located

  See also Phyllis Reynolds Naylor, "Media about Newbery/Caldecott Authors and illustrators."

Nothing But the Truth by Avi. Orchard, 1991. Newbery Honor Book.

  none located

The Wright Brothers: How They Invented the Airplane by Russell Freedman. Holiday, 1991. Newbery Honor Book.

  none located

  See also Russell Freedman, "Media about Newbery/Caldecott Authors and Illustrators."

1991 NEWBERY AWARDS

Maniac Magee by Jerry Spinelli. Little, 1990. Newbery Medal Book.

  none located

  See also Jerry Spinelli, "Media about Newbery/Caldecott Authors and Illustrators."

The True Confessions of Charlotte Doyle by Avi. Orchard, 1990. Newbery Honor Book.

  none located

1990 NEWBERY AWARDS

Number the Stars by Lois Lowry. Houghton, 1989. Newbery Medal Book.

  Braille: [BR8258] NLSBPH.

  See also Lois Lowry, "Media about Newbery/Caldecott Authors and Illustrators."

Afternoon of the Elves by Janet Taylor Lisle. Orchard, 1989. Newbery Honor Book.

  Talking book: [RC31277] NLSBPH.

Shabanu, Daughter of the Wind by Suzanne Fisher Staples. Knopf, 1989. Newbery Honor Book.

  Braille: [BR] NLSBPH.

The Winter Room by Gary Paulsen. Orchard, 1989. Newbery Honor Book.

  Braille: [BR] NLSBPH.

See also Gary Paulsen, "Media about Newbery/Caldecott Authors and Illustrators."

1989 NEWBERY AWARDS

Joyful Noise: Poems for Two Voices by Paul Fleischman. Illustrated by Eric Beddows. Harper, 1988. Newbery Medal Book.

> *Audio:* "Joyful Noise and I Am Phoenix: Poems for Two Voices" [cassette, 60 min] Caedmon, 1990.
> *Braille:* [BR7812] NLSBPH.
> *Filmstrip/sound:* [2 filmstrips/2 cassettes] American School, 1990.
> *Talking book:* [RC28922] NLSBPH.
> *Video:* [live-action, 18 min] American School, 1990. ALSC.

In the Beginning: Creation Stories from Around the World by Virginia Hamilton. Illustrated by Barry Moser. Harcourt, 1988. Newbery Honor Book.

> *Braille:* [BR7829] NLSBPH.

> *See also* Virginia Hamilton, "Media about Newbery/Caldecott Authors and Illustrators."

Scorpions by Walter Dean Myers. Harper, 1988. Newbery Honor Book.

> *Audio:* [cassette] American School, 1990. BKL 9/1/90
> *Filmstrip/sound:* [2 filmstrips/2 cassettes] American School, 1990. BKL 9/1/90.
> *Talking book:* [RC28940] NLSBPH.
> *Video:* [live-action, 37 min] American School, 1990. BKL 9/1/90, BKL/E

> *See also* Walter Dean Myers, "Media about Newbery/Caldecott Authors and Illustrators."

1988 NEWBERY AWARDS

Lincoln: A Photobiography by Russell Freedman. Clarion, 1987. Newbery Medal Book.

> *Braille:* [BR7349] NLSBPH.
> *Filmstrip/sound:* [4 filmstrips/4 cassettes, 66 min] American School, 1990.
> *Talking book:* [RC27881] NLSBPH.
> *Video:* [iconographic, 66 min] Random, 1990.

See also Russell Freedman, "Media about Newbery/Caldecott Authors and Illustrators."

After the Rain by Norma Fox Mazer. Morrow, 1987. Newbery Honor Book.

> *Audio:* [cassette, 12 min] American School, 1990. SLJ 2/91
> *Filmstrip/sound:* [2 filmstrips/2 cassettes, 263 fr/54 min] American School, 1990. BKL 11/15/90, BKL/E, SLJ 2/91
> *Large print:* G. K. Hall, 1989.
> *Talking book:* [RC28762] NLSBPH.
> *Video:* [filmstrip-on-video, 54 min] American School, 1990. BKL 11/15/90, SLJ 2/91

> *See also* Norma Fox Mazer, "Media about Newbery/Caldecott Authors and Illustrators."

Hatchet by Gary Paulsen. Bradbury, 1987. Newbery Honor Book.

> *Audio:* [cassette] McGraw-Hill, 1989. BKL 9/15/90, SLJ 12/90
> *Filmstrip/sound:* [2 filmstrips/2 cassettes, 280 fr/53 min] McGraw-Hill, 1989. BKL 9/15/90, BKL/E, SLJ 12/90
> *Large print:* Cornerstone, 198?.
> *Talking book:* [RC30535] NLSBPH.
> *Video:* [filmstrip-on-video, 49 min] McGraw-Hill, 1989. BKL 9/15/90, SLJ 12/90

> *About the Book:*

> *Filmstrip/sound:* "New Endings" includes discussion of *Hatchet* [Literature to enjoy and write about series 1, filmstrip/cassette, about 20 min] Pied Piper, 1989. SLJ 5/90
> *Video:* "New Endings" includes discussion of *Hatchet* [Literature to enjoy and write about series 1, about 20 min] Pied Piper, 1989. SLJ 5/90

> *See also* Gary Paulsen, "Media about Newbery/Caldecott Authors and Illustrators."

1987 NEWBERY AWARDS

The Whipping Boy by Sid Fleischman. Illustrated by Peter Sis. Greenwillow, 1986. Newbery Medal Book.

> *Audio:* [2 cassettes, 90 min] G. K. Hall, 1989.

Filmstrip/sound: [First choice: Authors and books series, 2 filmstrips/2 cassettes, 38 min] Pied Piper, 1988.
Large print: Cornerstone, 1989.
Poster: [17x22 in] Perfection Form, 198?.
Talking book: [RC25778] NLSBPH.
Video: [First choice: Authors and books series, 38 min] Pied Piper, 1988.
Video: [More books from cover to cover series, 15 min] PBS, 1987. ESLC

See also Sid Fleischman, "Media about Newbery/Caldecott Authors and Illustrators."

A Fine White Dust by Cynthia Rylant. Bradbury, 1986. Newbery Honor Book.

Audio: [dramatized, cassette] Miller-Brody, 198?.
Braille: [BR6809] NLSBPH. ESLC
Filmstrip/sound: [2 filmstrips/2 cassettes, 224 fr/42 min] Miller-Brody, 1988. SLJ 12/89
Video: [filmstrip-on-video, 34 min] McGraw-Hill, 1989. SLJ 12/89

See also Cynthia Rylant, "Media about Newbery/Caldecott Authors and Illustrators."

On My Honor by Marion Dane Bauer. Clarion, 1986. Newbery Honor Book.

Audio: [dramatized, cassette, 29 min] Miller-Brody, 1988.
Braille: [BR6959] NLSBPH.
Filmstrip/sound: [2 filmstrips/2 cassettes, 222 fr/29 min] Miller-Brody, 1988. SLJ 2/90
Large print: G. K. Hall, 1989.
Talking book: [RC26123] NLSBPH.
Video: [filmstrip-on-video, 28 min] McGraw-Hill, 1989. SLJ 2/90

About the Book:

Filmstrip/sound: "Friendly Letter/Realistic Fiction" includes discussion of *On My Honor* [Literature to enjoy and write about series 2, filmstrip/cassette, about 20 min] Pied Piper, 1989. SLJ 5/90
Video: "Friendly Letter/Realistic Fiction" includes discussion of *On My Honor* [Literature to enjoy and write about series 2, about 20 min] Pied Piper, 1989. SLJ 5/90

Volcano: The Eruption and Healing of Mount St. Helens by Patricia Lauber. Bradbury, 1986. Newbery Honor Book.

Braille: [BR7293] NLSBPH.
Filmstrip/sound: [filmstrip/cassette, 151 fr/23 min] Random, 1989. ALSC
Video: [filmstrip-on-video, 23 min] Random, 1989.

1986 NEWBERY AWARDS

Sarah, Plain and Tall by Patricia MacLachlan. Harper, 1985. Newbery Medal Book.

Audio: [unabridged, record or cassette, 61 min] Caedmon, 1986. ESLC, PC
Audio: [dramatized, cassette, 30 min] Miller-Brody, 1986.
Filmstrip/sound: [2 filmstrips/2 cassettes, 221 fr/30 min] Miller-Brody, 1986. SLJ 4/88
Large print: Cornerstone, 1988.
Poster: [17x22 in] Perfection Form, 198?.
Talking book: [RC23524] NLSBPH. ESLC
Television: [CBS Hallmark Hall of Fame, 120 min] Sarah Productions, 1990.
Video: [filmstrip-on-video, 30 min] Random, 1988.

About the Book:

Filmstrip/sound: "Readers Theatre/Historical Fiction" includes discussion of *Sarah, Plain and Tall* [Literature to enjoy and write about, filmstrip/cassette, about 20 min] Pied Piper, 1989. SLJ 5/90
Software: "Sarah, Plain and Tall: A Novel Study" [Write On! series] Humanities Software, 198?.
Video: "Readers Theatre/Historical Fiction" includes discussion of *Sarah, Plain and Tall* [Literature to enjoy and write about, about 20 min] Pied Piper, 1989. SLJ 5/90

See also Patricia MacLachlan, "Media about Newbery/Caldecott Authors and illustrators."

Commodore Perry in the Land of the Shogun by Rhoda Blumberg. Lothrop, 1985. Newbery Honor Book.

Audio: [cassette] Miller-Brody, 198?.
Braille: [BR6429] NLSBPH. ESLC

Filmstrip/sound: [filmstrip/cassette, 150 fr/28 min] Random, 1986. ESLC
Talking book: [RC23821] NLSBPH. ESLC

Dogsong by Gary Paulsen. Bradbury, 1985. Newbery Honor Book.

Audio: [cassette] Miller-Brody, 198?.
Braille: [BR6535] NLSBPH.
Filmstrip/sound: [2 filmstrips/2 cassettes, 40 min] Random, 1986. SLJ 5/88
Talking book: [RC24450] NLSBPH.
Video: [filmstrip-on-video, 40 min] Random, 1988. SLJ 5/88

See also Gary Paulsen, "Media about Newbery/Caldecott Authors and Illustrators."

1985 NEWBERY AWARDS

The Hero and the Crown by Robin McKinley. Greenwillow, 1984. Newbery Medal Book.

Audio: [2 cassettes] Random, 1986. ESLC
Large print: Cornerstone, 198?.
Poster: [17x22 in] Perfection Form, 198?.
Talking book: [RC25926] NLSBPH. ESLC

See also Robin McKinley, "Media about Newbery/Caldecott Authors and Illustrators."

Like Jake and Me by Mavis Jukes. Illustrated by Lloyd Bloom. Knopf, 1984. Newbery Honor Book.

Film: [live-action, 14 min] Disney, 1989. BKL 11/15/89, SLJ 3/90
Filmstrip/sound: [filmstrip/cassette, 16 min] McGraw-Hill, 1989. BKL 9/15/90, SLJ 1/91
Read-along: [cassette/book, 15 min] Random, 1986. ESLC
Talking book: [RC23104] NLSBPH. ESLC
Video: [live-action, cc, 14 min] Disney, 1989. BKL 11/15/89, SLJ 3/90
Video: [filmstrip-on-cassette, 16 min] McGraw-Hill, 1989. BKL 9/15/90, SLJ 1/91

See also Mavis Jukes, "Media about Newbery/Caldecott Authors and Illustrators."

The Moves Make the Man by Bruce Brooks. Harper, 1984. Newbery Honor Book.

Audio: [dramatized, cassette] Miller-Brody, 1988.
Filmstrip/sound: [2 filmstrips/2 cassettes] Miller-Brody, 1988.
Large print: Cornerstone, 1988.
Talking book: [RC23531] NLSBPH.

One-Eyed Cat by Paula Fox. Bradbury, 1984. Newbery Honor Book.

Audio: [cassette] Miller-Brody, 1988.
Filmstrip/sound: [2 filmstrips/2 cassettes] Miller-Brody, 1988.
Large print: Cornerstone, 198?.
Poster: [17x22 in] Perfection Form, 198?.
Talking book: [RC22756] NLSBPH.

See also Paula Fox, "Media about Newbery/Caldecott Authors and Illustrators."

1984 NEWBERY AWARDS

Dear Mr. Henshaw by Beverly Cleary. Illustrated by Paul O. Zelinsky. Morrow, 1983. Newbery Medal Book.

Audio: [dramatized, cassette, 34 min] Random, 1984. ALSC
Braille: [BR5629] NLSBPH. ESLC
Filmstrip/sound: [2 filmstrips/2 cassettes, 180 fr/40 min] Random, 1984. ALSC, ESLC
Filmstrip/sound: "Challenges" includes excerpt from *Dear Mr. Henshaw* [Reading for the fun of it: Getting hooked on books series, 2 filmstrips/2 cassettes, 30 min] Guidance Assoc, 198?.
Large print: Cornerstone, 1987. ESLC
Poster: [17x22 in] Perfection Form, 198?.
Talking book: [RC21309] NLSBPH. ESLC
Video: [filmstrip-on-video, 31 min] Random, 1989.
Video: "Challenges" includes excerpt from *Dear Mr. Henshaw* [Reading for the fun of it: Getting hooked on books series, filmstrip-on-video, 30 min] Guidance Assoc, 198?.

About the Book:

Filmstrip/sound: "Diary-Journal/Realistic Fiction" includes discussion of *Dear Mr. Henshaw* [Literature to enjoy and write about series 1, filmstrip/cassette, about 20 min] Pied Piper, 1989. SLJ 5/90
Video: "Diary-Journal/Realistic Fiction" includes discussion of *Dear Mr. Henshaw* [Literature to enjoy and write about series 1, about 20 min] Pied Piper, 1989. SLJ 5/90

See also Beverly Cleary, "Media about Newbery/Caldecott Authors and Illustrators."

The Sign of the Beaver by Elizabeth George Speare. Houghton, 1983. Newbery Honor Book.

Audio: [cassette] Miller-Brody, 1985. ESLC
Braille: [BR5697] NLSBPH. ESLC
Filmstrip/sound: [2 filmstrips/2 cassettes] Miller-Brody, 1985. ESLC
Large print: Cornerstone, 1988.
Poster: [17x22] Perfection Form, 198?.
Talking book: [RC21639] NLSBPH. ESLC
Video: [filmstrip-on-video, 36 min] Random, 1987.

About the Book:

Filmstrip/sound: "New Endings" includes discussion of *The Sign of the Beaver* [Literature to enjoy and write about series 1, filmstrip/cassette, about 20 min] Pied Piper, 1989. SLJ 5/90
Video: "New Endings" includes discussion of *The Sign of the Beaver* [Literature to enjoy and write about series 1, about 20 min] Pied Piper, 1989. SLJ 5/90

See also Elizabeth George Speare, "Media about Newbery/Caldecott Authors and illustrators."

Sugaring Time by Kathryn Lasky. Photographs by Christopher G. Knight. Macmillan, 1983. Newbery Honor Book.

Audio: [cassette, 23 min] Random, 1985. ALSC, ESLC, PC
Filmstrip/sound: [filmstrip/cassette, 137 fr/20 min] Random, 1984. ALSC, BKL 12/15/89, ESLC

Video: [filmstrip-on-video, 22 min] Random, 1989. ESLC

The Wish Giver: Three Tales of Coven Tree by Bill Brittain. Illustrated by Andrew Glass. Harper, 1983. Newbery Honor Book.

Audio: [cassette, 26 min] Random, 1984.
Filmstrip/sound: [2 filmstrips/2 cassettes, 38 min] Miller-Brody, 1984. ESLC
Talking book: [RC21758] NLSBPH. ESLC
Video: [More books from cover to cover series, 15 min] PBS, 1987. ESLC
Video: [filmstrip-on-video, 38 min] Random, 1987.

A Solitary Blue by Cynthia Voigt. Atheneum, 1983. Newbery Honor Book.

Braille: [BR5755] NLSBPH. ESLC
Talking book: [RC22123] NLSBPH. ESLC

See also Cynthia Voigt, "Media about Newbery/Caldecott Authors and Illustrators."

1983 NEWBERY AWARDS

Dicey's Song by Cynthia Voigt. Atheneum, 1982. Newbery Medal Book.

Braille: [BR5473] NLSBPH. ESLC
Filmstrip/sound: "Challenges" includes excerpt from *Dicey's Song* [Reading for the fun of it: Getting hooked on books series, 2 filmstrips/2 cassettes, 30 min] Guidance Assoc, 198?.
Large print: Cornerstone, 1990.
Poster: [17x22 in] Perfection Form, 198?.
Talking book: [RC21617] NLSBPH. ESLC
Video: "Challenges" includes excerpt from *Dicey's Song* [Reading for the fun of it: Getting hooked on books series, filmstrip-on-video, 30 min] Guidance Assoc, 198?.

See also Cynthia Voigt, "Media about Newbery/Caldecott Authors and Illustrators."

The Blue Sword by Robin McKinley. Greenwillow, 1983. Newbery Honor Book.

Audio: [2 cassettes, 93 min] Miller-Brody, 198?.
Talking book: [RC23523] NLSBPH.

See also Robin McKinley, "Media about New-bery/Caldecott Authors and Illustrators."

Doctor De Soto by William Steig. Farrar, 1982. New-bery Honor Book.

> *Audio:* "Dominic" includes *Doctor De Soto* [record or cassette, 42 min] Caedmon, 1983. ALSC
> *Audio:* [cassette, 9 min] Weston Woods, 1983. ALSC, ESLC
> *Audio:* "Doctor De Soto and Other Stories" [cassette] Caedmon, 198?.
> *Braille/print:* [BR5462] NLSBPH. ESLC
> *Film:* [animated, 10 min] Weston Woods, 1984. BKL 9/1/84
> *Filmstrip/sound:* [filmstrip/cassette, 47 fr/9 min] Weston Woods, 1983. ALSC, BKL 2/1/84, ESLC
> *Read-along:* [Blue ribbon series, cassette/book] Scholastic, 1984.
> *Read-along:* [cassette/book] Weston Woods, 198?.
> *Talking book:* [RD19505] NLSBPH. ESLC
> *Video:* "Doctor De Soto and Other Stories" [animated, 33 min] CC Studios, 1984. CINE
> *Video:* [animated, 10 min] Weston Woods, 1984. BVC, ESLC

Graven Images: 3 Stories by Paul Fleischman. Illus-trated by Andrew Glass. Harper, 1982. Newbery Honor Book.

> *Audio:* [cassette, 56 min] Miller-Brody, 198?.
> *Filmstrip/sound:* [filmstrip/cassette] Miller-Brody, 198?.
> *Talking book:* [RC22181] NLSBPH.

Homesick, My Own Story by Jean Fritz. Illustrated by Margot Tomes. Putnam, 1982. Newbery Honor Book.

> *Audio:* [Readings to remember series, 3 cas-settes, 260 min] Weston Woods, 1983. ALSC
> *Filmstrip/sound:* [2 filmstrips/2 cassettes] Mill-er-Brody, 1984. ESLC
> *Large print:* Cornerstone, 1987.
> *Read-along:* [3 cassettes/book] Weston Woods, 198?.
> *Talking book:* [RC19266] NLSBPH. ESLC

See also Jean Fritz, "Media about Newbery/ Caldecott Authors and Illustrators."

Sweet Whispers, Brother Rush by Virginia Hamilton. Philomel, 1982. Newbery Honor Book.

> *Audio:* [cassette] Miller-Brody, 198?.
> *Filmstrip/sound:* [2 filmstrips/2 cassettes, 285 fr/39 min] Miller-Brody, 1983. ALSC, BKL/ E, L
> *Talking book:* [RC19388] NLSBPH
> *Video:* [filmstrip-on-video, 40 min] Random, 1987.

See also Virginia Hamilton, "Media about New-bery/Caldecott Authors and Illustrators."

1982 NEWBERY AWARDS

A Visit to William Blake's Inn: Poems for Innocent and Experienced Travelers by Nancy Willard. Illustrated by Alice and Martin Provensen. Harcourt, 1981. Newbery Medal Book.

> *Braille/print:* [BR5501] NLSBPH. ESLC
> *Filmstrip/sound:* [filmstrip/cassette, 151 fr/17 min] Miller-Brody, 1982. ALSC, ESLC, L, MMA
> *Poster:* [17x22 in] Perfection Form, 198?.
> *Read-along:* [cassette/book, 22 min] Random, 1982. ESLC.
> *Talking book:* [RC19591] NLSBPH. ESLC
> *Video:* [filmstrip-on-video, 18 min] Random House, 1987.

See also Nancy Willard, "Media about New-bery/Caldecott Authors and Illustrators."

Ramona Quimby, Age 8 by Beverly Cleary. Illustrat-ed by Alan Tiegreen. Morrow, 1981. Newbery Honor Book

> *Audio:* [unabridged, 2 cassettes, 180 min] Lis-tening Library, 1988.
> *Audio:* [dramatized, cassette, 22 min] Miller-Brody, 1981. ALSC, ESLC, MMA
> *Bookmark:* "Libraries are Forever" ALA, 1984.
> *Braille:* [BR5155] NLSBPH. ESLC
> *Film:* "Ramona" [includes episodes from *Ra-mona Quimby, Age 8*, 10 programs, 27 min each] Churchill, 1987. ALSC, BKL 12/15/ 89, SLJ 4/89

Filmstrip/sound: [filmstrip/cassette, 142 fr/22 min] Miller-Brody, 1981. MMA
Large-print: Cornerstone Books, 1987. ESLC
Poster: "Libraries are Forever" [22x34 in] ALA, 1984.
Talking book: [RC19685] NLSBPH.
Video: "Ramona" includes episodes from *Ramona Quimby, Age 8* [live-action, 10 programs, 27 min each] Churchill, 1987. ALSC, BKL 12/15/89, BVC, SLJ 4/89
Video: "Ramona" includes episodes from *Ramona Quimby, Age 8* [live-action, 3 programs, 60 min each] Pied Piper, 1987.

See also Beverly Cleary, "Media about Newbery/Caldecott Authors and Illustrators."

Upon the Head of the Goat: A Childhood in Hungary 1939-1944 by Aranka Siegal. Farrar, 1981. Newbery Honor Book.

Audio: [cassette, 51 min] Miller-Brody, 198?.
Braille: [BR6524] NLSBPH.
Filmstrip/sound: [2 filmstrips/2 cassettes] Miller-Brody, 198?.

1981 NEWBERY AWARDS

Jacob Have I Loved by Katherine Paterson. Crowell, 1980. Newbery Medal Book

Audio: [dramatized, cassette] Miller-Brody, 198?.
Braille: [BR6264] NLSBPH.
Filmstrip/sound: [2 filmstrips/2 cassettes, 55 min] Miller-Brody, 198?.
Large print: Cornerstone, 1990.
Poster: [17x22 in] Perfection Form, 198?.
Talking book: [RC17690] NLSBPH.
Video: [WonderWorks collection, 55 min] Public Media, 1989. ALSC, BKL 10/1/90, BKL/E, PC, SLJ 6/91
Video: [filmstrip-on-video, 55 min] Random, 1988.

See also Katherine Paterson, "Media about Newbery/Caldecott Authors and Illustrators."

The Fledgling by Jane Langton. Illustrated by Erik Blegvad. Harper, 1980. Newbery Honor Book.

Audio: [cassette, 47 min] Miller-Brody, 1982.

Braille: [BR6681] NLSBPH. ESLC
Filmstrip/sound: [2 filmstrips/2 cassettes, 38 min] Miller-Brody, 198?.
Video: [filmstrip-on-video, 38 min] Random, 1988. ESLC

A Ring of Endless Light by Madeleine L'Engle. Farrar, 1980. Newbery Honor Book.

Audio: [dramatized, cassette] Miller-Brody, 1984.
Braille: [BR4975] NLSBPH. ESLC
Filmstrip/sound: [2 filmstrips/2 cassettes] Miller-Brody, 1984. ESLC, L
Talking book: [RC18375] NLSBPH. ESLC

See also Madeleine L'Engle, "Media about Newbery/Caldecott Authors and Illustrators."

1980 NEWBERY AWARDS

A Gathering of Days by Joan W. Blos. Scribner, 1979. Newbery Medal Book.

Audio: [cassette, 46 min] Miller-Brody, 1980. ESLC
Braille: [BR4546] NLSBPH.
Filmstrip/sound: [2 filmstrips/2 cassettes] Miller-Brody, 1982.
Poster: [17x22 in] Perfection Form, 198?.
Talking book: [RC16844] NLSBPH.

See also Joan W. Blos, "Media about Newbery/Caldecott Authors and Illustrators."

The Road from Home: The Story of an Armenian Girl by David Kherdian. Greenwillow, 1979. Newbery Honor Book.

Audio: [cassette, 44 min] Random House, 1980. ESLC
Talking book: [RC16607] NLSBPH.

1979 NEWBERY AWARDS

The Westing Game by Ellen Raskin. Dutton, 1978. Newbery Medal Book.

Braille: [BR6285] NLSBPH. ESLC
Filmstrip/sound: [First choice: Authors and books series, 2 filmstrips/cassette, 31 min] Pied Piper, 1986. ESLC

Large print: Cornerstone, 1988.
Poster: [17x22 in] Perfection Form, nd.
Talking book: [RC12787] NLSBPH. ESLC
Video: [First choice: Authors and books series, 31 min] Pied Piper, 198?.

About the Book:

Filmstrip/sound: "Mapping/Mysteries" includes discussion of *The Westing Game* [Literature to enjoy and write about series 1, filmstrip/cassette, about 20 min] Pied Piper, 1989. SLJ 5/90
Video: "Mapping/Mysteries" includes discussion of *The Westing Game* [Literature to enjoy and write about series 1, about 20 min] Pied Piper, 1989. SLJ 5/90

See also Ellen Raskin, "Media about Newbery/Caldecott Authors and Illustrators."

The Great Gilly Hopkins by Katherine Paterson. Crowell, 1978. Newbery Honor Book.

Audio: [dramatized, record or cassette, 46 min] Miller-Brody, 1979. MMA
Filmstrip/sound: [2 filmstrips/2 cassettes, 238 fr/32 min] Miller-Brody, 1980. L, MMA
Large print: Cornerstone, 1987. ESLC
Talking book: [RC12172] NLSBPH. ESLC
Video: [filmstrip-on-video, 32 min] Random, 1985.

See also Katherine Paterson, "Media about Newbery/Caldecott Authors and Illustrators."

1978 NEWBERY AWARD BOOKS

Bridge to Terabithia by Katherine Paterson. Illustrated by Donna Diamond. Crowell, 1977. Newbery Medal Book.

Audio: [dramatized, record or cassette, 51 min] Miller-Brody, 1979. ESLC, MMA
Filmstrip/sound: [2 filmstrips/2 cassettes, 263 fr/34 min] Miller-Brody, 1981. MMA
Filmstrip/sound: "Friendship" includes excerpt from *Bridge to Terabithia* [Reading for the fun of it: Getting hooked on books series, 2 filmstrips/2 cassettes, 11 min] Guidance Assoc, 197?.
Large print: [also Spanish] Cornerstone, 1987. ESLC

Poster: [17x22 in] Perfection Form, nd.
Talking book: [RC12343] NLSBPH. ESLC
Video: [WonderWorks collection, cc, 58 min] Public Media, 1985, released 1991. BKL 6/15/91
Video: [filmstrip-on-video, 33 min] Random, 198?.
Video: "Friendship" includes excerpt from *Bridge to Terabithia* [Reading for the fun of it: Getting hooked on books series, filmstrip-on-video, 11 min] Guidance Assoc, 197?.
Video: [Storybound series, 15 min] GPN, nd.

About the Book:

Filmstrip/sound: "Friendly Letter/Realistic Fiction" includes discussion of *Bridge to Terabithia* [Literature to enjoy and write about series 2, about 20 min] Pied Piper, 1989. SLJ 5/90
Video: "Friendly Letter/Realistic Fiction" includes discussion of *Bridge to Terabithia* [Literature to enjoy and write about series 2, about 20 min] Pied Piper, 1989. SLJ 5/90

See also Katherine Paterson, "Media about Newbery/Caldecott Authors and Illustrators."

Anpao: An American Indian Odyssey by Jamake Highwater. Illustrated by Fritz Scholder. Lippincott, 1977. Newbery Honor Book.

Audio: [cassette, 44 min] Miller-Brody, 1981. ESLC
Audio: [record] Folkways Records, 1978. op MMA
Filmstrip/sound: [2 filmstrips/2 cassettes] Miller-Brody, 1981. ESLC
Talking book: [RC12093] NLSBPH.

See also Jamake Highwater, "Media about Newbery/Caldecott Authors and Illustrators."

Ramona and Her Father by Beverly Cleary. Illustrated by Alan Tiegreen. Morrow, 1977. Newbery Honor Book.

Audio: [unabridged, 2 cassettes, 150 min] Listening Library, 1990.
Audio: [dramatized, record or cassette, 46 min] Miller-Brody, 1978. ESLC, MMA
Bookmark: "Libraries are Forever" ALA, 1984.
Braille: [BR3913] NLSBPH. ESLC
Filmstrip/sound: [2 filmstrips/2 cassettes, 204 fr/23 min] Miller-Brody, 1980. MMA

Filmstrip/sound: "Beverly Cleary" includes dramatized excerpt from *Ramona and Her Father* [Meet the Newbery author series, filmstrip/cassette, 112 fr/13 min] Miller-Brody, 1979. ESLC, MMA
Large print: Cornerstone, 1988.
Poster: "Libraries are Forever" [22x34 in] ALA, 1984.
Talking book: [RC12425] NLSBPH. ESLC

See also Beverly Cleary, "Media about Newbery/Caldecott Authors and Illustrators."

1977 NEWBERY AWARDS

Roll of Thunder, Hear My Cry by Mildred D. Taylor. Dial, 1976. Newbery Medal Book.

Audio: [dramatized, record or cassette, 54 min] Miller-Brody, 1978. ESLC, MMA
Braille: [BR6283] NLSBPH. ESLC
Film: [live-action, 110 min] Learning Corp, 1977. MMA
Filmstrip/sound: [2 filmstrips/2 cassettes, 290 fr/45 min] Miller-Brody, 1981. L, MMA
Large print: Cornerstone, 1989.
Poster: [17x22 in] Perfection Form, nd.
Talking book: [RC10893] NLSBPH. ESLC
Video: [filmstrip-on-video, 46 min] Random, 1988.
Video: [live-action, 150 min] International Video, 1978, released 1988. Note: a made-for-television movie
Video: [live-action, 110 min] Learning Corp, 1977.

See also Mildred D. Taylor, "Media about Newbery/Caldecott Authors and Illustrators."

Abel's Island by William Steig. Farrar, 1976. Newbery Honor Book.

Film: [animated, 29 min] Lucerne, 1988.
Poster: [17x22 in] Perfection Form, nd.
Read-along: [3 cassettes/book] Random, nd.
Talking book: [RC10693] NLSBPH. ESLC
Video: [animated, cc, 30 min] Lucerne, 1988. ALSC, BVC Note: home use version available from RH Home Video

A String in the Harp by Nancy Bond. Atheneum, 1976. Newbery Honor Book.

Braille: [BR6788] NLSBPH. ESLC
Talking book: [RC15269] NLSBPH.

1976 NEWBERY AWARDS

The Grey King by Susan Cooper. Illustrated by Michael Heslop. Atheneum, 1975. Newbery Medal Book.

Audio: [dramatized, 2 records or cassettes, 96 min] Miller-Brody, 1977. ESLC
Braille: [OCL-BPH(BCL520)BR] NLSBPH.
Large print: Cornerstone, 1988.
Poster: [17x22 in] Perfection Form, nd.
Talking book: [RC9196] NLSBPH. ESLC

See also Susan Cooper, "Media about Newbery/Caldecott Authors and Illustrators."

Dragonwings by Laurence Yep. Harper, 1975. Newbery Honor Book.

Audio: [dramatized, 2 records or cassettes, 86 min] Miller-Brody, 1977. ESLC, MMA
Filmstrip/sound: [4 filmstrips/4 cassettes, 512 fr/75 min] Miller-Brody, 1978. L, MMA
Large print: Cornerstone, 1990.
Talking book: [RC9784] NLSBPH. ESLC

See also Laurence Yep, "Media about Newbery/Caldecott Authors and Illustrators."

The Hundred Penny Box by Sharon Bell Mathis. Illustrated by Leo Dillon and Diane Dillon. Viking, 1975. Newbery Honor Book.

Audio: [record or cassette, 50 min] Miller-Brody, 1977. ALSC, ESLC
Film: [live-action, 18 min] Churchill, 1979. AFVF, ALSC, MMA
Filmstrip/sound: [2 filmstrips/2 cassettes, 189 fr/47 min] Miller-Brody, 1979. ALSC, L, MMA
Talking book: [RC10920] NLSBPH. ESLC
Video: [live-action, 18 min] Churchill, 1979. AFVF, ALSC
Video: [filmstrip-on-video, 47 min] Random, nd.

See also Leo and Diane Dillon, "Media about Newbery/Caldecott Authors and illustrators."

1975 NEWBERY AWARDS

M. C. Higgins, the Great by Virginia Hamilton. Macmillan, 1974. Newbery Medal Book.

> *Audio:* [dramatized, 2 records or 2 cassettes, 79 min] Miller-Brody, 1975. ALSC, ESLC, MMA
> *Braille:* [BR2749] NLSBPH. ESLC
> *Filmstrip/sound:* [2 filmstrips/2 cassettes, 287 fr/42 min] Miller-Brody, 1980. MMA
> *Filmstrip/sound:* "Virginia Hamilton" includes dramatized excerpt from *M. C. Higgins the Great* [Meet the Newbery author series, filmstrip/record or cassette, 101 fr/15 min] Miller-Brody, 1976. ALSC, BKL 12/1/76, CMCE, ESLC, L, MMA
> *Large print:* Cornerstone, 1988.
> *Poster:* [17x22 in] Perfection Form, nd.
> *Talking book:* [RD7696] NLSBPH. ESLC
> *Video:* [filmstrip-on-video, 42 min] Random, 1987.

> *See also* Virginia Hamilton, "Media about Newbery/Caldecott Authors and Illustrators."

Figgs & Phantoms by Ellen Raskin. Dutton, 1974. Newbery Honor Book.

> *Braille:* [BRA13769] NLSBPH.

> *See also* Ellen Raskin, "Media about Newbery/Caldecott Authors and Illustrators."

My Brother Sam Is Dead by James Lincoln Collier and Christopher Collier. Four Winds, 1973. Newbery Honor Book.

> *Audio:* [dramatized, record or cassette, 41 min] Miller-Brody, 1976. ALSC, BKL 9/15/77, CMCE, ESLC, MMA
> *Filmstrip/sound:* [2 filmstrips/2 cassettes, 26 min] Random, 1981. MMA
> *Filmstrip/sound:* "Challenges" includes excerpt from *My Brother Sam Is Dead* [Reading for the fun of it: Getting hooked on books series, 2 filmstrips/2 cassettes, 30 min] Guidance Assoc, 198?.

> *Large print:* Cornerstone, 1988.
> *Talking book:* [RD8094] NLSBPH. ESLC
> *Video:* [filmstrip-on-video, 25 min] Random, 1986.
> *Video:* "Challenges" includes excerpt from *My Brother Sam Is Dead* [Reading for the fun of it: Getting hooked on books series, filmstrip-on-video, 30 min] Guidance Assoc, 198?.

> *See also* Christopher Collier and James Lincoln Collier, "Media about Newbery/Caldecott Authors and Illustrators."

The Perilous Gard by Elizabeth Marie Pope. Illustrated by Richard Cuffari. Houghton, 1974. Newbery Honor Book.

> *Talking book:* [RC8842] NLSBPH. ESLC

Philip Hall Likes Me, I Reckon Maybe by Bette Greene. Illustrated by Charles Lilly. Dial, 1974. Newbery Honor Book.

> *Audio:* [dramatized, record or cassette, 58 min] Miller-Brody, 1976. BKL 9/15/77, CMCS, ESLC, MMA
> *Filmstrip/sound:* [2 filmstrips/2 records or cassettes, 195 fr/28 min] Miller-Brody, 1979. MMA
> *Large print:* Cornerstone, 1989.
> *Talking book:* [RC8748] NLSBPH. ESLC
> *Video:* [filmstrip-on-video, 29 min] Random, 1987.

> *See also* Bette Greene, "Media about Newbery/Caldecott Authors and Illustrators."

1974 NEWBERY AWARDS

The Slave Dancer by Paula Fox. Illustrated by Eros Keith. Bradbury, 1973. Newbery Medal Book.

> *Braille:* [BR2653] NLSBPH. ESLC
> *Filmstrip/sound:* "Adventure" includes excerpt from *The Slave Dancer* [Reading for the fun of it: Getting hooked on books series, filmstrip/cassette, 84 fr/15 min] Guidance Assoc, 1976.
> *Large print:* Cornerstone, 1988.
> *Poster:* [17x22 in] Perfection Form, nd.
> *Talking book:* [RC8551] NLSBPH. ESLC

Video: "Adventure" includes excerpt from *The Slave Dancer* [Reading for the fun of it: Getting hooked on books series, filmstrip-on-video, 15 min] Guidance Assoc, 1976.

See also Paula Fox, "Media about Newbery/ Caldecott Authors and Illustrators."

The Dark Is Rising by Susan Cooper. Illustrated by Alan E. Cober. Atheneum, 1973. Newbery Honor Book.

> *Audio:* [dramatized, 2 records or cassettes, 100 min] Miller-Brody, 1977. ESLC, MMA
> *Braille:* [OCL-BPH(BCL349)BR] NLSBPH.
> *Large print:* Cornerstone, 1988.
> *Talking book:* [RC8054] NLSBPH. ESLC
> *Video:* [More books from cover to cover series, 15 min] PBS, 1987. ESLC

See also Susan Cooper, "Media about Newbery/Caldecott Authors and Illustrators."

1973 NEWBERY AWARDS

Julie of the Wolves by Jean Craighead George. Illustrated by John Schoenherr. Harper, 1972. Newbery Medal Book.

> *Audio:* [abridged, record or cassette, 60 min] Caedmon, 1973. ALSC, BKL 5/1/74, CMCE, ESLC
> *Audio:* [dramatized, record or cassette, 40 min] Miller-Brody, 1973. ESLC, MMA
> *Audio:* [Book bag series, dramatized, cassette/book] Troll, nd.
> *Braille:* [BRA13071] NLSBPH. ESLC
> *Filmstrip/sound:* "Adventure" includes excerpt from *Julie of the Wolves* [Reading for the fun of it: Getting hooked on books series, filmstrip/cassette, 15 min] Guidance Assoc, 1976.
> *Filmstrip/sound:* [2 filmstrips/2 records or cassettes, 195 fr/40 min] Miller-Brody, 1975. MMA
> *Large print:* Cornerstone, 1987.
> *Poster:* [17x22 in] Perfection Form, nd.
> *Talking book:* [RD6776] NLSBPH. ESLC
> *Video:* [filmstrip-on-video, 38 min] Random, 1987.

Video: "Adventure" includes excerpt from *Julie of the Wolves* [Reading for the fun of it: Getting hooked on books series, filmstrip-on-video, 15 min] Guidance Assoc, 1976.

About the Book:

> *Filmstrip/sound:* "New Endings" includes discussion of *Julie of the Wolves* [Literature to enjoy and write about series 1, filmstrip/cassette, about 20 min] Pied Piper, 1989. SLJ 5/90
> *Filmstrip/sound:* "Newbery Medal Winners" includes discussion of *Julie of the Wolves* [4 filmstrips/4 cassettes] Meridian, 1986.
> *Video:* "New Endings" includes discussion of *Julie of the Wolves* [Literature to enjoy and write about series 1, about 20 min] Pied Piper, 1989. SLJ 5/90
> *Video:* "Newbery Medal Winners" includes discussion of *Julie of the Wolves* [filmstrip-on-video] Meridian, 1986.

See also Jean Craighead George and John Schoenherr, "Media about Newbery/Caldecott Authors and Illustrators."

Frog and Toad Together by Arnold Lobel. Harper, 1972. Newbery Honor Book.

> *Audio:* "Frog and Toad" includes *Frog and Toad Together* [Junior cassette library series, 2 cassettes] Listening Library, 1987. Note: read by the author
> *Audio:* [cassette] Miller-Brody, nd.
> *Film:* [animated, 18 min] Churchill, 1987. ALSC, CINE, PC, SLJ 4/89
> *Film:* [Words and pictures series, 15 min] Films Inc, nd.
> *Filmstrip/sound:* [5 filmstrips/5 records or cassettes, about 200 fr/30 min, also Spanish, Miller-Brody, 1976. BKL 8/15/77, CMCE, ESLC Note: available as individual filmstrips: "Cookies," "Dragons and Giants," "The Dream," "The Garden," and "The List"
> *Read-along:* [I can read series, cassette/book, 15 min] Caedmon, 1985. ESLC Note: read by the author
> *Talking book/print:* [record/book, TB4809] NLSBPH. ESLC
> *Video:* [animated, 18 min] Churchill, 1987. ALSC, BVC, CINE, PC, SLJ 4/89

Video: "Arnold Lobel Video Showcase" includes selections from *Frog and Toad Together* [filmstrip-on-video, 60 min] Random, 1985. ESLC, PC

Video: [15 min] Films Inc, nd.

About the Book:

Film: "Frog and Toad: Behind the Scenes" [10 min] Churchill, 1988.

Video: "Frog and Toad: Behind the Scenes" [10 min] Churchill, 1988.

See also Arnold Lobel, "Media about Newbery/ Caldecott Authors and Illustrators."

The Upstairs Room by Johanna Reiss. Crowell, 1972. Newbery Honor Book.

> *Audio:* [dramatized, record or cassette, 37 min] Miller-Brody, 1974. ESLC
>
> *Filmstrip/sound:* [2 filmstrips/2 records or cassettes, 212 fr/37 min] Miller-Brody, 1976.
>
> *Talking book:* [RD16930] NLSBPH. ESLC
>
> *Video:* [filmstrip-on-video, 37 min] Random, 1985.
>
> *Video:* [Best of cover to cover series, 15 min] WETA-TV, 1974. op

The Witches of Worm by Zilpha Keatley Snyder. Illustrated by Alton Raible. Atheneum, 1972. Newbery Honor Book,

> *Audio:* [dramatized, record or cassette, 50 min] Miller-Brody, 1978. ESLC, MMA
>
> *Filmstrip:* [2 filmstrips, script] Miller-Brody, 1979.
>
> *Filmstrip/sound:* [2 filmstrips/2 records or cassettes, 313 fr/38 min] Miller-Brody, 1979. MMA
>
> *Talking book:* [RD6168] NLSBPH. ESLC

1972 NEWBERY AWARD BOOKS

Mrs. Frisby and the Rats of NIMH by Robert C. O'Brien. Illustrated by Zena Bernstein. Atheneum, 1971. Newbery Medal Book.

> *Audio:* [dramatized, record or cassette, 48 min] Miller-Brody, 1972. ESLC
>
> *Braille:* [BRA12967 or IC-BPH(BIL4048)BR] NLSBPH. ESLC

Film: "The Secret of NIMH" [animated, 83 min] MGM-United Artists, 1982.

Filmstrip/sound: "Getting Hooked on Science Fiction" includes excerpts from *Mrs. Frisby and the Rats of NIMH* [filmstrip/cassette] Guidance Assoc, 1976.

Filmstrip/sound: [2 filmstrips/2 cassettes, 185 fr/49 min] Miller-Brody, 1973. L

Large print: G. K. Hall, 198?

Poster: [17x22 in] Perfection Form, nd.

Talking book: [RC23562] NLSBPH. ESLC

Video: [filmstrip-on-video, 49 min] Random, 1987.

Video: [animated, 83 min] MGM/UA Home Video, 1982.

Annie and the Old One by Miska Miles. Illustrated by Peter Parnall. Little, 1971. Newbery Honor Book.

> *Audio:* [record or cassette, 18 min] Miller-Brody, 1979. ALSC
>
> *Braille:* [BR2228] NLSBPH. ESLC
>
> *Film:* [15 min] Phoenix/BFA, 1976.
>
> *Filmstrip/sound:* [2 filmstrips/2 records or cassettes, 116 fr/14 min] Miller-Brody, 1979. MMA
>
> *Read-along:* [book/record or cassette] Random House, nd. MMA
>
> *Talking book:* [Mi-BPH(MSL4868)RM] NLSBPH.
>
> *Video:* [filmstrip-on-video, 14 min] Random, 198?.
>
> *Video:* [cc, 15 min] Phoenix/BFA, 1976.
>
> *Video:* "Coyote Cry/Annie and the Old One" [Best of cover to cover series, 15 min] WETA-TV, 197?. op
>
> *Video:* "Gabrielle and Selena/Annie and the Old One" [28 min] Phoenix/BFA, nd.

About the Book:

Filmstrip/sound: "Theme" includes discussion of *Annie and the Old One* [Literature for children series 9, filmstrip/cassette, about 19 min] Pied Piper, 198?.

Video: "Theme" includes discussion of *Annie and the Old One* [Literature for children series 9, about 19 min] Pied Piper, 198?.

The Headless Cupid by Zilpha Keatley Snyder. Illustrated by Alton Raible. Atheneum, 1971. Newbery Honor Book.

Audio: [record or cassette, 32 min] Miller-Brody, 1976. ALSC, ESLC, MMA
Braille: [BR13679] NLSBPH. ESLC
Filmstrip/sound: [First choice: Authors and books series, filmstrip/cassette, 110 fr/19 min] Pied Piper, 1980. MMA
Talking book: [RC24224] NLSBPH. ESLC
Video: [Best of cover to cover series, 15 min] WETA-TV, 1974. op

Incident at Hawk's Hill by Allan W. Eckert. Illustrated by John Schoenherr. Little, 1971. Newbery Honor Book.

Audio: [dramatized, record or cassette, 40 min] Miller-Brody, 1974. ESLC
Braille: [BR1771] NLSBPH. ESLC
Film: [Film as literature series 2, 29 min] Disney, 1979.
Filmstrip/sound: [Literary classics 5 series, 2 filmstrips/2 cassettes, 232 fr] Disney, 1980.
Television: "The Boy Who Talked to Badgers" [100 min] Disney, 1975.
Video: [Film as literature series 2, 29 min] Disney, 1979. Note: this is an edited version of made-for-TV movie listed above

See also John Schoenherr, "Media about Newbery/Caldecott Authors and Illustrators."

The Planet of Junior Brown by Virginia Hamilton. Macmillan, 1971. Newbery Honor Book.

Audio: [dramatized, record or cassette, 39 min] Miller-Brody, 1975. ESLC, MMA
Filmstrip/sound: [2 filmstrips/2 records or cassettes, 249 fr/39 min] Miller-Brody, 1977. ALSC, MMA
Large print: G. K. Hall, 1988.
Video: [filmstrip-on-video, 39 min] Random, 1987.

See also Virginia Hamilton, "Media about Newbery/Caldecott Authors and Illustrators."

The Tombs of Atuan by Ursula K. Le Guin. Illustrated by Gail Garraty. Atheneum, 1971. Newbery Honor Book.

Audio: [dramatized, record or cassette, 51 min] Miller-Brody, 1975. ESLC
Braille: [BR7771] NLSBPH.
Filmstrip/sound: [2 filmstrips/2 records or cassettes, 266 fr/42 min] Miller-Brody, 1979.
Large print: G. K. Hall, 1988.
Talking book: [RC24584] NLSBPH.

See also Ursula Le Guin, "Media about Newbery/Caldecott Authors and Illustrators."

1971 NEWBERY AWARDS

Summer of the Swans by Betsy Byars. Illustrated by Ted CoConis. Viking, 1970. Newbery Medal Book.

Audio: [dramatized, record or cassette, 51 min] Live Oak, 1972. ESLC, MMA
Audio: [cassette] Miller-Brody, nd.
Audio: [Book bag series, dramatized, cassette/book] Troll, nd.
Film: "Sara's Summer of the Swans" [Teenage years series, 33 min] Time-Life, 1976. distributed by Ambrose. CINE, MMA Note: originally shown on the ABC Afterschool Specials television series
Large print: Cornerstone, 1988.
Poster: [17x22 in] Perfection Form, nd.
Talking book: [RC23118] NLSBPH. ESLC
Video: "Sara's Summer of the Swans" [Teenage years series, 33 min] Time-Life, 1976, distributed by Ambrose. Note: originally shown on the ABC Afterschool Specials television series
Video: [Best of cover to cover series, 15 min] WETA-TV, 1974. op

About the Book:

Filmstrip/sound: "Friendly Letter/Realistic Fiction" includes discussion of *Summer of the Swans* [Literature to enjoy and write about series 2, filmstrip/cassette, about 20 min] Pied Piper, 1989. SLJ 5/90

Filmstrip/sound: "Newbery Medal Winners" includes discussion of *Summer of the Swans* [4 filmstrips/4 cassettes] Meridian, 1986.

Filmstrip/sound: "Realistic Fiction" includes discussion of *Summer of the Swans* [Literature for children series 6, filmstrip/cassette, 81 fr/12 min] Pied Piper, 1980.

Video: "Friendly Letter/Realistic Fiction" includes discussion of *Summer of the Swans* [Literature to enjoy and write about series 2, about 20 min] Pied Piper, 1989. SLJ 5/90

Video: "Newbery Medal Winners" includes discussion of *Summer of the Swans* [filmstrip-on-video] Meridian, 1986.

Video: "Realistic Fiction" includes discussion of *Summer of the Swans* [Literature for children series 6, about 12 min] Pied Piper, 198?.

See also Betsy Byars, "Media about Newbery/Caldecott Authors and Illustrators."

Enchantress from the Stars by Sylvia Louise Engdahl. Illustrated by Rodney Shackell. Atheneum, 1970. Newbery Honor Book.

Talking book: [TB4025] NLSBPH.

Knee Knock Rise by Natalie Babbitt. Farrar, 1970. Newbery Honor Book.

Audio: [dramatized, record or cassette, 33 min] Miller-Brody, 1973. ESLC

Filmstrip/sound: [2 filmstrips/2 records or cassettes, 201 fr] Miller-Brody, 1975.

Talking book: [TB3787] NLSBPH. ESLC

See also Natalie Babbitt, "Media about Newbery/Caldecott Authors and Illustrators."

Sing Down the Moon by Scott O'Dell. Houghton, 1970. Newbery Honor Book.

Audio: [dramatized, record or cassette, 45 min] Miller-Brody, 1973. ESLC, MMA

Filmstrip/sound: "Many Lands" includes excerpt from *Sing Down the Moon* [Reading for the fun of it: Getting hooked on books series, filmstrip/cassette, 90 fr/16 min] Guidance Assoc, 1976.

Filmstrip/sound: [2 filmstrips/2 records or cassettes, 205 fr/36 min] Miller-Brody, 1975. BKL 9/15/75, CMCE

Large print: Cornerstone, 1989.

Talking book: [Co-B(CC574)RC or RC25275] NLSBPH. ESLC

Video: [filmstrip-on-video, 36 min] Random, 1986.

See also Scott O'Dell, "Media about Newbery/Caldecott Authors and Illustrators."

1970 NEWBERY AWARD BOOKS

Sounder by William H. Armstrong. Illustrated by James Barkley. Harper, 1969. Newbery Medal Book.

Audio: [dramatized, record or cassette, 45 min] Miller-Brody, 1970. ESLC, MMA

Audio: [cassette] Listening Library, nd.

Audio: [Book bag series, dramatized, cassette/book] Troll, nd.

Braille: [BR6227 or BRA4842] NLSBPH. ESLC

Film: [live-action, 105 min] Paramount, 1972. MMA

Filmstrip/sound: "Nature" includes excerpt from *Sounder* [Reading for the fun of it: Getting hooked on books series, filmstrip/cassette, 15 min] Guidance Assoc, 1978.

Filmstrip/sound: "I Couldn't Put It Down: Hooked on Reading—Adolescent Novels" includes excerpt from *Sounder* [3 filmstrips/3 cassettes, 167 fr/37 min] Guidance Assoc, 1977.

Filmstrip/sound: [Learn to read by reading series, filmstrip/cassette] Eye Gate Media, nd. op

Large print: Cornerstone, 1987. ELSC

Poster: [17x22 in] Perfection Form, nd.

Talking book: [RC22898] NLSBPH. ESLC

Video: "Nature" includes excerpt from *Sounder* [Reading for the fun of it: Getting hooked on books series, filmstrip-on-video, 15 min] Guidance Assoc, 1978.

Video: "I Couldn't Put It Down: Hooked on Reading—Adolescent Novels" includes excerpt from *Sounder* [filmstrip-on-video, 37 min] Guidance Assoc, 1977.

Video: [live-action, cc, 105 min] Paramount, 1972, released Paramount Home Video 1984. PCGV, VM

Video: [Storybound series, 15 min] GPN, nd.

About the Book:

Filmstrip/sound: [filmstrip/cassette] Current Affairs, nd. op

See also William Armstrong, "Media about Newbery/Caldecott Authors and Illustrators."

Journey Outside by Mary Q. Steele. Illustrated by Rocco Negri. Viking, 1969. Newbery Honor Book.

> *Audio:* [dramatized, cassette, 53 min] Live Oak, 1976. ESLC, MMA

The Many Ways of Seeing: An Introduction to the Pleasures of Art by Janet Gaylord Moore. World, 1969. Newbery Honor Book.

> none located

Our Eddie by Sulamith Ish-Kishor. Pantheon, 1969. Newbery Honor Book.

> none located

1969 NEWBERY AWARDS

The High King by Lloyd Alexander. Holt, 1968. Newbery Medal Book.

> *Audio:* [cassette] Miller-Brody, 197?.
> *Braille:* [BRA5040] NLSBPH. ESLC
> *Filmstrip/sound:* [4 filmstrips/4 cassettes] Miller-Brody, 1974.
> *Poster:* [17x22 in] Perfection Form, nd.
> *Talking book:* [RC27715] NLSBPH. ESLC

About the Book:

Filmstrip/sound: "Lloyd Alexander" includes discussion of *The High King* [Meet the Newbery author series, filmstrip/record or cassette, 94 fr/13 min] Miller-Brody, 1974. ESLC, MMA

See also Lloyd Alexander, "Media about Newbery/Caldecott Authors and Illustrators."

To Be a Slave by Julius Lester. Illustrated by Tom Feelings. Dial, 1968. Newbery Honor Book.

> *Audio:* [2 cassettes] Caedmon, 1972.
> *Braille:* [BR7247 or BRA16729] NLSBPH.
> *Talking book:* [RC27538] NLSBPH.

See also Tom Feelings, "Media about Newbery/Caldecott Authors and Illustrators."

When Shlemiel Went to Warsaw and Other Stories by Isaac Bashevis Singer. Illustrated by Margot Zemach. Farrar, 1968. Newbery Honor Book.

> *Audio:* "Eli Wallach Reads Isaac Bashevis Singer" includes *When Shlemiel Went to Warsaw and Other Stories* [2 records or cassettes, 90 min] Miller-Brody, 1974. ESLC, MMA
> *Audio:* "Rabbi Leib/Shrewd Todie" includes stories from *When Shlemiel Went to Warsaw* [cassette] Miller-Brody, nd.
> *Braille:* [BR954] NLSBPH. ESLC
> *Filmstrip/sound:* "Eli Wallach Reads Isaac Bashevis Singer" includes *When Shlemiel Went to Warsaw and Other Stories* [filmstrip/record or cassette] Miller-Brody, 1975.
> *Filmstrip/sound:* [2 filmstrips/2 records or cassettes, 200 fr/45 min] Miller-Brody, 1974. MMA
> *Talking book:* [Nj-B(C1512m)RC or Tx-BPH(CBT1888)RC] NLSBPH.

See also Isaac Bashevis Singer, "Media about Newbery/Caldecott Authors and illustrators."

1968 NEWBERY AWARDS

From the Mixed-Up Files of Mrs. Basil E. Frankweiler by E. L. Konigsburg. Atheneum, 1967. Newbery Medal Book.

> *Audio:* [unabridged, 3 cassettes, 219 min] Listening Library, 1988.
> *Audio:* [dramatized, record or cassette, 49 min] Miller-Brody, 1969. ESLC. MMA
> *Braille:* [BRA4504] NLSBPH. ESLC
> *Film:* [live-action, 30 min] Phoenix/BFA, 1978. MMA
> *Film:* [live-action, 105 min] Films Inc, 1973. Note: Reissued as "The Hideaways"
> *Filmstrip/sound:* [2 filmstrips/2 cassettes, 356 fr] Films Inc, 1981. op
> *Filmstrip/sound:* [First choice: Authors and books series, 2 filmstrips/cassette, 154 fr/34 min] Pied Piper, 1980. MMA

Filmstrip/sound: "Challenges" includes excerpt from *From the Mixed-Up Files of Mrs. Basil E. Frankweiler* [Reading for the fun of it: Getting hooked on books series, 2 filmstrips/2 cassettes, 30 min] Guidance Assoc, 198?.
Large print: Cornerstone, 1988.
Poster: [17x22 in] Perfection Form, nd.
Read-along/large print: [Large print book/3 cassettes, 225 min] Listening Library, 1988. ESLC
Talking book: [RC22914] NLSBPH. ESLC
Video: "Challenges" includes excerpt from *From the Mixed-Up Files of Mrs. Basil E. Frankweiler* [Reading for the fun of it: Getting hooked on books series, filmstrip-on-video, 30 min] Guidance Assoc, 198?.
Video: [First choice: Authors and books series] Pied Piper, 198?.
Video: [live-action, 105 min] Films Inc, 1978.
Video: [live-action, 30 min] Phoenix/BFA, 1978.

See also E. L. Konigsburg, "Media about Newbery/Caldecott Authors and Illustrators."

The Black Pearl by Scott O'Dell. Illustrated by Milton Johnson. Houghton, 1967. Newbery Honor Book.

Audio: [dramatized, record or cassette, 43 min] Miller-Brody, 1973. ESLC
Braille: [BR764] NLSBPH. ESLC
Filmstrip/sound: [2 filmstrips/2 cassettes, 214 fr/37 min] Miller-Brody, 1974.
Talking book: [AZ-BPH(AZCB1039)RC or Mi-BPH(MSL2543)RM] NLSBPH
Video: [filmstrip-on-video, 37 min] Random, 1988.
Video: "Bookbag" includes excerpt from *The Black Pearl* [Matter of fiction series, 20 min] AIT, 1969.

See also Scott O'Dell, "Media about Newbery/Caldecott Authors and Illustrators."

The Egypt Game by Zilpha Keatley Snyder. Illustrated by Alton Raible. Atheneum, 1967. Newbery Honor Book.

Audio: [dramatized, record or cassette, 40 min] Miller-Brody, 1975. ESLC
Braille: [BRA2704] NLSBPH. ESLC
Talking book: [TB2108] NLSBPH.

About the Book:

Filmstrip/sound: "Mysteries" includes discussion of *The Egypt Game* [Literature for children series 6, filmstrip/cassette, 77 fr/12 min] Pied Piper, 1980.
Video: "Mysteries" includes discussion of *The Egypt Game* [Literature for children series 6, about 12 min] Pied Piper, 198?.

The Fearsome Inn by Isaac Bashevis Singer. Illustrated by Nonny Hogrogian. Scribner, 1967. Newbery Honor Book.

Talking book: [TB2242] NLSBPH.

See also Isaac Bashevis Singer, "Media about Newbery/Caldecott Authors and illustrators."

Jennifer, Hecate, Macbeth, William McKinley, and Me, Elizabeth by E. L. Konigsburg. Atheneum, 1967. Newbery Honor Book.

Filmstrip/sound: "Humor" includes excerpt from *Jennifer, Hecate, Macbeth, William McKinley, and Me, Elizabeth* [Reading for the fun of it: Getting hooked on books series, filmstrip/cassette, 15 min] Guidance Assoc, nd.
Large print: Cornerstone, 1989.
Read-along: [Cliffhanger series, cassette/book, 46 min] Listening Library, 1986.
Talking book: [TB2048] NLSBPH.
Video: [Best of cover to cover series, 15 min] WETA-TV, 1974. op
Video: "Humor" includes excerpt from *Jennifer, Hecate, Macbeth, William McKinley, and Me, Elizabeth* [Reading for the fun of it: Getting hooked on books series, filmstrip-on-video, 15 min] Guidance Assoc, nd.

About the Book:

Filmstrip/sound: "Character" includes discussion of *Jennifer, Hecate, Macbeth, William McKinley, and Me, Elizabeth* [Literature for children series 9, filmstrip/cassette, about 19 min] Pied Piper, 198?.
Video: "Character" includes discussion of *Jennifer, Hecate, Macbeth, William McKinley, and Me, Elizabeth* [Literature for children series 9, about 19 min] Pied Piper, 198?.

See also E. L. Konigsburg, "Media about Newbery/Caldecott Authors and Illustrators."

1967 NEWBERY AWARDS

Up a Road Slowly by Irene Hunt. Follett, 1966. Newbery Medal Book.

> *Audio:* [dramatized, record or cassette, 43 min] Miller-Brody, 1972. ESLC, MMA
> *Braille:* [BRA14015 or BRA14781] NLSBPH. ESLC
> *Filmstrip/sound:* [2 filmstrips/2 cassettes, 249 fr/40 min] Miller-Brody, 1980. MMA
> *Talking book:* [Ct-BPH(CTC5616)RC or RC22915] NLSBPH. ESLC
>
> *See also* Irene Hunt, "Media about Newbery/Caldecott Authors and Illustrators."

The Jazz Man by Mary Hays Weik. Illustrated by Ann Grifalconi. Atheneum, 1966. Newbery Honor Book.

> *Talking book:* [Mi-BPH(MSL4388)RM or RC19127] NLSBPH.

The King's Fifth by Scott O'Dell. Illustrated by Samuel Bryant. Houghton, 1966. Newbery Honor Book.

> *Audio:* [dramatized, record or cassette, 43 min] Miller-Brody, 1974. ALSC, ESLC
> *Braille:* [BRA2444] NLSBPH.
> *Filmstrip/sound:* [2 filmstrips/2 records or cassettes, 262 fr/34 min] Miller-Brody, 1976. BKL 4/15/77, CMCE
> *Filmstrip/sound:* "Scott O'Dell" includes dramatized excerpt from *The King's Fifth* [Meet the Newbery author series, filmstrip/record or cassette, 85 fr/13 min] Miller-Brody, 1974. ESLC, MMA
> *Talking book:* [TB1661] NLSBPH.
>
> *See also* Scott O'Dell, "Media about Newbery/Caldecott Authors and Illustrators."

Zlateh the Goat and Other Stories by Isaac Bashevis Singer. Illustrated by Maurice Sendak. Harper, 1966. Newbery Honor Book.

> *Audio:* [cassette, 62 min] Caedmon, 1989. ALSC, SLJ 8/90

> *Audio:* "Eli Wallach Reads Isaac Bashevis Singer" includes *Zlateh the Goat and Other Stories* [2 records or cassettes, 90 min] Miller-Brody, 1974. ESLC, MMA
> *Audio:* [cassette, 43 min] Miller-Brody, nd.
> *Braille:* [BRA11122] NLSBPH. ESLC
> *Film:* [live-action, 20 min, also Danish/French/German] Weston Woods, 1974. CMCS, MMA
> *Filmstrip/sound:* "Isaac Bashevis Singer" includes dramatized excerpt from *Zlateh the Goat* [Meet the Newbery author series, filmstrip/record or cassette, 88 fr/18 min] Miller-Brody, 1976. BKL 10/15/76, CMCE, ESLC, L, MMA
> *Filmstrip/sound:* [2 filmstrips/2 records or cassettes, 200 fr/43 min, script] Miller-Brody, 1974. MMS
> *Talking book:* [RC25902] NLSBPH. ESLC
> *Video:* [live-action, 20 min, also Danish/French/German] Weston Woods, 1974. ESLC, MMA
>
> *See also* Isaac Bashevis Singer and Maurice Sendak, "Media about Newbery/Caldecott Authors and Illustrators."

1966 NEWBERY AWARDS

I, Juan de Pareja by Elizabeth Borton de Treviño. Farrar, 1965. Newbery Medal Book.

> *Audio:* [dramatized, record or cassette, 42 min] Miller-Brody, 1973. ESLC
> *Braille:* [BRA1727] NLSBPH.
> *Filmstrip/sound:* [2 filmstrips/2 records or cassettes, 194 fr, script] Miller-Brody, 1975.
> *Talking book:* [RC23338] NLSBPH.
>
> *See also* Elizabeth Borton de Treviño, "Media about Newbery/Caldecott Authors and Illustrators."

The Animal Family by Randall Jarrell. Illustrated by Maurice Sendak. Pantheon, 1965. Newbery Honor Book.

> *Braille:* [BRA1670] NLSBPH. ESLC
> *Talking book:* [CT-BPH(CTC5637)RC or RC25834] NLSBPH. ESLC

See also Randall Jarrell and Maurice Sendak, "Media about Newbery/Caldecott Authors and Illustrators."

The Black Cauldron by Lloyd Alexander. Holt, 1965. Newbery Honor Book.

Braille: [BRA513] NLSBPH. ESLC
Talking book: [Co-B(CC763)RC or RC25014] NLSBPH. ESLC
Video: [animated, 81 min] Disney, 1985.

About the Book:

Filmstrip/sound: "Book Review/Fantasy" includes discussion of *The Black Cauldron* [Literature to enjoy and write about series 2, filmstrip/cassette, about 20 min] Pied Piper, 1989. SLJ 5/90
Video: "Book Review/Fantasy" includes discussion of *The Black Cauldron* [Literature to enjoy and write about series 2, about 20 min] Pied Piper, 1989. SLJ 5/90

See also Lloyd Alexander, "Media about Newbery/Caldecott Authors and Illustrators."

The Noonday Friends by Mary Stolz. Illustrated by Louis S. Glanzman. Harper, 1965. Newbery Honor Book.

Audio: [dramatized, record or cassette] Miller-Brody, 1975. ESLC, MMA
Braille: [BR279] NLSBPH. ESLC
Filmstrip/sound: [2 filmstrips/record or 2 cassettes, 244 fr/42 min] Miller-Brody, 1977. MMA
Talking book: [RD6455] NLSBPH. ESLC

See also Mary Stolz, "Media about Newbery/Caldecott Authors and Illustrators."

1965 NEWBERY AWARDS

Shadow of a Bull by Maia Wojciechowska. Illustrated by Alvin Smith. Atheneum, 1964. Newbery Medal Book.

Audio: [dramatized, record or cassette, 41 min] Miller-Brody, 1970. ESLC. MMA

Audio: [2 cassettes] Caedmon, nd.
Audio: [cassette] Listening Library, nd.
Audio: [Book bag series, dramatized, cassette/book] Troll, nd.
Filmstrip/sound: [2 filmstrips/2 records or cassettes, 255 fr/39 min] Miller-Brody, 1978. MMA
Filmstrip/sound: "Many Lands" includes excerpt from *Shadow of a Bull* [Reading for the fun of it: Getting hooked on books series, filmstrip/cassette, 16 min] Guidance Assoc, 1976.
Poster: [Study prints set 4, 17x24 in] Horn Book Magazine, 1971-1974. op ESLC
Talking book: [RC23786] NLSBPH. ESLC
Video: [Books from cover to cover series, b&w, 20 min] WETA-TV, nd. op

See also Maia Wojciechowska, "Media about Newbery/Caldecott Authors and Illustrators."

Across Five Aprils by Irene Hunt. Follett, 1964. Newbery Honor Book.

Audio: [dramatized, record or cassette, 38 min] Miller-Brody, 1973. BKL 9/15/74, CMCE, ESLC, L, MMA
Audio: [Book bag series, dramatized, cassette/book] Troll, nd.
Braille: [BRA14637 or BRJ1696] NLSBPH. ESLC
Film: [live-action, 2 films, 66 min] Coronet/MTI, 1990. BKL 10/1/90, BKL/E, SLJ 10/90
Filmstrip/sound: [2 filmstrips/2 cassettes, 165 fr/29 min] Miller-Brody, 1974. L
Poster: [17x22 in] Perfection Form, nd.
Talking book: [IC-BPH(CIL30)RC or RC26336] NLSBPH. ESLC
Video: [live-action, 2 videos, 66 min] Coronet/MTI, 1990. BKL 10/1/90, BKL/E, SLJ 10/90
Video: [filmstrip-on-video, 29 min] Random, 1987.
Video: [Matter of fiction series, 20 min] AIT, 1969.

See also Irene Hunt, "Media about Newbery/ Caldecott Authors and Illustrators."

1964 NEWBERY AWARDS

It's Like This, Cat by Emily Neville. Illustrated by Emil Weiss. Harper, 1963. Newbery Medal Book.

> *Audio:* [dramatized, record or cassette, 42 min] Miller-Brody, 1970. ESLC, MMA
> *Audio:* [cassette] Listening Library, nd.
> *Audio:* [Book bag series, dramatized, cassette/ book] Troll, nd.
> *Braille:* [BRA9431 or BRA9617] NLSBPH. ESLC
> *Filmstrip/sound:* [2 filmstrips/record or 2 cassettes, 251 fr/34 min] Miller-Brody, 1978. MMA
> *Talking book:* [RC22850] NLSBPH. ESLC
> *Video:* [filmstrip-on-video, 34 min] Random, 1988.

The Loner by Ester Wier. Illustrated by Christine Price. McKay, 1963. Newbery Honor Book.

> *Audio:* [dramatized, record or cassette, 44 min] Miller-Brody, 1973. ESLC
> *Braille:* [BR33] NLSBPH. ESLC
> *Filmstrip/sound:* [2 filmstrips/2 records or cassettes, 203 fr, script] Miller-Brody, 1975.
> *Talking book:* [Nj-B(C1740m)RC] NLSBPH.
> *Video:* [Books from cover to cover series, b&w, 20 min] WETA-TV, nd. op

> *See also* Ester Wier, "Media about Newbery/ Caldecott Authors and Illustrators."

Rascal: A Memoir of a Better Era by Sterling North. Illustrated by John Schoenherr. Dutton, 1963. Newbery Honor Book.

> *Audio:* [dramatized, record or cassette, 40 min] Miller-Brody, 1975. ESLC, MMA
> *Braille:* [BRA9787] NLSBPH. ESLC
> *Film:* [Film as literature series 3, 15 min] Disney, 1980.
> *Film:* [live-action, 85 min] Disney, 1969. MMA
> *Talking book:* [CT-BPH(CTC5676)RC or RD7202] NLSBPH. ESLC
> *Video:* [Film as literature series 3, 15 min] Disney, 1980.

See also John Schoenherr, "Media about Newbery/Caldecott Authors and Illustrators."

1963 NEWBERY AWARDS

A Wrinkle in Time by Madeleine L'Engle. Farrar, 1962. Newbery Medal Book.

> *Audio:* [dramatized, record or cassette, 40 min] Miller-Brody, 1972. ESLC
> *Audio:* [I open the door series, 3-3/4 ips tape, 15 min] National Center for Audio Tapes, nd. op
> *Audio:* [Book bag series, dramatized, cassette/ book] Troll, nd.
> *Braille:* [BR1546] NLSBPH. ESLC
> *Filmstrip/sound:* [2 filmstrips/2 cassettes, 214 fr] Miller-Brody, 1974.
> *Filmstrip/sound:* "Madeleine L'Engle" includes dramatized excerpt from *A Wrinkle in Time* [Meet the Newbery author series, 102 fr/16 min] Miller-Brody, 1974. ESLC, MMA
> *Large print:* Cornerstone, 1987.
> *Poster:* [17x22 in] Perfection Form, nd.
> *Talking book:* [RC9768] NLSBPH. ESLC
> *Video:* [Storybound series, 15 min] GPN, nd.
> *Video:* [Books from cover to cover series, b&w, 20 min] WETA-TV, nd. op
> *Video:* "Earthfasts" includes excerpt from *A Wrinkle in Time* [Books from cover to cover series, b&w, 20 min] WETA-TV, nd. op

About the Book:

> *Filmstrip/sound:* "Newbery Medal Winners" includes discussion of *A Wrinkle in Time* [4 filmstrips/4 cassettes] Meridian, 1986.
> *Filmstrip/sound:* "Science Fiction" includes discussion of *A Wrinkle in Time* [Literature for children series 6, filmstrip/cassette, 90 fr/ 12 min] Pied Piper, 1980.
> *Software:* "Character Sketch I" includes discussion of *A Wrinkle in Time* [Write On! series] Humanities Software, 198?.
> *Software:* "Character Sketch II" includes discussion of *A Wrinkle in Time* [Write On! series] Humanities Software, 198?.
> *Software:* "Finding a Writing Style I" includes discussion of *A Wrinkle in Time* [Write On! series] Humanities Software, 198?.

Software: "The Literary Mapper: Level 2" includes discussion of *A Wrinkle in Time* Teacher Support Software, 198?.

Software: "Observe and Describe" includes discussion of *A Wrinkle in Time* [Write On! series] Humanities Software, 198?.

Video: "Newbery Medal Winners" includes discussion of *A Wrinkle in Time* [filmstrip-on-video] Meridian, 1986.

Video: "Science Fiction" includes discussion of *A Wrinkle in Time* [Literature for children series 6, about 12 min] Pied Piper, 198?.

See also Madeleine L'Engle, "Media about Newbery/Caldecott Authors and Illustrators."

Men of Athens by Olivia Coolidge. Illustrated by Milton Johnson. Houghton, 1962. Newbery Honor Book.

Audio: [Book detective series, 3-3/4 ips tape, 15 min] National Center for Audio Tapes, nd. op

Braille: [BRA12291] NLSBPH.

Talking book: [Tx-BPH(CBT1460)RC] NLSBPH.

Thistle and Thyme: Tales and Legends from Scotland by Sorche Nic Leodhas, pseud. (Leclaire Alger). Illustrated by Evaline Ness. Holt, 1962. Newbery Honor Book.

Braille: [BRA12272] NLSBPH.

See also Evaline Ness, "Media about Newbery/Caldecott Authors and Illustrators."

1962 NEWBERY AWARDS

The Bronze Bow by Elizabeth George Speare. Houghton, 1961. Newbery Medal Book.

Audio: [dramatized, record or cassette, 42 min] Miller-Brody, 1972. ESLC, MMA

Audio: [Book bag series, dramatized, cassette/book] Troll, nd.

Braille: [BRA46] NLSBPH. ESLC

Filmstrip/sound: [2 filmstrips/2 records or cassettes, 232 fr/41 min] Miller-Brody, 1978. MMA

Talking book: [RC17367] NLSBPH. ESLC

See also Elizabeth George Speare, "Media about Newbery/Caldecott Authors and illustrators."

Belling the Tiger by Mary Stolz. Illustrated by Beni Montresor. Harper, 1961. Newbery Honor Book.

Video: [Books from cover to cover series, b&w, 20 min] WETA-TV, nd. op

See also Mary Stolz, "Media about Newbery/Caldecott Authors and Illustrators."

Frontier Living by Edwin Tunis. World, 1961. Newbery Honor Book.

Braille: [BRA7157] NLSBPH.

Talking book: [TB2678] NLSBPH.

See also Edwin Tunis, "Media about Newbery/Caldecott Authors and Illustrators."

The Golden Goblet by Eloise Jarvis McGraw. Coward, 1961. Newbery Honor Book.

Audio: [dramatized, record or cassette, 36 min] Miller-Brody, 1973. ESLC

Filmstrip/sound: [2 filmstrips/2 cassettes, 252 fr] Miller-Brody, 1974.

Talking book: [RC27542] NLSBPH

1961 NEWBERY AWARDS

Island of the Blue Dolphins by Scott O'Dell. Houghton, 1960. Newbery Medal Book.

Braille: [BR6230 or BRA1649] NLSBPH. ESLC

Film: [live-action, 99 min] Universal, 1964. MMA

Film: [live-action, 20 min] Universal, 1964. Note: this is an excerpt from 99 min feature film listed above

Filmstrip/sound: "Living with Nature" [filmstrip/cassette, 181 fr] Films Inc, 1981. op

Filmstrip/sound: "A Young Girl Stranded" [filmstrip/cassette, 162 fr] Films Inc, 1981. op

Filmstrip/sound: "Adventure" includes excerpt from *Island of the Blue Dolphins* [Reading for the fun of it: Getting hooked on books series, filmstrip/cassette, 15 min] Guidance Assoc, 1976.

Filmstrip/sound: "Scott O'Dell" includes excerpt from *Island of the Blue Dolphins* filmstrip [Meet the Newbery author series, filmstrip/record or cassette, 85 fr/13 min] Miller-Brody, 1974. ESLC, MMA

Large print: G. K. Hall, 1974; Cornerstone, 1987. ESLC

Poster: [17x22 in] Perfection Form, nd.

Talking book: [RC22397, also Spanish RC15317] NLSBPH. ESLC

Video: "Adventure" includes excerpt from *Island of the Blue Dolphins* [Reading for the fun of it: Getting hooked on books series, filmstrip-on-video, 15 min] Guidance Assoc, 1976.

Video: [live-action, 99 min] Universal, 1964, released MCA/Universal Home Video, 1985.

Video: [Storybound series, 15 min] GPN, nd.

About the Book:

Filmstrip/sound: "Historical Fiction (rev ed)" includes discussion of *Island of the Blue Dolphins* [Literature for children series 3, filmstrip/cassette, about 12 min] Pied Piper, 1983.

Software: "Finding a Writing Style I" includes discussion of *Island of the Blue Dolphins* [Write On! series] Humanities Software, 198?.

Software: "Island of the Blue Dolphins: A Novel Study" [Write On! series] Humanities Software, 198?.

Video: "Historical Fiction" includes discussion of *Island of the Blue Dolphins* [Literature for children series 3, about 12 min] Pied Piper, 198?.

See also Scott O'Dell, "Media about Newbery/Caldecott Authors and Illustrators."

America Moves Forward: A History for Peter by Gerald W. Johnson. Illustrated by Leonard Everett Fisher. Morrow, 1960. Newbery Honor Book.

Braille: [BRA4008] NLSBPH.

Talking book: [TB1718] NLSBPH.

The Cricket in Times Square by George Selden, pseud. (George Thompson.) Illustrated by Garth Williams. Farrar, 1960. Newbery Honor Book.

Audio: [dramatized, record or cassette, 45 min] Miller-Brody, 1971. ESLC

Audio: [unabridged, 3 cassettes] Random, nd.

Audio: [Book bag series, dramatized, cassette/book] Troll, nd.

Braille: [BR5850 or BRA2579] NLSBPH. ESLC

Film: [animated, 26 min] Xerox, 1973, released 1976.

Filmstrip/sound: "Friendship" includes excerpt from *The Cricket in Times Square* [Reading for the fun of it: Getting hooked on books series, 2 filmstrips/2 cassettes, 11 min] Guidance Assoc, 197?.

Filmstrip/sound: [2 filmstrips/2 records or cassettes, 153 fr] Miller-Brody, 197?.

Large print: Cornerstone, 1990.

Talking book: [RC16458] NLSBPH.

Video: [animated, 26 min] Family Home, 1973, released 1985. PCGV

Video: "Friendship" includes excerpt from *The Cricket in Times Square* [Reading for the fun of it: Getting hooked on books series, filmstrip-on-video, 11 min] Guidance Assoc, 197?.

Video: [Book bird series, 15 min] GPN, nd.

Video: [Books from cover to cover series, b&w, 20 min] WETA-TV, nd. op

About the Book:

Filmstrip/sound: "Fantasy (rev ed)" includes discussion of *The Cricket in Times Square* [Literature for children series 1, filmstrip/cassette, about 12 min] Pied Piper, 1983.

Video: "Fantasy" includes discussion of *The Cricket in Times Square* [Literature for children series 1, about 12 min] Pied Piper, 1983.

See also George Thompson, "Media about Newbery/Caldecott Authors and Illustrators."

Old Ramon by Jack Schaefer. Illustrated by Harold West. Houghton, 1960. Newbery Honor Book.

Audio: [dramatized, record or cassette, 42 min] Miller-Brody, 1973. ESLC

Braille: [BRA5131] NLSBPH.

Filmstrip/sound: [2 filmstrips/2 cassettes, 204 fr/33 min] Miller-Brody, 1974. MMA

1960 NEWBERY AWARDS

Onion John by Joseph Krumgold. Illustrated by Symeon Shimin. Crowell, 1959. Newbery Medal Book.

> *Audio:* [dramatized, record or cassette, 35 min] Miller-Brody, 1972. ESLC, MMA
> *Braille:* [BRA2670 or BRA6088] NLSBPH. ESLC
> *Filmstrip/sound:* [2 filmstrips/2 records or cassettes, 236 fr/27 min] Miller-Brody, 1978. MMA
> *Talking book:* [RC18347] NLSBPH. ESLC

> *About the Book:*

> *Film:* "Reading Stories: Characters and Settings" includes discussion of *Onion John* [11 min] Coronet/MTI, 1969.
> *Video:* "Reading Stories: Characters and Settings" includes discussion of *Onion John* [11 min] Coronet/MTI, 1969.

> *See also* Joseph Krumgold, "Media about Newbery/Caldecott Authors and Illustrators."

America Is Born: A History for Peter by Gerald W. Johnson. Illustrated by Leonard Everett Fisher. Morrow, 1959. Newbery Honor Book.

> *Braille:* [BRA4104] NLSBPH.
> *Talking book:* [TB1716] NLSBPH.

The Gammage Cup by Carol Kendall. Illustrated by Erik Blegvad. Harcourt, 1959. Newbery Honor Book.

> *Audio:* [dramatized, record or cassette] Miller-Brody, 1976. ESLC, MMA
> *Braille:* [BRA1613] NLSBPH. ESLC
> *Filmstrip/sound:* [2 filmstrips/record or 2 cassettes, 263 fr/45 min] Miller-Brody, 1976. CMCS, MMA
> *Talking book:* [TB1387] NLSBPH. ESLC

My Side of the Mountain by Jean Craighead George. Dutton, 1959. Newbery Honor Book.

> *Braille:* [BRA5078] NLSBPH. ESLC
> *Film:* [Great literature film classics series, live-action, 38 min] AIMS, 1979. Note: this is an edited version of 100 min film listed below
> *Film:* [100 min] Paramount, 1969, distributed by Films Inc. MMA
> *Filmstrip/sound:* "Nature" includes excerpt from *My Side of the Mountain* [Reading for the fun of it: Getting hooked on books series, filmstrip/cassette, 15 min] Guidance Assoc, 1978.
> *Filmstrip/sound:* "Skillstrip—Classification" [*My Side of the Mountain* learning kit series, filmstrip/cassette, 130 fr, activity cards] Films Inc, 1976. op
> *Filmstrip/sound:* "Storystrip 1—Boy in the Wilderness" [*My Side of the Mountain* learning kit series, filmstrip/cassette, 128 fr, activity cards] Films Inc, 1976. op
> *Filmstrip/sound:* "Storystrip 2—To Stay or Go Home" [*My Side of the Mountain* learning kit series, filmstrip/cassette, 138 fr, activity cards] Films Inc, 1976. op
> *Poster:* [17x22 in] Perfection Form, nd.
> *Talking book:* [RC9825] NLSBPH. ESLC
> *Video:* [Great literature film classics series, live-action, 38 min] AIMS, 1979. Note: this is an edited version of 100 min video listed below
> *Video:* "Nature" includes excerpt from *My Side of the Mountain* [Reading for the fun of it: Getting hooked on books series, filmstrip-on-video, 15 min] Guidance Assoc, 1978.
> *Video:* [live-action, 100 min] Paramount, 1969, released Paramount Home Video, 19??.
> *Video:* [Books from cover to cover series, b&w, 20 min] WETA-TV, nd. op

> *About the Book:*

> *Software:* "Finding a Writing Style I" includes discussion of *My Side of the Mountain* [Write On! series] Humanities Software, 198?.

Video: "Jean George, Writing" [Pass it along series, 15 min] GPN, 1985.

See also Jean Craighead George, "Media about Newbery/Caldecott Authors and illustrators."

1959 NEWBERY AWARDS

The Witch of Blackbird Pond by Elizabeth George Speare. Houghton, 1958. Newbery Medal Book.

Audio: [dramatized, record or cassette, 43 min] Miller-Brody, 1970. ESLC, MMA
Audio: [cassette] Listening Library, nd.
Audio: [Book bag series, dramatized, cassette/book] Troll, nd.
Braille: [BR1427] NLSBPH. ESLC
Filmstrip/sound: "Adventure" includes excerpt from *The Witch of Blackbird Pond* [Time out for reading series, filmstrip/cassette] Guidance Assoc, 197?.
Large print: Cornerstone, 1989.
Poster: [17x22 in] Perfection Form, nd.
Talking book: [Ct-BPH(CTC5018)RC or RC22927 or Sd-BPH(CB-2154)RC] NLSBPH. ESLC
Video: "Adventure" includes excerpt from *The Witch of Blackbird Pond* [Time out for reading series, filmstrip-on-video] Guidance Assoc, 197?.
Video: [Storybound series, 15 min] GPN, nd.

See also Elizabeth George Speare, "Media about Newbery/Caldecott Authors and illustrators."

Along Came a Dog by Meindert DeJong. Illustrated by Maurice Sendak. Harper, 1958. Newbery Honor Book.

Braille: [BRA5977] NLSBPH.
Video: [Book bird series, 15 min] GPN, nd.

See also Maurice Sendak, "Media about Newbery/Caldecott Authors and Illustrators."

Chúcaro: Wild Pony of the Pampa by Francis Kalnay. Illustrated by Julian DeMiskey. Harcourt, 1958. Newbery Honor Book.

Audio: [dramatized, record or cassette] Miller-Brody, 1975. ESLC

Filmstrip/sound: [2 filmstrips/2 records or cassettes, 210 fr] Miller-Brody, 1977.

The Family under the Bridge by Natalie Savage Carlson. Illustrated by Garth Williams. Harper, 1958. Newbery Honor Book.

Audio: [dramatized, record or cassette, 40 min] Miller-Brody, 1974. ESLC, MMA
Braille: [BRA9321] NLSBPH. ESLC
Filmstrip/sound: [2 filmstrips/2 records or cassettes, 260 fr/39 min] Miller-Brody, 1978. MMA
Talking book: [RC18427] NLSBPH. ESLC

The Perilous Road by William O. Steele. Illustrated by Paul Galdone. Harcourt, 1958. Newbery Honor Book.

Audio: [dramatized, record or cassette] Miller-Brody, 1977. ESLC, MMA
Filmstrip/sound: [2 filmstrips/2 records or cassettes, 211 fr/35 min] Miller-Brody, 1976. MMA

About the Book:

Filmstrip: "Historical Fiction" includes discussion of *The Perilous Road* [Literature for children series 3, filmstrip/script, 82 fr] Pied Piper, 1971.
Filmstrip/sound: "Historical Fiction (rev ed)" includes discussion of *The Perilous Road* [Literature for children series 3, filmstrip/cassette, about 12 min] Pied Piper, 1983.
Video: "Historical Fiction" includes discussion of *The Perilous Road* [Literature for children series 3, about 12 min] Pied Piper, 198?.

See also William O. Steele, "Media about Newbery/Caldecott Authors and Illustrators."

1958 NEWBERY AWARDS

Rifles for Watie by Harold Keith. Crowell, 1957. Newbery Medal Book.

Audio: [dramatized, record or cassette, about 40 min] Miller-Brody, 1971. MMA
Filmstrip/sound: [2 filmstrips/2 cassettes, 192 fr] Miller-Brody, 1972.
Talking book: [RC16572] NLSBPH.

About the Book:

Filmstrip/sound: "Historical Fiction" includes excerpt from *Rifles for Watie* [Reading for the fun of it: Getting hooked on books series, filmstrip/cassette, 96 fr/16 min] Guidance Assoc, 1976.

Gone-Away Lake by Elizabeth Enright. Illustrated by Beth and Joe Krush. Harcourt, 1957. Newbery Honor Book.

> *Talking book:* [RC10042] NLSBPH.

> *See also* Elizabeth Enright, "Media about Newbery/Caldecott Authors and Illustrators."

The Great Wheel by Robert Lawson. Viking, 1957. Newbery Honor Book.

> *Braille:* [BRA6092] NLSBPH.

> *See also* Robert Lawson, "Media about Newbery/Caldecott Authors and Illustrators."

The Horsecatcher by Mari Sandoz. Westminster, 1957. Newbery Honor Book.

> *Audio:* [abridged, cassette or record, 35 min] Miller-Brody, 1973. ESLC
> *Braille:* [BRA2297] NLSBPH.
> *Filmstrip/sound:* [2 filmstrips/2 cassettes, 199 fr] Miller-Brody, 1974.
> *Talking book:* [TB1149] NLSBPH.

> *See also* Mari Sandoz, "Media about Newbery/Caldecott Authors and Illustrators."

Tom Paine: Freedom's Apostle by Leo Gurko. Illustrated by Fritz Kredel. Crowell, 1957. Newbery Honor Book.

> *Braille:* [BRA1538] NLSBPH.
> *Talking book:* [TB1434] NLSBPH.

1957 NEWBERY AWARDS

Miracles on Maple Hill by Virginia Sorensen. Illustrated by Beth and Joe Krush. Harcourt, 1956. Newbery Medal Book.

> *Audio:* [dramatized, record or cassette, 45 min] Miller-Brody, 1972. ESLC, MMA
> *Braille:* [BRA5797] NLSBPH.

> *Filmstrip/sound:* [2 filmstrips/2 cassettes, 264 fr/33 min] Miller-Brody, 1980. MMA
> *Talking book:* [RC23479] NLSBPH.

The Black Fox of Lorne by Marguerite de Angeli. Doubleday, 1956. Newbery Honor Book.

> *Braille:* [BRA6156] NLSBPH.

> *See also* Marguerite de Angeli, "Media about Newbery/Caldecott Authors and illustrators."

The Corn Grows Ripe by Dorothy Rhoads. Illustrated by Jean Charlot. Viking, 1956. Newbery Honor Book.

> none located

The House of Sixty Fathers by Meindert DeJong. Illustrated by Maurice Sendak. Harper, 1956. Newbery Honor Book.

> *Audio:* [dramatized, record or cassette, 44 min] Miller-Brody, 1973. ESLC
> *Filmstrip/sound:* [2 filmstrips/2 cassettes, 250 fr] Miller-Brody, 1974.
> *Talking book:* [RC16612] NLSBPH. ESLC
> *Video:* [Books from cover to cover series, b&w, 20 min] WETA-TV, nd. op

> *See also* Maurice Sendak, "Media about Newbery/Caldecott Authors and Illustrators."

Mr. Justice Holmes by Clara Ingram Judson. Illustrated by Robert Todd. Follett, 1956. Newbery Honor Book.

> *Talking book:* [TB1486] NLSBPH.

Old Yeller by Fred Gipson. Illustrated by Carl Burger. Harper, 1956. Newbery Honor Book.

> *Audio:* [unabridged, 5 cassettes, 300 min] Books on Tape, 1989. LJ 2/1/90
> *Audio:* [dramatized, cassette or record, 42 min] Miller-Brody, 1973. ESLC, MMA
> *Audio:* [Book bag series, dramatized, cassette/book] Troll, nd.
> *Braille:* [BR7798 or BRA1734] NLSBPH. ESLC
> *Film:* [Film as literature series 2, live-action, 28 min] Disney, 1979. Note: this is an edited version of 83 min film listed below

Film: "Love and Duty, Which Comes First?" [Questions/answers series set 1, live-action, 18 min] Disney, 1975. Note: this is an excerpt from 83 min film listed below

Film: [live-action, 83 min] Disney, 1957.

Filmstrip: [Literary classics series set 1, 2 filmstrips/captions, 134 fr] Disney, 1972.

Filmstrip: [61 fr] Encyclopedia Britannica, 1961. op ESLC

Filmstrip: [Famous stories retold series, 62 fr] Disney, 1961.

Filmstrip/sound: [Literary classics series set 1, 2 filmstrips/2 records, 232 fr] Disney, 1970.

Filmstrip/sound: "Adventure" includes excerpt from *Old Yeller* [Time out for reading series, filmstrip/cassette] Guidance Assoc, 197?.

Poster: [17x22 in] Perfection Form, nd.

Talking book: [RC15325] NLSBPH. ESLC

Video: [Film as literature series 2, live-action, 28 min] Disney, 1979. Note: this is an edited version of 83 min video listed below

Video: "Adventure" includes excerpt from *Old Yeller* [Time out for reading series, Filmstrip-on-video] Guidance Assoc, 197?.

Video: [live-action, 83 min] Disney, 1957, released 1981. PCGV, VM

See also Fred Gipson, "Media about Newbery/ Caldecott Authors and Illustrators."

1956 NEWBERY AWARDS

Carry On, Mr. Bowditch by Jean Lee Latham. Illustrated by John O'Hara Cosgrave. Houghton, 1955. Newbery Medal Book.

Audio: [record or cassette, 42 min] Miller-Brody, 1971. ESLC

Audio: [Book fair series, cassette, 15 min] National Center for Audio Tapes, nd. op

Audio: [Book bag series, dramatized, cassette/ book] Troll, nd.

Braille: [BRA6105] NLSBPH.

Filmstrip/sound: [2 filmstrips/2 cassettes, 197 fr] Miller-Brody, 1972.

Talking book: [RC17659] NLSBPH.

See also Jean Lee Latham, "Media about Newbery/Caldecott Authors and Illustrators."

The Golden Name Day by Jennie Lindquist. Illustrated by Garth Williams. Harper, 1955. Newbery Honor Book.

Braille: [BRA6091] NLSBPH.

Men, Microscopes, and Living Things by Katherine B. Shippen. Illustrated by Anthony Ravielli. Viking, 1955. Newbery Honor Book.

Braille: [BRA3190] NLSBPH.

The Secret River by Marjorie Kinnan Rawlings. Illustrated by Leonard Weisgard. Scribner, 1955. Newbery Honor Book.

Talking book: [RC11956] NLSBPH.

See also Marjorie Kinnan Rawlings, "Media about Newbery/Caldecott Authors and illustrators."

1955 NEWBERY AWARDS

The Wheel on the School by Meindert DeJong. Illustrated by Maurice Sendak. Harper, 1954. Newbery Medal Book.

Audio: [dramatized, record or cassette, 38 min] Miller-Brody, 1969. ESLC, MMA

Audio: [cassette] Listening Library, nd.

Audio: [Book fair series, cassette, 15 min] National Center for Audio Tapes, nd. op

Braille: [BRA6215] NLSBPH. ESLC

Filmstrip/sound: [2 filmstrips/2 records or cassettes, 172 fr/about 45 min] Miller-Brody, 1971. MMA

Talking book: [RC23202] NLSBPH. ESLC

See also Maurice Sendak, "Media about Newbery/Caldecott Authors and Illustrators."

Banner in the Sky by James Ramsey Ullman. Lippincott, 1954. Newbery Honor Book.

Audio: [dramatized, record or cassette, 43 min] Miller-Brody, 1972. ESLC

Braille: [BRA1811 or BRA16194] NLSBPH. ESLC

Film: [Film as literature series 2, 36 min] Disney, 1980. Note: this is an edited version of 105 min film listed below

Film: "Third Man on the Mountain" [105 min] Disney, 1959.

Filmstrip: "Third Man on the Mountain" [Walt Disney stories of yesterday series, 85 fr] Encyclopedia Britannica, 1964. op

Filmstrip: "Two Men on a Mountain" [Walt Disney stories of yesterday series, 71 fr] Encyclopedia Britannica, 1964. op

Talking book: [RC18958] NLSBPH. ESLC

Video: [Film as literature series 2, 36 min] Disney, 1980.

Video: [Books from cover to cover series, 20 min] WETA-TV, nd. op

The Courage of Sarah Noble by Alice Dalgliesh. Illustrated by Leonard Weisgard. Scribner, 1954. Newbery Honor Book.

Audio: [dramatized, record or cassette, 49 min] Miller-Brody, 1978. ALSC, ESLC, MMA

Braille: [BRA8354] NLSBPH. ESLC

Filmstrip/sound: [2 filmstrips/2 cassettes, 200 fr/33 min] Miller-Brody, 1980. MMA

Talking book: [RC26124] NLSBPH. ESLC

Video: [filmstrip-on-video, 49 min] Random, 1987.

About the Book:

Software: "The Literary Mapper: Level 1" includes discussion of *The Courage of Sarah Noble* Teacher Support Software, 198?.

1954 NEWBERY AWARDS

. . . And Now Miguel by Joseph Krumgold. Illustrated by Jean Charlot. Crowell, 1953. Newbery Medal Book.

Audio: [dramatized, cassette or record, 38 min] Miller-Brody, 1973. ESLC, MMA

Audio: [Book fair series, cassette, 15 min] National Center for Audio Tapes, nd. op

Braille: [BRA6089] NLSBPH. ESLC

Film: [live-action, 95 min] Universal, 1966. op MMA

Film: [b&w, 63 min] U. S. Information Agency, 1953. op

Filmstrip/sound: [2 filmstrips/2 cassettes, 190 fr/27 min] Miller-Brody, 1980. MMA

Filmstrip/sound: "Many Lands" includes excerpt from *And Now Miguel* [Reading for the fun of it: Getting hooked on books series, filmstrip/cassette, 16 min] Guidance Assoc, 1976.

Talking book: [RC23489] NLSBPH. ESLC

Video: [Books from cover to cover series, b&w, 20 min] WETA-TV, nd. op

See also Joseph Krumgold, "Media about Newbery/Caldecott Authors and Illustrators."

All Alone by Claire Huchet Bishop. Illustrated by Feodor Rojankovsky. Viking, 1953. Newbery Honor Book.

Braille: [BRA6944] NLSBPH.

Hurry Home, Candy by Meindert DeJong. Illustrated by Maurice Sendak. Harper, 1953. Newbery Honor Book.

Audio: [dramatized, record or cassette, 40 min] Miller-Brody, 1976. ESLC

Braille: [BRA6357] NLSBPH. ESLC

Filmstrip/sound: [2 filmstrips/2 records or cassettes, 242 fr] Miller-Brody, 1977.

See also Maurice Sendak, "Media about Newbery/Caldecott Authors and Illustrators."

Magic Maize by Mary and Conrad Buff. Houghton, 1953. Newbery Honor Book.

none located

Shadrach by Meindert DeJong. Illustrated by Maurice Sendak. Harper, 1953. Newbery Honor Book.

Talking book: [TB1131] NLSBPH. ESLC

See also Maurice Sendak, "Media about Newbery/Caldecott Authors and Illustrators."

Theodore Roosevelt, Fighting Patriot by Clara Ingram Judson. Illustrated by Lorence F. Bjorklund. Follett, 1953. Newbery Honor Book.

none located

1953 NEWBERY AWARDS

Secret of the Andes by Ann Nolan Clark. Illustrated by Jean Charlot. Viking, 1952. Newbery Medal Book.

> *Braille:* [BRA6344] NLSBPH. ESLC
> *Talking book:* [RC11319] NLSBPH. ESLC

The Bears on Hemlock Mountain by Alice Dalgliesh. Illustrated by Helen Sewell. Scribner, 1952. Newbery Honor Book.

> *Braille:* [BRA2477] NLSBPH.
> *Talking book:* [RD6249] NLSBPH.
> *Video:* [Magic pages series, 15 min] AIT, 1976.

Birthdays of Freedom, Vol. 1 by Genevieve Foster. Scribner, 1952. Newbery Honor Book.

> none located

> *See also* Genevieve Foster, "Media about Newbery/Caldecott Authors and Illustrators."

Charlotte's Web by E. B. White. Illustrated by Garth Williams. Harper, 1952. Newbery Honor Book.

> *Audio:* [unabridged, CD or cassette] Bantam, 1991.
> *Audio:* [unabridged, 4 records or 10 cassettes, 192 min] Pathways of Sound, 1970, cassettes released 1976. BKL 5/15/77, CMCE, ESLC, MMA Note: read by the author
> *Audio:* "E. B. White" includes excerpt from *Charlotte's Web* [Books and around series, 3-3/4 ips tape, 30 min] KUOM Radio-University of Minnesota, nd. op
> *Audio:* [I open the door series, 3-3/4 ips tape, 15 min] National Center for Audio Tapes, nd. op
> *Braille:* [BR1318] NLSBPH. ESLC
> *Film:* "Runt of the Litter" [Peppermint stick selection series, cc, 13 min] Films Inc, 1976.
> *Film:* "Wilbur's Story" [Peppermint stick selection series, cc, 15 min] Films Inc, 1976.
> *Film:* [animated, 90 min] Films Inc, 1972. MMA
> *Filmstrip/sound:* "Skillstrip—Sequencing" [*Charlotte's Web* learning kit series, filmstrip/cassette, 90 fr] Films Inc, 1976. op

> *Filmstrip/sound:* "Storystrip 1—Charlotte, A True Friend" [*Charlotte's Web* learning kit series, filmstrip/cassette, 163 fr] Films Inc, 1976. op
> *Filmstrip/sound:* "Storystrip 2—Wilbur, A Terrific Pig" [*Charlotte's Web* learning kit series, filmstrip/cassette, 181 fr] Films Inc, 1976. op
> *Filmstrip/sound:* [unabridged, 18 filmstrips/6 records or 18 cassettes, 1240 fr] Bosustow, 1974. op CMCE, MMA Note: read by the author
> *Filmstrip/sound:* "Fantasy" includes excerpt from *Charlotte's Web* [Reading for the fun of it: Getting hooked on books series, filmstrip/cassette, 15 min] Guidance Assoc, 197?.
> *Large print:* G. K. Hall, 198?
> *Poster:* [21x15 in] Peaceable Kingdom, nd.
> *Poster:* [17x22 in] Perfection Form, nd.
> *Talking book:* [FD7107 or RC7107 or RC8723] NLSBPH. ESLC
> *Video:* [animated, 90 min] Paramount, 1972, released Paramount Home Video 1979. PCGV, VM
> *Video:* "Fantasy" includes excerpt from *Charlotte's Web* [Reading for the fun of it: Getting hooked on books series, filmstrip-on-video, 15 min] Guidance Assoc, 197?.

> *See also* E. B. White, "Media about Newbery/Caldecott Authors and Illustrators."

Moccasin Trail by Eloise Jarvis McGraw. Illustrated by Paul Galdone. Coward, 1952. Newbery Honor Book.

> *Audio:* [cassette, 49 min] Miller-Brody, nd.
> *Braille:* [BRA8714] NLSBPH.

Red Sails to Capri by Ann Weil. Illustrated by C. B. Falls. Viking, 1952. Newbery Honor Book.

> none located

1952 NEWBERY AWARDS

Ginger Pye by Eleanor Estes. Harcourt, 1951. Newbery Medal Book.

> *Audio:* [dramatized, record or cassette, 47 min] Miller-Brody, 1969. ESLC, MMA

Audio: [Book fair series, cassette, 15 min] National Center for Audio Tapes, nd. op
Audio: [Book bag series, dramatized, cassette/book] Troll, nd.
Braille: [BR5962 or BRA5963] NLSBPH. ESLC
Filmstrip/sound: [2 filmstrips/2 records or cassettes, 232 fr, script] Miller-Brody, 1974. MMA
Large print: Cornerstone, 1987.
Talking book: [RC10550] NLSBPH. ESLC
Video: [filmstrip-on-video, 40 min] Random, 1987.

> *See also* Eleanor Estes, "Media about Newbery/Caldecott Authors and Illustrators."

Americans before Columbus by Elizabeth Chesley Baity. Illustrated by C. B. Falls. Viking, 1951. Newbery Honor Book.

> none located

The Apple and the Arrow by Mary and Conrad Buff. Houghton, 1951. Newbery Honor Book.

> *Braille:* [BRA7420] NLSBPH.

The Defender by Nicholas Kalashnikoff. Illustrated by Claire and George Louden. Scribner, 1951. Newbery Honor Book.

> *Braille:* [BRJ1493] NLSBPH.

The Light at Tern Rock by Julia L. Sauer. Illustrated by Georges Schreiber. Viking, 1951. Newbery Honor Book.

> *Braille:* [BRA6641] NLSBPH.

Minn of the Mississippi by Holling C. Holling. Houghton, 1951. Newbery Honor Book.

> *Braille:* [BR1848] NLSBPH. ESLC

> *See also* Holling C. Holling, "Media about Newbery/Caldecott Authors and Illustrators."

1951 NEWBERY AWARDS

Amos Fortune, Free Man by Elizabeth Yates. Illustrated by Nora S. Unwin. Aladdin, 1950. Newbery Medal Book.

> *Audio:* [cassette] Listening Library, nd.

Audio: [dramatized, record or cassette, 44 min] Miller-Brody, nd. ESLC
Audio: [Reading is adventure series, cassette, 12 min] National Center for Audio Tapes, nd. op
Braille: [BRA6930] NLSBPH. ESLC
Filmstrip/sound: "Elizabeth Yates" includes dramatized excerpt from *Amos Fortune* [Meet the Newbery author series, filmstrip/record or cassette, 113 fr/19 min] Miller-Brody, 1976. BKL 12/15/76, CMCE, ESLC
Filmstrip/sound: [2 filmstrips/record or 2 cassettes, 178 fr/46 min] Miller-Brody, 1970.
Talking book: [RC23596] NLSBPH. ESLC
Video: [filmstrip-on-video, 46 min] Random, 1986.

> *See also* Elizabeth Yates, "Media about Newbery/Caldecott Authors and Illustrators."

Abraham Lincoln, Friend of the People by Clara Ingram Judson. Illustrated by Robert Frankenberg. Wilcox, 1950. Newbery Honor Book.

> *Braille:* [BRA5114] NLSBPH.

Better Known as Johnny Appleseed by Mabel Leigh Hunt. Illustrated by James Daugherty. Lippincott, 1950. Newbery Honor Book.

> *Braille:* [BRA5821] NLSBPH.

> *See also* James Daugherty, "Media about Newbery/Caldecott Authors and Illustrators."

Gandhi, Fighter without a Sword by Jeanette Eaton. Illustrated by Ralph Ray. Morrow, 1950. Newbery Honor Book.

> *Audio:* [Reading is adventure series, cassette, 12 min] National Center for Audio Tapes, nd. op
> *Braille:* [BRA396] NLSBPH.

The Story of Appleby Capple by Anne Parrish. Harper, 1950. Newbery Honor Book.

> none located

1950 NEWBERY AWARDS

The Door in the Wall by Marguerite de Angeli. Doubleday, 1949. Newbery Medal Book.

>*Audio:* [dramatized, record or cassette, 39 min] Miller-Brody, 1970. ESLC, MMA
>*Audio:* [cassette] Listening Library, nd.
>*Audio:* [Reading is adventure series, cassette, 12 min] National Center for Audio Tapes, nd. op
>*Braille:* [BRA6074] NLSBPH.
>*Filmstrip/sound:* [2 filmstrips/2 records or cassettes, 182 fr/40 min] Miller-Brody, 1972. MMA
>*Talking book:* [RC22885] NLSBPH.
>*Video:* [filmstrip-on-cassette, 40 min] Random, 1987.

>*See also* Marguerite de Angeli, "Media about Newbery/Caldecott Authors and illustrators."

The Blue Cat of Castle Town by Catherine Cate Coblentz. Illustrated by Janice Holland. Longmans, 1949. Newbery Honor Book.

>none located

George Washington by Genevieve Foster. Scribner, 1949. Newbery Honor Book.

>none located

>*See also* Genevieve Foster, "Media about Newbery/Caldecott Authors and Illustrators."

Kildee House by Rutherford Montgomery. Illustrated by Barbara Cooney. Doubleday, 1949. Newbery Honor Book.

>*Braille:* [BRA6222] NLSBPH.
>*Talking book:* [Nj-B(C1672m)RC] NLSBPH.

>*See also* Barbara Cooney, "Media about Newbery/Caldecott Authors and Illustrators."

Song of the Pines: A Story of Norwegian Lumbering in Wisconsin by Walter and Marion Havighurst. Illustrated by Richard Floethe. Winston, 1949. Newbery Honor Book.

>none located

Tree of Freedom by Rebecca Caudill. Illustrated by Dorothy B. Morse. Viking, 1949. Newbery Honor Book.

>none located

>*See also* Rebecca Caudill, "Media about Newbery/Caldecott Authors and Illustrators."

1949 NEWBERY AWARDS

King of the Wind by Marguerite Henry. Illustrated by Wesley Dennis. Rand McNally, 1948. Newbery Medal Book.

>*Audio:* [dramatized, record or cassette, about 45 min] Miller-Brody, 1971. ESLC, MMA
>*Audio:* [Book bag series, dramatized, cassette/book] Troll, nd.
>*Braille:* [BRA5965] NLSBPH. ESLC
>*Filmstrip/sound:* "Nature" includes excerpt from *King of the Wind* [Reading for the fun of it: Getting hooked on books series, filmstrip/cassette, 93 fr/15 min] Guidance Assoc, 1978.
>*Filmstrip/sound:* "Marguerite Henry" includes dramatized excerpt from *King of the Wind* [Meet the Newbery author series, filmstrip/record or cassette, 85 fr/18 min] Miller-Brody, 1974. ESLC
>*Filmstrip/sound:* [2 filmstrips/2 cassettes, 217 fr/44 min] Miller-Brody, 1973.
>*Talking book:* [RC16570] NLSBPH. ESLC
>*Video:* [filmstrip-on-cassette, 44 min] Random, 1987.
>*Video:* "Nature" includes excerpt from *King of the Wind* [Reading for the fun of it: Getting hooked on books series, filmstrip-on-video, 15 min] Guidance Assoc, 1978.
>*Video:* [Books from cover to cover series, b&w, 20 min] WETA-TV, nd. op

>*About the Book:*

>*Filmstrip/sound:* "Animals (rev ed)" includes discussion of *King of the Wind* [Literature for children series 2, filmstrip/cassette, about 12 min] Pied Piper, 1983.
>*Video:* "Animals" includes discussion of *King of the Wind* [Literature for children series 2, about 12 min] Pied Piper, 198?.

See also Marguerite Henry, "Media about New-bery/Caldecott Authors and Illustrators."

Daughter of the Mountains by Louise Rankin. Illustrated by Kurt Wiese. Viking, 1948. Newbery Honor Book.

> *Braille:* [BRA6115 or IC-BPH(BIL4432)BR] NLSBPH.

My Father's Dragon by Ruth Stiles Gannett. Illustrated by Ruth Chrisman Gannett. Random, 1948. Newbery Honor Book.

> *Audio:* [Stories are for fun series, 3-3/4 ips tape, 12 min] National Center for Audio Tapes, nd. op
> *Braille:* [BRA7124] NLSBPH. ESLC
> *Talking book:* [RC25589] NLSBPH. ESLC
> *Video:* [Readit series, 15 min] AIT, 1982.
> *Video:* "My Father's Dragon and The Hundred Dresses" [Magic pages series, 15 min] AIT, 1976.

Seabird by Holling C. Holling. Houghton, 1948. Newbery Honor Book.

> *Braille:* [BRA6007] NLSBPH. ESLC
> *Talking book:* [Mi-BPH(MSL1115)RM or RC10317] NLSBPH. ESLC
>
> *See also* Holling C. Holling, "Media about New-bery/Caldecott Authors and Illustrators."

Story of the Negro by Arna Bontemps. Illustrated by Raymond Lufkin. Knopf, 1948. Newbery Honor Book.

> *Braille:* [BRA9452] NLSBPH.
>
> *See also* Arna Bontemps, "Media about New-bery/Caldecott Authors and Illustrators."

1948 NEWBERY AWARDS

The Twenty-One Balloons by William Pène du Bois. Viking, 1947. Newbery Medal Book.

> *Audio:* [dramatized, record or cassette, 49 min] Live Oak, 1972. ESLC, MMA
> *Audio:* [cassette] Miller-Brody, nd.
> *Audio:* [Book bag series, dramatized, cassette/ book] Troll, nd.

Braille: [BRA3561] NLSBPH. ESLC
Talking book: [RC23467] NLSBPH. ESLC

The Cow-Tail Switch, and Other West African Stories by Harold Courlander and George Herzog. Illustrated by Madye Lee Chastain. Holt, 1947. Newbery Honor Book.

> *Audio:* "Folk Tales from West Africa" [record] Folkways Records, 1951. op ESLC, MMA
> Note: narrated by Harold Courlander
> *Film:* [Tales for the very young series, animated, 8 min, also Spanish] Learning Corp, 1970.
> *Talking book:* [RC27932] NLSBPH.
> *Video:* [animated, 8 min, also Spanish] Learning Corp, 1970.

Li Lun, Lad of Courage by Carolyn Treffinger. Illustrated by Kurt Wiese. Abingdon, 1947. Newbery Honor Book.

> *Braille:* [BR1782 or BRA10594] NLSBPH.
> *Talking book:* [Nj-B(C84m)RC] NLSBPH.

Misty of Chincoteague by Marguerite Henry. Illustrated by Wesley Dennis. Rand McNally, 1947. Newbery Honor Book.

> *Audio:* [dramatized, record or cassette, 35 min] Miller-Brody, 1973. ESLC
> *Braille:* [BRA14544] NLSBPH. ESLC
> *Film:* "Misty" [live-action, 92 min] 20th Century-Fox, 1961, distributed by Films Inc. MMA
> *Filmstrip/sound:* [2 filmstrips/2 cassettes, 184 fr/27 min] Miller-Brody, 1974.
> *Talking book:* [RC25353] NLSBPH. ESLC
> *Video:* [filmstrip-on-video, 27 min] Random, 1988. ESLC
> *Video:* [Book bird series, 15 min] GPN, nd.
>
> *See also* Marguerite Henry, "Media about New-bery/Caldecott Authors and Illustrators."

Pancakes-Paris by Claire Huchet Bishop. Illustrated by Georges Schreiber. Viking, 1947. Newbery Honor Book.

> *Braille:* [BRA63392] NLSBPH.

The Quaint and Curious Quest of Johnny Longfoot, the Shoe-King's Son by Catherine Besterman. Illustrated by Warren Chappell. Bobbs Merrill, 1947. Newbery Honor Book.

none located

1947 NEWBERY AWARDS

Miss Hickory by Carolyn Sherwin Bailey. Illustrated by Ruth Gannett. Viking, 1946. Newbery Medal Book.

> *Audio:* [dramatized, record or cassette, 49 min] Live Oak, 1972. ESLC, MMA
> *Audio:* [cassette] Miller-Brody, nd.
> *Audio:* [Book bag series, dramatized, cassette/book] Troll, nd.
> *Braille:* [BRA7058] NLSBPH.
> *Poster:* [Study prints set 4, 17x24 in] Horn Book Magazine, 1971-1974. op ESLC
> *Talking book:* [RC22824] NLSBPH. ESLC

The Avion My Uncle Flew by Cyrus Fisher, pseud. (Darwin L. Teilhet). Illustrated by Richard Floethe. Appleton, 1946. Newbery Honor Book.

none located

Big Tree by Mary and Conrad Buff. Viking, 1946. Newbery Honor Book.

none located

The Heavenly Tenants by William Maxwell. Illustrated by Ilonka Karasz. Harper, 1946. Newbery Honor Book.

none located

The Hidden Treasure of Glaston by Eleanore M. Jewett. Illustrated by Frederick T. Chapman. Viking, 1946. Newbery Honor Book.

> *Talking book:* [TB2682] NLSBPH.

The Wonderful Year by Nancy Barnes. Illustrated by Kate Seredy. Messner, 1946. Newbery Honor Book.

none located

See also Kate Seredy, "Media about Newbery/Caldecott Authors and Illustrators."

1946 NEWBERY AWARDS

Strawberry Girl by Lois Lenski. Lippincott, 1945. Newbery Medal Book.

> *Audio:* [dramatized, record or cassette, about 45 min] Miller-Brody, 1971. ESLC, MMA
> *Audio:* [Book bag series, dramatized, cassette/book] Troll, nd.
> *Braille:* [BRA6065] NLSBPH.
> *Filmstrip/sound:* [2 filmstrips/2 cassettes, 199 fr] Miller-Brody, 1973.
> *Talking book:* [RC15118] NLSBPH. ESLC
> *Video:* [filmstrip-on-video, 42 min] Random, 1988.

See also Lois Lenski, "Media about Newbery/Caldecott Authors and Illustrators."

Bhimsa, the Dancing Bear by Christine Weston. Illustrated by Roger Duvoisin. Scribner, 1945. Newbery Honor Book.

none located

Justin Morgan Had a Horse by Marguerite Henry. Illustrated by Wesley Dennis. Wilcox, 1945. Newbery Honor Book.

> *Audio:* [dramatized, record or cassette, 45 min] Miller-Brody, 1975. ESLC
> *Film:* [91 min] Disney, 1972.
> *Filmstrip/sound:* [2 filmstrips/2 records or cassettes, 233 fr] Miller-Brody, 1976.
> *Talking book:* [RC10772] NLSBPH. ESLC
> *Video:* [91 min] Disney, 1972, released 1981.

See also Marguerite Henry, "Media about Newbery/Caldecott Authors and Illustrators."

The Moved-Outers by Florence Crannell Means. Illustrated by Helen Blair. Houghton, 1945. Newbery Honor Book.

none located

New Found World by Katherine B. Shippen. Illustrated by C. B. Falls. Viking, 1945. Newbery Honor Book.

none located

1945 NEWBERY AWARDS

Rabbit Hill by Robert Lawson. Viking, 1944. Newbery Medal Book.

> *Audio:* [dramatized, record or cassette, 50 min] Live Oak, 1972. ESLC, MMA
> *Audio:* [cassette] Miller-Brody, nd.
> *Audio:* [Book bag series, dramatized, cassette/ book] Troll, nd.
> *Braille:* [BRA13266] NLSBPH. ESLC
> *Film:* [live-action, 53 min] NBC, 1968, distributed by CRM. MMA
> *Talking book:* [RC23114] NLSBPH. ESLC
> *Video:* [live-action, 53 min] NBC, 1968, distributed by CRM.

> *See also* Robert Lawson, "Media about Newbery/Caldecott Authors and Illustrators."

Abraham Lincoln's World by Genevieve Foster. Scribner, 1944. Newbery Honor Book.

> *Talking book:* [RC14602] NLSBPH.

> *See also* Genevieve Foster, "Media about Newbery/Caldecott Authors and Illustrators."

The Hundred Dresses by Eleanor Estes. Illustrated by Louis Slobodkin. Harcourt, 1944. Newbery Honor Book.

> *Audio:* [unabridged, record or cassette, 46 min] Miller-Brody, 1975. ESLC, MMA
> *Audio:* [I open the door series, 3-3/4 ips tape, 15 min] National Center for Audio Tapes, nd. op
> *Braille:* [BR1416] NLSBPH. ESLC
> *Filmstrip/sound:* [2 filmstrips/record or 2 cassettes, 222 fr/46 min] Miller-Brody, 1978. MMA
> *Video:* [filmstrip-on-video, 36 min] Random, 1987.
> *Video:* "My Father's Dragon and The Hundred Dresses" [Magic pages series, 15 min] AIT, 1976.

See also Eleanor Estes and Louis Slobodkin, "Media about Newbery/Caldecott Authors and Illustrators."

Lone Journey: The Life of Roger Williams by Jeanette Eaton. Illustrated by Woodi Ishmael. Harcourt, 1944. Newbery Honor Book.

none located

The Silver Pencil by Alice Dalgliesh. Illustrated by Katherine Milhous. Scribner, 1944. Newbery Honor Book.

none located

1944 NEWBERY AWARDS

Johnny Tremain by Esther Forbes. Illustrated by Lynd Ward. Houghton, 1943. Newbery Medal Book.

> *Audio:* [abridged, 2 records or cassettes, 99 min] Caedmon, 1974. ESLC, MMA
> *Audio:* [dramatized, record or cassette, 42 min] Miller-Brody, 1969.
> *Audio:* "American History" includes excerpt from *Johnny Tremain* [Books and around series, 3-3/4 ips tape, 30 min] KUOM Radio-University of Minnesota, nd. op
> *Audio:* [cassette] Listening Library, nd.
> *Audio:* [Book bag series, dramatized, cassette/ book] Troll, nd.
> *Braille:* [BR6225 or BRA8887] NLSBPH. ESLC
> *Film:* "The Boston Tea Party" [Johnny Tremain series, 30 min] Disney, 1966. Note: this is an excerpt from 80 min film listed below
> *Film:* "The Shot Heard 'Round the World" [Johnny Tremain series, 32 min] Disney, 1966. Note: this is an excerpt from 80 min film listed below
> *Film:* [live-action, 80 min] Disney, 1957. MMA
> *Filmstrip:* "Johnny Tremain, Minuteman" [Action stories series, 51 fr] Disney, 1960.
> *Filmstrip/sound:* "Johnny Tremain and the Boston Tea Party" [Stories in American history series, set 1, filmstrip/record, 73 fr] Disney, 1972.
> *Filmstrip/sound:* "Johnny Tremain—Minuteman" [Stories in American history series, set 1, filmstrip/record, 69 fr] Disney, 1972.

Filmstrip/sound: "Adventure" includes excerpt from *Johnny Tremain* [Time out for reading series, filmstrip/cassette] Guidance Assoc, 197?.

Filmstrip/sound: [Learn to read by reading series, filmstrip/cassette] Eye Gate Media, nd. op

Large print: Cornerstone, 1987.

Poster: [17x22 in] Perfection Form, nd.

Talking book: [Ct-BPH(CTC5244)RC or RC22808] NLSBPH. ESLC

Video: "Adventure" includes excerpt from *Johnny Tremain* [Time out for reading series, filmstrip-on-video] Guidance Assoc, 197?.

Video: "The Boston Tea Party" [Johnny Tremain series, 30 min] Disney, 1966. Note: this is an excerpt from 80 min film listed above

Video: "The Shot Heard 'Round the World" [Johnny Tremain series, 32 min] Disney, 1966. Note: this is an excerpt from 80 min film listed above

About the Book:

Filmstrip/sound: [filmstrip/cassette] Current Affairs, nd. op

Software: "Character Sketch I" includes discussion of *Johnny Tremain* [Write On! series] Humanities Software, 198?.

See also Lynd Ward, "Media about Newbery/Caldecott Authors and Illustrators."

Fog Magic by Julia L. Sauer. Illustrated by Lynd Ward. Viking, 1943. Newbery Honor Book.

none located

See also Lynd Ward, "Media about Newbery/Caldecott Authors and Illustrators."

Mountain Born by Elizabeth Yates. Illustrated by Nora S. Unwin. Coward, 1943. Newbery Honor Book.

Audio: [dramatized, 19 min] Miller-Brody, nd.

See also Elizabeth Yates, "Media about Newbery/Caldecott Authors and Illustrators."

Rufus M. by Eleanor Estes. Illustrated by Louis Slobodkin. Harcourt, 1943. Newbery Honor Book.

Braille: [BR6069 or BRA7008] NLSBPH.

Film: "Rufus M., Try Again" [live-action, 13 min] Phoenix/BFA, 1977.

Talking book: [Nj-B(C2055m)RC or RC22091] NLSBPH.

Video: "Rufus M., Try Again" [live-action, 13 min] Phoenix/BFA, 1977.

Video: "Rufus M., Try Again/Ira Sleeps Over" [20 min] Phoenix/BFA, nd.

See also Eleanor Estes and Louis Slobodkin, "Media about Newbery/Caldecott Authors and Illustrators."

These Happy Golden Years by Laura Ingalls Wilder. Illustrated by Helen Sewell and Mildred Boyle. Harper, 1943. Newbery Honor Book.

Braille: [BR4443] NLSBPH. ESLC

Talking book: [RC21200] NLSBPH. ESLC

Television: "Little House on the Prairie" NBC-TV, September 1974-September 1982.

See also Laura Ingalls Wilder, "Media about Newbery/Caldecott Authors and illustrators."

1943 NEWBERY AWARDS

Adam of the Road by Elizabeth Janet Gray. Illustrated by Robert Lawson. Viking, 1942. Newbery Medal Book.

Audio: [dramatized, record or cassette, 61 min] Live Oak, 1980. ESLC, MMA

Audio: [cassette] Miller-Brody, nd.

Braille: [BRA7490] NLSBPH. ESLC

Talking book: [RC23486] NLSBPH. ESLC

See also Elizabeth Janet Gray and Robert Lawson, "Media about Newbery/Caldecott Authors and Illustrators."

"Have You Seen Tom Thumb?" by Mabel Leigh Hunt. Illustrated by Fritz Eichenberg. Stokes, 1942. Newbery Honor Book.

none located

The Middle Moffat by Eleanor Estes. Illustrated by Louis Slobodkin. Harcourt, 1942. Newbery Honor Book.

Braille: [BR5937] NLSBPH.

Talking book: [RC22557] NLSBPH.

See also Eleanor Estes and Louis Slobodkin, "Media about Newbery/Caldecott Authors and Illustrators."

1942 NEWBERY AWARDS

The Matchlock Gun by Walter D. Edmonds. Illustrated by Paul Lantz. Dodd, 1941. Newbery Medal Book.

> *Audio:* [dramatized, record or cassette, 35 min] Miller-Brody, 1969. ESLC
> *Audio:* [cassette] Listening Library, nd.
> *Braille:* [BR6718 or BRA2221] NLSBPH. ESLC
> *Filmstrip/sound:* [2 filmstrips/2 records or cassettes, 125 fr/35 min] Miller-Brody, 1971. MMA
> *Talking book:* [RC10418] NLSBPH. ESLC
> *Video:* [filmstrip-on-video, 35 min] Random, 198?.
>
> *See also* Walter D. Edmonds, "Media about Newbery/Caldecott Authors and illustrators."

Down Ryton Water by Eva Roe Gaggin. Illustrated by Elmer Hader. Viking, 1941. Newbery Honor Book.

> none located

George Washington's World by Genevieve Foster. Scribner, 1941. Newbery Honor Book.

> *Talking book:* [RC15696] NLSBPH.
>
> *See also* Genevieve Foster, "Media about Newbery/Caldecott Authors and Illustrators."

Indian Captive: The Story of Mary Jemison by Lois Lenski. Stokes, 1941. Newbery Honor Book.

> *Braille:* [BRA8753] NLSBPH.
>
> *See also* Lois Lenski, "Media about Newbery/Caldecott Authors and Illustrators."

Little Town on the Prairie by Laura Ingalls Wilder. Illustrated by Helen Sewell and Mildred Boyle. Harper, 1941. Newbery Honor Book.

> *Braille:* [BR4237] NLSBPH.

Talking book: [RC21199] NLSBPH. ESLC
Television: "Little House on the Prairie" NBC-TV, September 1974-September 1982

See also Laura Ingalls Wilder, "Media about Newbery/Caldecott Authors and illustrators."

1941 NEWBERY AWARDS

Call It Courage by Armstrong Sperry. Macmillan, 1940. Newbery Medal Book.

> *Audio:* [unabridged, 7 cassettes, 630 min] Books on Tape, 1987.
> *Audio:* [dramatized, record or cassette, 43 min] Miller-Brody, 1969. ESLC, MMA
> *Audio:* [cassette] Listening Library, nd.
> *Audio:* [Book fair series, cassette, 15 min] National Center for Audio Tapes, nd. op
> *Audio:* [Book bag series, dramatized, cassette/book] Troll, nd.
> *Braille:* [BRA2042] NLSBPH.
> *Film:* [live-action, 24 min] Disney, 1980.
> *Filmstrip/sound:* [2 filmstrips/2 records or cassettes, 195 fr/43 min] Miller-Brody, 1972. MMA
> *Filmstrip/sound:* [Literary classics series, set 6, 2 filmstrips/2 cassettes] Disney, nd.
> *Large print:* Cornerstone, 1989.
> *Poster:* [Study prints set 4, 17x24 in] Horn Book Magazine, 1971-1974. op ESLC
> *Poster:* [17x22 in] Perfection Form, nd.
> *Talking book:* [RC22825] NLSBPH.
> *Video:* [filmstrip-on-video, 50 min] Random, 1987.
> *Video:* [live-action, 24 min] Disney, 1980.
> *Video:* [Storybound series, 15 min] GPN, nd.
> *Video:* [Books from cover to cover series, 20 min] WETA-TV, nd. op

About the Book:

> *Filmstrip:* "Adventure" includes discussion of *Call It Courage* [Literature for children series 3, filmstrip/script, 78 fr] Pied Piper, 1971.
> *Filmstrip/sound:* "Adventure (rev ed)" includes discussion of *Call It Courage* [Literature for children series 3, filmstrip/cassette, about 12 min] Pied Piper, 1983.

Video: "Adventure" includes discussion of *Call It Courage* [Literature for children series 3, about 12 min] Pied Piper, 198?.

Blue Willow by Doris Gates. Illustrated by Paul Lantz. Viking, 1940. Newbery Honor Book.

> *Audio:* [dramatized, record or cassette, 51 min] Live Oak, 1972. ESLC
> *Audio:* "People and Places in the United States" includes excerpt from *Blue Willow* [Books and around series, 3-3/4 ips tape, 30 min] KUOM Radio-University of Minnesota, nd. op
> *Audio:* [cassette] Miller-Brody, nd.
> *Audio:* [I open the door series, 3-3/4 ips tape, 15 min] National Center for Audio Tapes, nd. op
> *Audio:* [Book bag series, dramatized, cassette/book] Troll, nd.
> *Braille:* [BRA6062] NLSBPH. ESLC
> *Poster:* [17x22 in] Perfection Form, nd.
> *Video:* "Roosevelt Grady" includes excerpt from *Blue Willow* [Books from cover to cover series, b&w, 20 min] WETA-TV, nd. op

The Long Winter by Laura Ingalls Wilder. Illustrated by Helen Sewell and Mildred Boyle. Harper, 1940. Newbery Honor Book.

> *Audio:* [Book fair series, cassette, 15 min] National Center for Audio Tapes, nd. op
> *Braille:* [BR4445 or BRA14018] NLSBPH. ESLC
> *Poster:* [17x22 in] Perfection Form, nd.
> *Talking book:* [RC21198] NLSBPH. ESLC
> *Television:* "Little House on the Prairie" NBC-TV, September 1972-September 1984.
> *Video:* [Books from cover to cover series, b&w, 20 min] WETA-TV, nd. op

> *See also* Laura Ingalls Wilder, "Media about Newbery/Caldecott Authors and illustrators."

Nansen by Anna Gertrude Hall. Illustrated by Boris Artzybasheff. Viking, 1940. Newbery Honor Book.

> *Talking book:* [Nj-B(C1957m)RC] NLSBPH.

Young Mac of Fort Vancouver by Mary Jane Carr. Illustrated by Richard Holberg. Crowell, 1940. Newbery Honor Book.

none located

1940 NEWBERY AWARDS

Daniel Boone by James Daugherty. Viking, 1939. Newbery Medal Book.

> *Audio:* [I open the door series, 3-3/4 ips tape, 15 min] National Center for Audio Tapes, nd. op
> *Braille:* [BRA8444] NLSBPH.
> *Talking book:* [Tx-BPH(CBT1271)RC] NLSBPH.

> *See also* James Daugherty, "Media about Newbery/Caldecott Authors and Illustrators."

Boy with a Pack by Stephen W. Meader. Illustrated by Edward Shenton. Harcourt, 1939. Newbery Honor Book.

> *Braille:* [BRA1615] NLSBPH.
> *Talking book:* [TB1156] NLSBPH.

By the Shores of Silver Lake by Laura Ingalls Wilder. Illustrated by Helen Sewell and Mildred Boyle. Harper, 1939. Newbery Honor Book.

> *Audio:* [record or cassette, 44 min] Miller-Brody, 1979. ALSC
> *Braille:* [BR4444 or BRA6196 or BRA14241] NLSBPH. ESLC
> *Large print:* Cornerstone, 1990.
> *Talking book:* [RC21197] NLSBPH. ESLC
> *Television:* "Little House on the Prairie" NBC-TV, September 1974-September 1982

> *See also* Laura Ingalls Wilder, "Media about Newbery/Caldecott Authors and illustrators."

Runner of the Mountain Tops: The Life of Louis Agassiz by Mabel L. Robinson. Illustrated by Lynd Ward. Random, 1939. Newbery Honor Book.

none located

See also Lynd Ward, "Media about Newbery/ Caldecott Authors and Illustrators."

The Singing Tree by Kate Seredy. Viking, 1939. Newbery Honor Book.

none located

See also Kate Seredy, "Media about Newbery/ Caldecott Authors and Illustrators."

1939 NEWBERY AWARDS

Thimble Summer by Elizabeth Enright. Rinehart, 1938. Newbery Medal Book.

Audio: [dramatized, record or cassette, 42 min] Miller-Brody, 1969. ESLC, MMA
Audio: [cassette] Listening Library, nd.
Braille: [BRA8998] NLSBPH.
Filmstrip/sound: [2 filmstrips/record or 2 cassettes, 263 fr/33 min] Miller-Brody, 1978. MMA
Talking book: [RC23207] NLSBPH. ESLC

See also Elizabeth Enright, "Media about Newbery/Caldecott Authors and Illustrators."

"Hello the Boat!" by Phyllis Crawford. Illustrated by Edward Laning. Holt, 1938. Newbery Honor Book.

Talking book: [Tx-BPH(CBT3543)RC] NLSBPH.

Leader by Destiny: George Washington, Man and Patriot by Jeanette Eaton. Illustrated by Jack Manley Rosé. Harcourt, 1938. Newbery Honor Book.

none located

Mr. Popper's Penguins by Richard and Florence Atwater. Illustrated by Robert Lawson. Little, 1938. Newbery Honor Book.

Audio: [unabridged, 2 records or 2 cassettes, 103 min] Miller-Brody, 1975. ALSC, ESLC, MMA
Audio: [I open the door series, 3-3/4 ips tape, 15 min] National Center for Audio Tapes, nd. op
Braille: [BR1297] NLSBPH.
Filmstrip/sound: [2 filmstrips/2 cassettes, 310 fr/41 min] Miller-Brody, 1979. MMA

Talking book: [RC23301 or Tx-BPH(CBT850)RC] NLSBPH. ESLC
Video: [filmstrip-on-video, 42 min] Random, 1985.

About the Book:

Filmstrip/sound: "Humor (rev ed)" includes discussion of *Mr. Popper's Penguins* [Literature for children series 2, filmstrip/cassette, about 12 min] Pied Piper, 1983.
Video: "Humor" includes discussion of *Mr. Popper's Penguins* [Literature for children series 2, about 12 min] Pied Piper, 198?.

See also Robert Lawson, "Media about Newbery/Caldecott Authors and Illustrators."

Nino by Valenti Angelo. Viking, 1938. Newbery Honor Book.

none located

Penn by Elizabeth Janet Gray. Illustrated by George Gillett Whitney. Viking, 1938. Newbery Honor Book.

none located

See also Elizabeth Janet Gray, "Media about Newbery/Caldecott Authors and illustrators."

1938 NEWBERY AWARDS

The White Stag by Kate Seredy. Viking, 1937. Newbery Medal Book.

Braille: [BRA1680] NLSBPH. ESLC
Talking book: [RC23270] NLSBPH. ESLC

See also Kate Seredy, "Media about Newbery/ Caldecott Authors and Illustrators."

Bright Island by Mabel L. Robinson. Illustrated by Lynd Ward. Random, 1937. Newbery Honor Book.

none located

See also Lynd Ward, "Media about Newbery/Caldecott Authors and Illustrators."

On the Banks of Plum Creek by Laura Ingalls Wilder. Illustrated by Helen Sewell and Mildred Boyle. Harper, 1937. Newbery Honor Book.

> *Audio:* [abridged, record or cassette, 45 min] Miller-Brody, 1979. ASLC Notable
> *Braille:* [BR4261] NLSBPH. ESLC
> *Large print:* Cornerstone, 1988.
> *Talking book:* [RC21196] NLSBPH. ESLC
> *Television:* "Little House on the Prairie" NBC-TV, September 1974-September 1982.

> *See also* Laura Ingalls Wilder, "Media about Newbery/Caldecott Authors and illustrators."

Pecos Bill: The Greatest Cowboy of All Time by James Cloyd Bowman. Illustrated by Laura Bannon. Little, 1937. Newbery Honor Book.

> *Audio:* [Folk tales retold series, cassette] ALA, 1971. op ESLC
> *Braille:* [BRA6299 or BRA13445] NLSBPH.
> *Talking book:* [TB1976] NLSBPH.

1937 NEWBERY AWARDS

Roller Skates by Ruth Sawyer. Illustrated by Valenti Angelo. Viking, 1936. Newbery Medal Book.

> *Talking book:* [RC23119] NLSBPH.

> *See also* Ruth Sawyer, "Media about Newbery/Caldecott Authors and Illustrators."

Audubon by Constance Rourke. Illustrated by James MacDonald. Harcourt, 1936. Newbery Honor Book.

> *Braille:* [BRA1195] NLSBPH.

The Codfish Musket by Agnes Danforth Hewes. Illustrated by Armstrong Sperry. Doubleday, 1936. Newbery Honor Book.

> none located

Golden Basket by Ludwig Bemelmans. Viking, 1936. Newbery Honor Book.

> none located

Phebe Fairchild: Her Book by Lois Lenski. Stokes, 1936. Newbery Honor Book.

> none located

> *See also* Lois Lenski, "Media about Newbery/Caldecott Authors and Illustrators."

Whistler's Van by Idwal Jones. Illustrated by Zhenya Gay. Viking, 1936. Newbery Honor Book.

> none located

Winterbound by Margery Bianco. Viking, 1936. Newbery Honor Book.

> none located

1936 NEWBERY AWARDS

Caddie Woodlawn by Carol Ryrie Brink. Illustrated by Kate Seredy. Macmillan, 1935. Newbery Medal Book.

> *Audio:* [dramatized, record or cassette, 45 min] Miller-Brody, 1969. ESLC, MMA
> *Audio:* [cassette] Listening Library, nd.
> *Audio:* [Book bag series, dramatized, cassette/book] Troll, nd.
> *Braille:* [BR7669 or BRA7293 or BRA14346] NLSBPH.
> *Film:* [Wonderworks series, live-action, 104 min] Churchill, 1989. BKL 12/1/89
> *Filmstrip/sound:* "Carol Ryrie Brink" includes excerpt from *Caddie Woodlawn* filmstrip [Meet the Newbery author series, filmstrip/record or cassette, 86 fr/15 min] Miller-Brody, 1976. CMCE, ESLC, MMA
> *Filmstrip/sound:* [2 filmstrips/2 records or cassettes, 193 fr/38 min] Miller-Brody, 1972. MMA
> *Large print:* Cornerstone, 1988.
> *Poster:* [17x22 in] Perfection Form, nd.
> *Talking book:* [Ms-BPH(RC404x)RC or RC22917] NLSBPH.
> *Video:* [Wonderworks series, live-action, 104 min] Churchill, 1989. BKL 12/1/89
> *Video:* [filmstrip-on-video, 38 min] Random, 1986.
> *Video:* [Book bird series, 15 min] GPN, nd.
> *Video:* [Books from cover to cover series, b&w, 20 min] WETA-TV, nd. op

About the Book:

Software: "The Literary Mapper: Level 2" includes discussion of *Caddie Woodlawn* Teacher Support Software, 198?.

See also Carol Ryrie Brink, "Media about Newbery/Caldecott Authors and Illustrators."

All Sail Set: A Romance of the Flying Cloud by Armstrong Sperry. Winston, 1935. Newbery Honor Book.

> *Audio:* [unabridged, 5 cassettes, 300 min] Books on Tape, 1986.

The Good Master by Kate Seredy. Viking, 1935. Newbery Honor Book.

> *Audio:* [I open the door series, 3-3/4 ips tape, 15 min] National Center for Audio Tapes, nd. op
> *Braille:* [BRA4487 or BRA5814] NLSBPH. ESLC
> *Talking book:* [RC25471] NLSBPH. ESLC

> *See also* Kate Seredy, "Media about Newbery/Caldecott Authors and Illustrators."

Honk, the Moose by Phil Stong. Illustrated by Kurt Wiese. Dodd, 1935. Newbery Honor Book.

> *Braille:* [BRA7098] NLSBPH.

Young Walter Scott by Elizabeth Janet Gray. Viking, 1935. Newbery Honor Book.

> none located

> *See also* Elizabeth Janet Gray. "Media about Newbery/Caldecott Authors and illustrators."

1935 NEWBERY AWARDS

Dobry by Monica Shannon. Illustrated by Atanas Katchamakoff. Viking, 1934. Newbery Medal Book.

> *Braille:* [BRA6219] NLSBPH.
> *Talking book:* [RC23168] NLSBPH.

Davy Crockett by Constance Rourke. Illustrated by James MacDonald. Harcourt, 1934. Newbery Honor Book.

> none located

A Day on Skates: The Story of a Dutch Picnic by Hilda Van Stockum. Harper, 1934. Newbery Honor Book.

> none located

The Pageant of Chinese History by Elizabeth Seeger. Illustrated by Bernard Watkins. Longmans, 1934. Newbery Honor Book.

> none located

1934 NEWBERY AWARDS

Invincible Louisa: The Story of the Author of "Little Women" by Cornelia Meigs. Little, 1933. Newbery Medal Book.

> *Audio:* [dramatized, record or cassette, 44 min] Miller-Brody, 1969. MMA
> *Audio:* [cassette] Listening Library, nd.
> *Braille:* [BR6305] NLSBPH. ESLC
> *Talking book:* [RC23477] NLSBPH. ESLC

The ABC Bunny by Wanda Gág. Coward, 1933. Newbery Honor Book.

> *Talking book:* [TB4814] NLSBPH. ESLC

> *See also* Wanda Gág, "Media about Newbery/Caldecott Authors and Illustrators."

The Apprentice of Florence by Anne Kyle. Illustrated by Erick Berry. Houghton, 1933. Newbery Honor Book.

> none located

The Big Tree of Bunlahy: Stories of My Own Countryside by Padraic Colum. Illustrated by Jack Yeats. Macmillan, 1933. Newbery Honor Book.

> none located

The Forgotten Daughter by Caroline Dale Snedeker. Illustrated by Dorothy P. Lathrop. Doubleday, 1933. Newbery Honor Book.

  none located

Glory of the Seas by Agnes Danforth Hewes. Illustrated by N. C. Wyeth. Knopf, 1933. Newbery Honor Book.

  none located

New Land by Sarah Lindsay Schmidt. Illustrated by Frank Dobias. McBride, 1933. Newbery Honor Book.

  none located

Swords of Steel by Elsie Singmaster. Illustrated by David Hendrickson. Houghton, 1933. Newbery Honor Book.

  none located

The Winged Girl of Knossos by Allena Best, pseud. (Erick Berry). Appleton, 1933. Newbery Honor Book.

  none located

1933 NEWBERY AWARDS

Young Fu of the Upper Yangtze by Elizabeth Foreman Lewis. Illustrated by Kurt Wiese. Winston, 1932. Newbery Medal Book.

  Audio: [dramatized, record or cassette, 38 min] Miller-Brody, 1972. ESLC
  Braille: [BRA6084] NLSBPH. ESLC
  Filmstrip/sound: [2 filmstrips/2 cassettes, 203 fr] Miller-Brody, 1973.
  Talking book: [RC23364] NLSBPH. ESLC

Children of the Soil: A Story of Scandinavia by Nora Burglon. Illustrated by E. Parin D'Aulaire. Doubleday, 1932. Newbery Honor Book.

  none located

See also Edgar Parin D'Aulaire, "Media about Newbery/Caldecott Authors and illustrators."

Railroad to Freedom: A Story of the Civil War by Hildegarde Hoyt Swift. Illustrated by James Daugherty. Harcourt, 1932. Newbery Honor Book.

  none located

See also James Daugherty, "Media about Newbery/Caldecott Authors and Illustrators."

Swift Rivers by Cornelia Meigs. Illustrated by Forrest W. Orr. Little, 1932. Newbery Honor Book.

  none located

1932 NEWBERY AWARDS

Waterless Mountain by Laura Adams Armer. Illustrated by Sidney and Laura Armer. Longmans, 1931. Newbery Medal Book.

  Braille: [BRA1927] NLSBPH.
  Talking book: [RC16608] NLSBPH.

Boy of the South Seas by Eunice Tietjens. Illustrated by Myrtle Sheldon. Coward, 1931. Newbery Honor Book.

  none located

Calico Bush by Rachel Field. Illustrated by Allen Lewis. Macmillan, 1931. Newbery Honor Book.

  Braille: [BRA6158] NLSBPH.
  Talking book: [TB4207] NLSBPH.

The Fairy Circus by Dorothy P. Lathrop. Macmillan, 1931. Newbery Honor Book.

  none located

Jane's Island by Marjorie Hill Allee. Illustrated by Maitland de Gorgoza. Houghton, 1931. Newbery Honor Book.

  none located

Out of the Flame by Eloise Lownsbery. Illustrated by Elizabeth Tyler Wolcott. Longmans, 1931. Newbery Honor Book.

>   none located

The Truce of the Wolf and Other Tales of Old Italy by Mary Gould Davis. Illustrated by Jay Van Everen. Harcourt, 1931. Newbery Honor Book.

>   none located

1931 NEWBERY AWARDS

The Cat Who Went to Heaven by Elizabeth Coatsworth. Illustrated by Lynd Ward. Macmillan, 1930. Newbery Medal Book.

>   *Audio:* [dramatized, record or cassette, 45 min] Miller-Brody, 1969. ESLC, MMA
>   *Audio:* [cassette] Listening Library, nd.
>   *Braille:* [BR6277] NLSBPH.
>   *Filmstrip/sound:* [2 filmstrips/2 records or cassettes, 187 fr/45 min] Miller-Brody, 1971. MMA
>   *Talking book:* [Me-BPH(MEC56)RC or RC10555] NLSBPH.
>
>   *See also* Lynd Ward, "Media about Newbery/ Caldecott Authors and Illustrators."

The Dark Star of Itza: The Story of a Pagan Princess by Alida Sims Malkus. Illustrated by Lowell Houser. Harcourt, 1930. Newbery Honor Book.

>   none located

Floating Island by Anne Parrish. Harper, 1930. Newbery Honor Book.

>   *Audio:* "Doll Stories" includes excerpt from *Floating Island* [Books and around series, 3-3/4 ips tape, 30 min] KUOM Radio-University of Minnesota, nd. op

Garram the Hunter: A Boy of the Hill Tribes by Herbert Best. Illustrated by Allena Best, pseud. (Erick Berry). Doubleday, 1930. Newbery Honor Book.

>   none located

Meggy Macintosh by Elizabeth Janet Gray. Illustrated by Marguerite de Angeli. Doubleday, 1930. Newbery Honor Book.

>   none located
>
>   *See also* Elizabeth Janet Gray and Marguerite de Angeli, "Media about Newbery/Caldecott Authors and Illustrators."

Mountains Are Free by Julia Davis Adams. Illustrated by Theodore Nadejen. Dutton, 1930. Newbery Honor Book.

>   none located

Ood-le-uk, the Wanderer by Alice Alison Lide and Margaret Alison Johansen. Illustrated by Raymond Lufkin. Little, 1930. Newbery Honor Book.

>   none located

Queer Person by Ralph Hubbard. Illustrated by Harold von Schmidt. Doubleday, 1930. Newbery Honor Book.

>   none located

Spice and the Devil's Cave by Agnes Danforth Hewes. Illustrated by Lynd Ward. Knopf, 1930. Newbery Honor Book.

>   none located
>
>   *See also* Lynd Ward, "Media about Newbery/ Caldecott Authors and Illustrators."

1930 NEWBERY AWARDS

Hitty: Her First Hundred Years by Rachel Field. Illustrated by Dorothy P. Lathrop. Macmillan, 1929. Newbery Medal Book.

>   *Braille:* [BR6224] NLSBPH. ESLC
>   *Poster:* [Study prints set 4, 17x24 in] Horn Book Magazine, 1971-1974. op ESLC
>   *Talking book:* [RC11649] NLSBPH. ESLC

A Daughter of the Seine: The Life of Madame Roland by Jeanette Eaton. Harper, 1929. Newbery Honor Book.

>   none located

The Jumping-Off Place by Marian McNeely. Illustrated by William Siegel. Longmans, 1929. Newbery Honor Book.

none located

Little Blacknose: The Story of a Pioneer by Hildegarde Hoyt Swift. Illustrated by Lynd Ward. Harcourt, 1929. Newbery Honor Book.

none located

See also Lynd Ward, "Media about Newbery/Caldecott Authors and Illustrators."

Pran of Albania by Elizabeth Cleveland Miller. Illustrated by Maud and Miska Petersham. Doubleday, 1929. Newbery Honor Book.

none located

The Tangle-Coated Horse and Other Tales: Episodes from the Fionn Saga by Ella Young. Illustrated by Vera Brock. Longmans, 1929. Newbery Honor Book.

none located

Vaino: A Boy of New Finland by Julia Davis Adams. Illustrated by Lempi Ostman. Dutton, 1929. Newbery Honor Book.

none located

1929 NEWBERY AWARDS

The Trumpeter of Krakow by Eric P. Kelly. Illustrated by Angela Pruszynska. Macmillan, 1928. Newbery Medal Book.

Audio: [dramatized, record or cassete, 42 min] Miller-Brody, 1969. ESLC, MMA
Audio: [cassette] Listening Library, nd.
Audio: [Reading is adventure series, cassette, 12 min] National Center for Audio Tapes, nd. op
Filmstrip/sound: [2 filmstrips/2 records or cassettes, 194 fr] Miller-Brody, 1977.
Talking book: [RC22916] NLSBPH. ESLC

The Boy Who Was by Grace T. Hallock. Illustrated by Harrie Wood. Dutton, 1928. Newbery Honor Book.

none located

Clearing Weather by Cornelia Meigs. Illustrated by Frank Dobias. Little, 1928. Newbery Honor Book.

none located

Millions of Cats by Wanda Gág. Coward, 1928. Newbery Honor Book.

Audio: [Stories are for fun series, 3-3/4 ips tape, 15 min] National Center for Audio Tapes, 1961. op
Audio: [record or cassette, 10 min, also Spanish] Weston Woods, nd. MMA
Audio: "Picture Book Parade: Beloved Stories in Words and Music 101" includes *Millions of Cats* [record or cassette] Weston Woods, nd. ESLC, MMA
Braille/print: [BR1738] NLSBPH. ESLC
Film: [Picture book parade series, iconographic, also 8mm, b&w, 10 min, also Spanish] Weston Woods, 1955. MMA
Filmstrip: [Picture book parade series 1, b&w, 44 fr, script] Weston Woods, 1957. ESLC
Filmstrip/sound: [filmstrip/record or cassette, 44 fr/10 min, also Spanish or Italian] Weston Woods, 1968. ESLC, MMA
Read-along: [cassette/book] Weston Woods, nd.
Video: [Picture book parade series, iconographic, cc, b&w, 10 min, also Spanish or Italian] Weston Woods, 1955, released 1984. ESLC

About the Book:

Video: [Imagine that series, b&w, 15 min] Twenty-One Inch Classroom, nd. op

See also Wanda Gág, "Media about Newbery/Caldecott Authors and Illustrators."

The Pigtail of Ah Lee Ben Loo by John Bennett. Longmans, 1928. Newbery Honor Book.

none located

The Runaway Papoose by Grace Moon. Illustrated by Carl Moon. Doubleday, 1928. Newbery Honor Book.

   none located

Tod of the Fens by Elinor Whitney. Illustrated by Warwick Goble. Macmillan, 1928. Newbery Honor Book.

   none located

1928 NEWBERY AWARDS

Gay-Neck: The Story of a Pigeon by Dhan Gopal Mukerji. Illustrated by Boris Artzybasheff. Dutton, 1927. Newbery Medal Book.

   Audio: [abridged, record or cassette, 27 min] Miller-Brody, 1973. ESLC
   Filmstrip/sound: [2 filmstrips/2 cassettes, 165 fr] Miller-Brody, 1973.

Downright Dencey by Caroline Dale Snedeker. Illustrated by Maginel Wright Barney. Doubleday, 1927. Newbery Honor Book.

   Braille: [BRA5076] NLSBPH.

The Wonder-Smith and His Son: A Tale from the Golden Childhood of the World retold by Ella Young. Illustrated by Boris Artzybasheff. Longmans, 1927. Newbery Honor Book.

   Audio: [Miami Beach storytelling festival series, 3-3/4 ips tape, 31 min] National Center for Audio Tapes, nd. op
   Braille: [BRA10604] NLSBPH.

1927 NEWBERY AWARDS

Smoky, the Cowhorse by Will James. Scribner, 1926. Newbery Medal Book.

   Audio: [unabridged, 5 cassettes, 450 min] Books on Tape, 1984.
   Audio: [Books and around series, 3-3/4 ips tape, 30 min] KUOM Radio-University of Minnesota, nd. op
   Braille: [BRA6477 or BRA10128] NLSBPH.
   Film: [live-action, b&w, 103 min] 20th Century-Fox, 1946. op MMA

Film: "The Education of Smoky" [live-action, b&w, 11 min] 20th Century-Fox, nd. op MMA Note: this is an excerpt from 103 min film listed above
   Talking book: [RC23452] NLSBPH.
   Video: [Books from cover to cover series, b&w, 20 min] WETA-TV, nd. op
   Video: "The Wild Heart" includes excerpt from *Smoky, the Cowhorse* [Books from cover to cover series, b&w, 20 min] WETA-TV, nd. op

See also Will James, "Media about Newbery/ Caldecott Authors and Illustrators."

1927 NEWBERY HONOR BOOKS

   no record

1926 NEWBERY AWARDS

Shen of the Sea by Arthur Bowie Chrisman. Illustrated by Else Hasselriis. Dutton, 1925. Newbery Medal Book.

   Audio: "Rain King's Daughter and Other Tales from Shen of the Sea" [record or cassette, 41 min] Miller-Brody, 1973. ESLC
   Audio: [dramatized, record or cassette, 45 min] Miller-Brody, 1971. ESLC
   Braille: [BR6324] NLSBPH.
   Filmstrip/sound: [series 1, 2 filmstrips/2 cassettes, 124 fr] Miller-Brody, 1971.
   Filmstrip/sound: [series 2, 2 filmstrips/2 cassettes, 168 fr] Miller-Brody, 1974.
   Filmstrip/sound: [series 3, 2 filmstrips/2 cassettes, 148 fr] Miller-Brody, 1974.
   Talking book: [RC16323] NLSBPH.

Voyagers: Being Legends and Romances of Atlantic Discovery by Padraic Colum. Illustrated by Wilfred Jones. Macmillan, 1925. Newbery Honor Book.

   none located

1925 NEWBERY AWARDS

Tales from Silver Lands by Charles Finger. Illustrated by Paul Honoré. Doubleday, 1924. Newbery Medal Book.

> *Audio:* "Calabash Man and Other Tales from Silver Lands" [record or cassette, 45 min] Miller-Brody, 1973. ESLC
>
> *Audio:* "Magic Ball and Other Tales from Silver Lands" [record or cassette, 21 min] Miller-Brody, 1970. ESLC
>
> *Audio:* [cassette] Listening Library, nd.
>
> *Braille:* [BRA9540] NLSBPH. ESLC
>
> *Filmstrip/sound:* "The Magic Ball and Other Tales from Silver Lands" [2 Filmstrips/2 cassettes, 150 fr] Miller-Brody, 1972.
>
> *Talking book:* [RC24830] NLSBPH. ESLC

The Dream Coach by Anne Parrish and Dillwyn Parrish. Macmillan, 1924. Newbery Honor Book.

> none located

Nicholas: A Manhattan Christmas Story by Anne Carroll Moore. Illustrated by Jay Van Everen. Putnam, 1924. Newbery Honor Book.

> none located

1924 NEWBERY AWARDS

The Dark Frigate by Charles Boardman Hawes. Illustrated by Anton Otto Fischer. Atlantic, 1923. Newbery Medal Book.

> *Audio:* [dramatized, record or cassette, 44 min] Miller-Brody, 1972. ESLC
>
> *Braille:* [BRA1242] NLSBPH.
>
> *Filmstrip/sound:* [2 filmstrips/2 records or cassettes, 235 fr] Miller-Brody, 1976.
>
> *Talking book:* [Ct-BPH(CTC5343)RC or RC23407]. NLSBPH.

1924 NEWBERY HONOR BOOKS

no record

1923 NEWBERY AWARDS

The Voyages of Doctor Dolittle by Hugh Lofting. Stokes, 1922. Newbery Medal Book.

> *Audio:* [cassette, 45 min] Miller-Brody, nd.
>
> *Braille:* [BR4017 or BRA55 or BRA13521] NLSBPH.
>
> *Film:* "Talk to the Animals" [live-action, Peppermint stick selection series, 10 min] Films Inc, 1978. Note: this is an excerpt from 152 min film listed below
>
> *Film:* "Pushmi-Pullyu" [live-action, Peppermint stick selection series, 11 min] Films Inc, 1976. Note: this is an excerpt from 152 min film listed below
>
> *Film:* "Doctor Dolittle" [live-action, 152 min] 20th Century-Fox, 1968.
>
> *Filmstrip:* "Dr. Dolittle: The Man Who Talks with Animals" [73 fr] Encyclopedia Britannica, 1967. op
>
> *Filmstrip/sound:* "Skillstrip—Note Taking" [Doctor Dolittle learning kit series, filmstrip/cassette, 100 fr] Films Inc, 1976. op
>
> *Filmstrip/sound:* "Storystrip 1—Talk to the Animals" [Doctor Dolittle learning kit series, filmstrip/cassette, 179 fr] Films Inc, 1976. op
>
> *Filmstrip/sound:* "Storystrip 2—In Search of Adventure" [Doctor Dolittle learning kit series, filmstrip/cassette, 183 fr] Films Inc, 1976. op
>
> *Filmstrip/sound:* [2 filmstrips/2 records or cassettes, 237 fr/46 min] Miller-Brody, 1976. BKL 5/15/77, CMCE, L
>
> *Filmstrip/sound:* [Classics for younger children series, 2 filmstrips/cassette, 39 min] Encyclopedia Britannica, nd. op
>
> *Talking book:* [RC28256] NLSBPH.
>
> *Video:* "Doctor Dolittle" [live-action, 144 min] 20th Century-Fox, 1968, released CBS/FOX Video, nd.

About the Book:

> *Filmstrip/sound:* "Fantasy (rev ed)" includes discussion of *The Voyages of Doctor Dolittle* [Literature for children series 1, filmstrip/cassette, about 12 min] Pied Piper, 1983.
>
> *Video:* "Fantasy" includes discussion of *The Voyages of Doctor Dolittle* [Literature for children series 1, about 12 min] Pied Piper, 198?.

1923 NEWBERY HONOR BOOKS

no record

1922 NEWBERY AWARDS

The Story of Mankind by Hendrik Willem Van Loon. Boni, 1921. Newbery Medal Book.

> *Audio:* [12 cassettes] Random, nd.
> *Braille:* [BR1626 or BRA10625] NLSBPH.
> *Talking book:* [RC17628] NLSBPH.

Cedric the Forester by Bernard G. Marshall. Appleton, 1921. Newbery Honor Book.

> none located

The Golden Fleece and the Heroes Who Lived before Achilles by Padraic Colum. Illustrated by Willy Pogany. Macmillan, 1921. Newbery Honor Book.

> *Audio:* "The Twelve Labors of Hercules" [abridged, record or cassette] Caedmon, 1968. ESLC, MMA
> *Talking book:* [RC14881] NLSBPH. ESLC

The Great Quest by Charles B. Hawes. Illustrated by George Varian. Little, 1921. Newbery Honor Book.

> none located

The Old Tobacco Shop: A True Account of What Befell a Little Boy in Search of Adventure by William Bowen. Illustrated by Reginald Birch. Macmillan, 1921. Newbery Honor Book.

> none located

The Windy Hill by Cornelia Meigs. Macmillan, 1921. Newbery Honor Book.

> none located

CALDECOTT MEDIA: MEDAL AND HONOR BOOKS
1992-1938

1992 CALDECOTT AWARDS

Tuesday by David Wiesner. Clarion, 1991. Caldecott Medal Book.

> none located

Tar Beach by Faith Ringgold. Crown, 1991. Caldecott Honor Book.

> none located

1991 CALDECOTT AWARDS

Black and White by David Macaulay. Houghton, 1990. Caldecott Medal Book.

> none located

> *See also* David Macaulay, "Media about Newbery/Caldecott Authors and Illustrators."

"More, More, More," Said the Baby: 3 Love Stories by Vera B. Williams. Greenwillow, 1990. Caldecott Honor Book.

> none located

> *See also* Vera B. Williams, "Media about Newbery/Caldecott Authors and Illustrators."

Puss in Boots translated from the French of Charles Perrault by Malcolm Arthur. Illustrated by Fred Marcellino. Farrar, 1990. Caldecott Honor Book.

> none located

1990 CALDECOTT AWARDS

Lon Po Po: A Red-Riding Hood Story from China translated and illustrated by Ed Young. Philomel, 1989. Caldecott Medal Book.

> none located

Bill Peet: An Autobiography by Bill Peet. Houghton, 1989. Caldecott Honor Book.

> *Talking book:* [RC31287] NLSBPH.

> *See also* Bill Peet, "Media about Newbery/Caldecott Authors and Illustrators."

Color Zoo by Lois Ehlert. Lippincott, 1989. Caldecott Honor Book.

> none located

Hershel and the Hanukkah Goblins by Eric Kimmel. Illustrated by Trina Schart Hyman. Holiday, 1989. Caldecott Honor Book.

> *Talking book:* [RC31281] NLSBPH.

> *See also* Trina Schart Hyman, "Media about Newbery/Caldecott Authors and illustrators."

The Talking Eggs: A Folktale from the American South retold by Robert D. San Souci. Illustrated by Jerry Pinkney. Dial, 1989. Caldecott Honor Book.

> *Filmstrip/sound:* [filmstrip/cassette] American School, 1991. BKL 6/15/91

Read-along: [cassette/book] Random, 1990.
Video: [iconographic, 21 min] American School, 1991. BKL 6/15/91

See also Jerry Pinkney, "Media about Newbery/ Caldecott Authors and Illustrators."

1989 CALDECOTT AWARDS

Song and Dance Man by Karen Ackerman. Illustrated by Stephen Gammell. Knopf, 1988. Caldecott Medal Book.

> *Audio:* [cassette, 8 min] American School, 1990. ALSC
> *Braille:* [BR7544] NLSBPH.
> *Filmstrip/sound:* [filmstrip/cassette, 80 fr/8 min] American School, 1990. ALSC, BKL 9/ 15/90, SLJ 1/91
> *Read-along:* [cassette/book, 8 min] American School, 1990. ALSC
> *Video:* [iconographic, 8 min] American School, 1990. BKL 9/15/90, SLJ 1/91

The Boy of the Three-Year Nap by Dianne Snyder. Illustrated by Allen Say. Houghton, 1988. Caldecott Honor Book.

> *Braille/print:* [PB/BR7542] NLSBPH.

Free Fall. Illustrated by David Wiesner. Lothrop, 1988. Caldecott Honor Book.

> *Filmstrip/sound:* [filmstrip/cassette, 10 min] American School, 1990. SLJ 1/91
> *Video:* [iconographic, 10 min] American School, 1990. SLJ 1/91

Goldilocks and the Three Bears retold and illustrated by James Marshall. Dial, 1988. Caldecott Honor Book.

> *Film:* [animated, 8 min] Weston Woods, 1990.
> *Video:* [animated, 8 min] Weston Woods, 1990.

See also James Marshall, "Media about Newbery/Caldecott Authors and Illustrators."

Mirandy and Brother Wind by Patricia McKissack. Illustrated by Jerry Pinkney. Knopf, 1988. Caldecott Honor Book.

> *Braille/print:* [PB/BR7545] NLSBPH.

See also Jerry Pinkney, "Media about Newbery/ Caldecott Authors and Illustrators."

1988 CALDECOTT AWARDS

Owl Moon by Jane Yolen. Illustrated by John Schoenherr. Philomel, 1987. Caldecott Medal Book.

> *Audio:* [cassette] Weston Woods, 198?.
> *Film:* [iconographic, 9 min] Weston Woods, 1989. BKL 7/90, BKL/E, SLJ 10/90
> *Filmstrip/sound:* [filmstrip/cassette, 43 fr/8 min] Weston Woods, 1989. ALSC, BKL 3/ 15/90, ESLC
> *Read-along:* [cassette/book, 9 min] Weston Woods, 1989. ALSC
> *Video:* "Owl Moon and Other Stories" [35 min] Children's Circle, 1990.
> *Video:* [iconographic, 9 min] Weston Woods, 1989. BKL 7/90, BKL/E, SLJ 10/90

See also Jane Yolen and John Schoenherr, "Media about Newbery/Caldecott Authors and Illustrators."

Mufaro's Beautiful Daughters: An African Tale retold and illustrated by John Steptoe. Lothrop, 1987. Caldecott Honor Book.

> *Audio:* [cassette] Weston Woods, 198?.
> *Film:* [iconographic, 14 min] Weston Woods, 1988. SLJ 10/89, VRG Winter 1990
> *Filmstrip/sound:* [filmstrip/cassette, 60 fr/14 min] Weston Woods, 1989. ALSC, BKL 3/ 15/90
> *Read-along:* [cassette/book, 14 min] Weston Woods, 1988. ALSC
> *Talking book:* [RC26453] NLSBPH.
> *Video:* [iconographic, 14 min] Weston Woods, 1988. ESLC, SLJ 10/89, VRG Winter 1990
> *Video:* [Reading rainbow series, 30 min] GPN, 198?.

1987 CALDECOTT AWARDS

Hey, Al by Arthur Yorinks. Illustrated by Richard Egielski. Farrar, 1986. Caldecott Medal Book.

> *Braille/print:* [BR7117] NLSBPH. ESLC

Filmstrip/sound: [filmstrip/cassette, 67 fr/10 min] Random, 1988. ALSC, BKL 9/15/89
Read-along: [cassette/book] Random, 198?.

See also Richard Egielski, "Media about Newbery/Caldecott Authors and Illustrators."

Alphabatics by Suse MacDonald. Bradbury, 1986. Caldecott Honor Book.

Braille/print: [BR7141] NLSBPH.
Filmstrip/sound: [filmstrip/cassette, 142 fr/16 min] Miller-Brody, 1988. ALSC, BKL/E
Read-along: [cassette/book] Random, 198?.
Video: [filmstrip-on-video, 16 min] Random, 1988. BKL/E

Rumpelstiltskin retold and illustrated by Paul O. Zelinsky. Dutton, 1986. Caldecott Honor Book.

Braille/print: [BR7108] NLSBPH. ESLC
Filmstrip/sound: [filmstrip/cassette, 86 fr/11 min] Random, 1988. ALSC, ESLC
Read-along: [cassette/book] Random, 198?.
Talking book: [RC25470] NLSBPH. ESLC
Video: [filmstrip-on-video, 10 min] Random, 1989. ESLC
Video: [Reading rainbow series, 30 min] GPN, 198?.

The Village of Round and Square Houses by Ann Grifalconi. Little, 1986. Caldecott Honor Book.

Audio: [cassette] Weston Woods, 198?.
Film: [iconographic, 12 min] Weston Woods, 1989. BKL 5/15/90, SLJ 8/90
Filmstrip/sound: [filmstrip/cassette, 90 fr/16 min] Weston Woods, 1988. ALSC, ESLC
Read-along: [cassette/book] Weston Woods, 198?.
Talking book: [RC26440] NLSBPH.
Video: [iconographic, 12 min] Weston Woods, 1989. BKL 5/15/90, SLJ 8/90

1986 CALDECOTT AWARDS

The Polar Express by Chris Van Allsburg. Houghton, 1985. Caldecott Medal Book.

Braille: [BR6467] NLSBPH. ESLC
Filmstrip/sound: [filmstrip/cassette, 70 fr/12 min] Random, 1987. ALSC, SLJ 10/90

Poster: [18x24 in] Peaceable Kingdom, 198?.
Read-along: [cassette/book, 10 min] Listening Library, 1989.
Read-along: [cassette/book, 12 min] Random, 1986. ESLC
Talking book: [RC23625] NLSBPH. ESLC
Video: [filmstrip-on-video, 12 min] Random, 1988. SLJ 10/90

See also Chris Van Allsburg, "Media about Newbery/Caldecott Authors and Illustrators."

King Bidgood's in the Bathtub by Audrey Wood. Illustrated by Don Wood. Harcourt, 1985. Caldecott Honor Book.

Audio: [cassette] Harcourt 1991.
Audio: "The Napping House" includes *King Bidgood's in the Bathtub* [cassette] Caedmon, 1987.
Filmstrip/sound: [filmstrip/cassette, 79 fr/8 min] Random, 1987. ALSC, ESLC
Poster: [18x24 in] Peaceable Kingdom, 198?.
Read-along: [book/cassette, 8 min] Random, 1986. ESLC
Talking book: [RC24651] NLSBPH. ESLC
Video: [filmstrip-on-video, 8 min] Random, 1988. ESLC

The Relatives Came by Cynthia Rylant. Illustrated by Stephen Gammell. Bradbury, 1985. Caldecott Honor Book.

Braille/print: [BR6124] NLSBPH.
Filmstrip/sound: [filmstrip/cassette, 70 fr/8 min] Miller-Brody, 1986. ALSC, SLJ 4/88
Read-along: [cassette/book] Random, 198?.
Video: [filmstrip-on-video, 8 min] Random, 1988.

See also Cynthia Rylant, "Media about Newbery/Caldecott Authors and Illustrators."

1985 CALDECOTT AWARDS

Saint George and the Dragon retold by Margaret Hodges. Illustrated by Trina Schart Hyman. Little, 1984. Caldecott Medal Book.

Filmstrip/sound: [filmstrip/cassette, 89 fr/12 min] Miller-Brody, 1985. ALSC, ESLC
Poster: [18x24 in] Peaceable Kingdom, 198?.

Read-along: [cassette/book] Random, 198?.
Talking book: [RC22236] NLSBPH. ESLC
Video: [filmstrip-on-video, 12 min] Random, 1987.

> *See also* Trina Schart Hyman, "Media about Newbery/Caldecott Authors and illustrators."

Hansel and Gretel retold by Rika Lesser. Illustrated by Paul O. Zelinsky. Dodd, 1984. Caldecott Honor Book.

> *Audio:* [cassette] Random, 198?.
> *Filmstrip/sound:* [filmstrip/cassette, 92 fr/15 min] Miller-Brody, 1985. ALSC, ESLC
> *Read-along:* [cassette/book, 15 min] Random, 198?. ESLC
> *Talking book:* [RC22393] NLSBPH. ESLC
> *Video:* [filmstrip-on-video, 15 min] Random, 198?.

Have You Seen My Duckling? by Nancy Tafuri. Greenwillow, 1984. Caldecott Honor Book.

> *Filmstrip/sound:* [filmstrip/cassette, 61 fr/5 min] Miller-Brody, 1985. ESLC

The Story of Jumping Mouse: A Native American Legend retold and illustrated by John Steptoe. Lothrop, 1984. Caldecott Honor Book.

> *Filmstrip/sound:* [filmstrip/cassette, 91 fr/14 min] Miller-Brody, 1985. BKL/E, ESLC
> *Read-along:* [cassette/book, 15 min] Random, 198?. ESLC
> *Talking book:* [RC23246] NLSBPH. ESLC

1984 CALDECOTT AWARDS

The Glorious Flight: Across the Channel with Louis Blériot by Alice and Martin Provensen. Viking, 1983. Caldecott Medal Book.

> *Filmstrip/sound:* [filmstrip/cassette, 52 fr/10 min] Live Oak, 1984. ESLC
> *Read-along:* [cassette/book, 8 min] Live Oak, 1987. ESLC
> *Video:* [iconographic, 10 min] Live Oak, 1988. ESLC
> *Video:* [filmstrip-on-video, 10 min] Random, 198?.

Little Red Riding Hood retold and illustrated by Trina Schart Hyman. Holiday, 1983. Caldecott Honor Book.

> *Braille:* [BR3030] NLSBPH. ESLC
> *Filmstrip/sound:* [filmstrip/cassette, 54 fr/13 min] Listening Library, 1984. ESLC

> *See also* Trina Schart Hyman, "Media about Newbery/Caldecott Authors and illustrators."

Ten, Nine, Eight by Molly Bang. Greenwillow, 1983. Caldecott Honor Book.

> *Audio:* [cassette, 3 min] Miller-Brody, 1984. ESLC
> *Filmstrip/sound:* [filmstrip/cassette, 37 fr/4 min] Miller-Brody, 1984. ALSC, ESLC
> *Read-along:* [cassette/book] American School, 198?.
> *Video:* "Introduction to Letters and Numbers" includes *Ten, Nine, Eight* [17 min] Random, 1985. ESLC

1983 CALDECOTT AWARDS

Shadow translated from the French of Blaise Cendrars and illustrated by Marcia Brown. Scribner, 1982. Caldecott Medal Book.

> *Audio:* [cassette, 9 min] Weston Woods, 1983. ALSC Note: read by Marcia Brown
> *Filmstrip/sound:* [filmstrip/cassette, 33 fr/9 min] Weston Woods, 1983. ALSC
> *Read-along:* [cassette/book] Weston Woods, 198?.

> *See also* Marcia Brown, "Media about Newbery/Caldecott Authors and Illustrators."

A Chair for My Mother by Vera B. Williams. Greenwillow, 1982. Caldecott Honor Book.

> *Filmstrip/sound:* [filmstrip/cassette, 81 fr/8 min] Miller-Brody, 1983. ALSC, ESLC, L
> *Read-along:* [Read-with-me series, cassette/book, 10 min] Morrow, 1988. ALSC
> *Read-along:* [cassette/book, 8 min] Random, 1983. ALSC
> *Talking book:* [RC22879] NLSBPH.
> *Video:* [Reading rainbow series, 30 min] GPN, 1984.

Video: [filmstrip-on-video, 9 min] Random, 198?.

See also Vera B. Williams, "Media about Newbery/Caldecott Authors and Illustrators."

When I Was Young in the Mountains by Cynthia Rylant. Illustrated by Diane Goode. Dutton, 1982. Caldecott Honor Book.

Filmstrip/sound: [filmstrip/cassette, 58 fr/6 min] Miller-Brody, 1983. ALSC, ESLC, L
Read-along: [cassette/book, 6 min] Random, 1983. ALSC, ESLC
Talking book: [Co-B(CC2336)RC] NLSBPH.
Video: [filmstrip-on-video, 7 min] Random, 1986.

See also Cynthia Rylant, "Media about Newbery/Caldecott Authors and Illustrators."

1982 CALDECOTT AWARDS

Jumanji by Chris Van Allsburg. Houghton, 1981. Caldecott Medal Book.

Braille: [BR5317] NLSBPH. ESLC
Filmstrip/sound: [filmstrip/cassette, 13 min] Miller-Brody, 198?.
Read-along: [cassette/book, 13 min] Random, 1982.
Talking book: [RD18720] NLSBPH. ESLC
Video: [filmstrip-on-video, 13 min] Random, 1986.

About the Book:

Video: [Through the pages series, 15 min] GPN, 1982.

See also Chris Van Allsburg, "Media about Newbery/Caldecott Authors and Illustrators."

On Market Street by Arnold Lobel. Illustrated by Anita Lobel. Greenwillow, 1981. Caldecott Honor Book.

Filmstrip/sound: [filmstrip/cassette, 115 fr/13 min] Miller-Brody, 1982. ESLC
Read-along: [cassette/book, 12 min] Random, 198?. ESLC
Video: "Introduction to Letters and Numbers" includes *On Market Street* [15 min] Random, 1985. ESLC

See also Arnold Lobel, "Media about Newbery/Caldecott Authors and Illustrators."

Outside Over There by Maurice Sendak. Harper, 1981. Caldecott Honor Book.

Audio: "Where the Wild Things Are and Other Stories" includes *Outside Over There* [record or cassette, 42 min] Caedmon, 1977. ALSC, ESLC

See also Maurice Sendak, "Media about Newbery/Caldecott Authors and Illustrators."

A Visit to William Blake's Inn: Poems for Innocent and Experienced Travelers by Nancy Willard. Illustrated by Alice and Martin Provensen. Harcourt, 1981. Caldecott Honor Book.

Braille/print: [BR5501] NLSBPH. ESLC
Filmstrip/sound: [filmstrip/cassette, 151 fr/17 min] Miller-Brody, 1982. ALSC, ESLC, L, MMA
Read-along: [cassette/book, 22 min] Random, 1982. ESLC.
Talking book: [RC19591] NLSBPH. ESLC
Video: [filmstrip-on-video, 18 min] Random House, 1987.

See also Nancy Willard, "Media about Newbery/Caldecott Authors and Illustrators."

Where the Buffaloes Begin by Olaf Baker. Illustrated by Stephen Gammell. Warne, 1981. Caldecott Honor Book.

Filmstrip/sound: [filmstrip/cassette, 110 fr/14 min] Random, 1982. ESLC, L, MMA
Read-along: [cassette/book] Random, 198?. MMA
Talking book: [RC18900] NLSBPH. ESLC
Video: [filmstrip-on-video, 14 min] Random, 1985.

1981 CALDECOTT AWARDS

Fables by Arnold Lobel. Harper, 1980. Caldecott Medal Book.

Braille/print: [BR5081] NLSBPH.
Filmstrip/sound: "Fables II" [filmstrip/cassette, 78 fr/12 min] Miller-Brody, 1985. ESLC

Filmstrip/sound: [filmstrip/cassette, 135 fr/18 min] Miller-Brody, 1981. ALSC, ESLC, MMA
Poster: [18x24 in] Peaceable Kingdom, 198?.
Read-along: [cassette/book, 21 min] Random, 1981. ESLC, MMA
Talking book: [RD17237] NLSBPH. ESLC
Video: [filmstrip-on-video, 18 min] Random, 1987.
Video: "Arnold Lobel Video Showcase" includes *Fables* [filmstrip-on-video, 60 min] Random, 1985. ESLC, PC
Video: "Children's Classics Video Collection" includes *Fables* [filmstrip-on-video, 39 min] Random, 198?.

See also Arnold Lobel, "Media about Newbery/Caldecott Authors and Illustrators."

The Bremen-Town Musicians retold and illustrated by Ilse Plume. Doubleday, 1980. Caldecott Honor Book.

Audio: [Read along library series 8, cassette] Disney, 198?.
Filmstrip/sound: [filmstrip/cassette, 74 fr/11 min] Miller-Brody, 1981. ESLC, MMA
Read-along: [cassette/book, 10 min] Random, 198?. MMA
Video: [filmstrip-on-video, 11 min] Random, 1988.

The Grey Lady and the Strawberry Snatcher by Molly Bang. Four Winds, 1980. Caldecott Honor Book.

Filmstrip/sound: [filmstrip/cassette, 109 fr/10 min] Miller-Brody, 1981. ALSC, MMA
Video: [filmstrip-on-video, 10 min] Random, 1988.
Video: "Children's Classics Video Collection" includes *The Grey Lady and the Strawberry Snatcher* [filmstrip-on-video, 39 min] Random, 198?.

Mice Twice by Joseph Low. Atheneum, 1980. Caldecott Honor Book.

Filmstrip/sound: [filmstrip/cassette, 92 fr/9 min] Miller-Brody, 1981. MMA
Read-along: [cassette/book, 8 min] Random, 198?. MMA
Video: [filmstrip-on-video, 9 min] Random, 1985.

Truck by Donald Crews. Greenwillow, 1980. Caldecott Honor Book.

Filmstrip/sound: [filmstrip/cassette, 32 fr/6 min] Live Oak, 1981. ESLC, MMA
Filmstrip/sound: [filmstrip/cassette] Miller-Brody, 198?.

1980 CALDECOTT AWARDS

Ox-Cart Man by Donald Hall. Illustrated by Barbara Cooney. Viking, 1979. Caldecott Medal Book.

Braille: [BR5914] NLSBPH. ESLC
Filmstrip/sound: [filmstrip/cassette, 34 fr/6 min] Live Oak, 1980. ESLC, MMA
Read-along: [cassette/book, 7 min] Live Oak, 1984. ESLC
Talking book: [RC21584] NLSBPH. ESLC
Video: [iconographic, 8 min] Live Oak, 1988. ESLC
Video: [Reading rainbow series, 30 min] GPN, 1984.

See also Donald Hall and Barbara Cooney, "Media about Newbery/Caldecott Authors and Illustrators."

Ben's Trumpet by Rachel Isadora. Greenwillow, 1979. Caldecott Honor Book.

Filmstrip/sound: [filmstrip/cassette, 120 fr/11 min] Miller-Brody, 1980. ALSC, ESLC, L, MMA
Video: [filmstrip-on-video, 11 min] Random, 1988.
Video: "Children's Classics Video Collection" includes *Ben's Trumpet* [filmstrip-on-video, 39 min] Random, 198?.

The Garden of Abdul Gasazi by Chris Van Allsburg. Houghton, 1979. Caldecott Honor Book.

Filmstrip/sound: [filmstrip/cassette, 64 fr/9 min] Miller-Brody, 1983. ESLC, L
Read-along: [cassette/book, 9 min] Random, 198?. ESLC
Video: [filmstrip-on-video, 8 min] Random, 1987.

See also Chris Van Allsburg, "Media about Newbery/Caldecott Authors and Illustrators."

The Treasure retold and illustrated by Uri Shulevitz. Farrar, 1979. Caldecott Honor Book.

> *Audio:* "Stories from Many Lands from the Picture Book Parade" includes *The Treasure* [cassette] Weston Woods, 1986.
>
> *Audio:* [cassette, 6 min] Weston Woods, 1980. MMA
>
> *Filmstrip/sound:* [filmstrip/cassette, 26 fr/6 min] Weston Woods, 1980. ALSC, ESLC, MMA

1979 CALDECOTT AWARDS

The Girl Who Loved Wild Horses by Paul Goble. Bradbury, 1978. Caldecott Medal Book.

> *Filmstrip/sound:* [filmstrip/cassette, 62 fr/9 min] Miller-Brody, 1979. ESLC, L, MMA
>
> *Read-along:* [cassette/book] Random, nd. MMA
>
> *Video:* [filmstrip-on-video, 9 min] Random, 1985.

See also Paul Goble, "Media about Newbery/Caldecott Authors and Illustrators."

Freight Train by Donald Crews. Greenwillow, 1978. Caldecott Honor Book.

> *Filmstrip/sound:* [filmstrip/cassette, 63 fr/5 min] Miller-Brody, 1980. ESLC, MMA

The Way to Start a Day by Byrd Baylor. Illustrated by Peter Parnall. Scribner, 1978. Caldecott Honor Book.

> *Audio:* [cassette, also Spanish] Southwest Series, 1988.
>
> *Talking book:* [Az-BPH(AZCB1363)RC] NLSBPH.
>
> *Video:* [animated, 10 min, also Spanish] Southwest Series, 1988. CINE, SLJ 4/89, VRG Winter 90

1978 CALDECOTT AWARDS

Noah's Ark by Peter Spier. Doubleday, 1977. Caldecott Medal Book.

> *Audio:* [Stories to remember series, CD or cassette] Lightyear, 1990.
>
> *Audio:* [cassette] Weston Woods, 198?.
>
> *Filmstrip/sound:* [filmstrip/cassette, 67 fr/11 min] Weston Woods, 1978. ALSC
>
> *Read-along:* [cassette/book, 30 min] Dutton, 1989. BKL 1/15/90
>
> *Read-along:* [cassette/book] Weston Woods, nd.
>
> *Video:* "What's a Good Story?: Noah's Ark" [20 min] Coronet/MTI, 1990. SLJ 11/90
>
> *Video:* [Stories to remember series, animated, cc, 28 min] Lightyear, 1989. BKL 12/15/89, BKL/E

See also Peter Spier, "Media about Newbery/Caldecott Authors and Illustrators."

Castle by David Macaulay. Houghton, 1977. Caldecott Honor Book.

> *Film:* [animated with live-action, 58 min] Lucerne, 1983. AFVF, ALSC, CINE
>
> *Film:* [animated with live-action, 34 min] Lucerne, 1983. ALSC Note: this is an edited version of 58 min film listed above
>
> *Filmstrip/sound:* [First choice: Authors and books series, filmstrip/cassette, 35 min] Pied Piper, 1984. ESLC
>
> *Kit:* "The Middle Ages School Kit" [videos/student background materials] PBS, 198?.
>
> *Video:* [animated with live-action, b&w/color, 58 min] PBS, 1983. AFVF, ALSC, BVC, CINE
>
> *Video:* [animated with live-action, b&w/color, 34 min] PBS, 1983. ALSC, BVC Note: this is an edited version of 58 min video listed above

See also David Macaulay, "Media about Newbery/Caldecott Authors and Illustrators."

It Could Always Be Worse retold and illustrated by Margot Zemach. Farrar, 1977. Caldecott Honor Book.

> *Filmstrip/sound:* [filmstrip/cassette, 72 fr/13 min] Miller-Brody, 1978. ESLC, MMA

Read-along: [cassette/book] Random, nd.
Talking book: [RC26910] NLSBPH.
Video: [filmstrip-on-video, 9 min] Random, 1984.

1977 CALDECOTT AWARDS

Ashanti to Zulu: African Traditions by Margaret Musgrove. Illustrated by Leo and Diane Dillon. Dial, 1976. Caldecott Medal Book.

> *Audio:* [cassette, 17 min] Weston Woods, 1977. MMA
> *Filmstrip/sound:* [filmstrip/cassette, 32 fr/17 min] Weston Woods, 1977. ESLC, MMA
> *Read-along:* [cassette/book] Weston Woods, nd.

> *See also* Leo and Diane Dillon, "Media about Newbery/Caldecott Authors and illustrators."

The Amazing Bone by William Steig. Farrar, 1976. Caldecott Honor Book.

> *Film:* [animated, 11 min] Weston Woods, 1985. ALSC, BKL 2/15/86, CINE
> *Filmstrip/sound:* [filmstrip/record or cassette, 111 fr/17 min] Miller-Brody, 1978. L, MMA
> *Read-along:* [Famous author/illustrator series, cassette/book, 17 min] Miller-Brody, 1978. ESLC, MMA
> *Talking book:* [RC11455] NLSBPH. ESLC
> *Video:* "The Amazing Bone and Other Stories" [40 min] Children's Circle, 1989.
> *Video:* [animated, 11 min] Weston Woods, 1985. ALSC, BKL 2/15/86, BVC, ESLC

The Contest adapted and illustrated by Nonny Hogrogian. Greenwillow, 1976. Caldecott Honor Book.

> *Filmstrip/sound:* [Visual anthology of literature series, filmstrip/cassette] Phoenix/BFA, nd.

Fish for Supper by M. B. Goffstein. Dial, 1976. Caldecott Honor Book.

> none located

The Golem: A Jewish Legend retold and illustrated by Beverly Brodsky McDermott. Lippincott, 1976. Caldecott Honor Book.

> *Audio:* [cassette, 10 min] Weston Woods, 1979. ALSC, MMA
> *Filmstrip/sound:* [filmstrip/cassette, 60 fr/10 min] Weston Woods, 1979. ALSC, ESLC, MMA

Hawk, I'm Your Brother by Byrd Baylor. Illustrated by Peter Parnall. Scribner, 1976. Caldecott Honor Book.

> *Audio:* [cassette, also Spanish] Southwest Series, 1988. SLJ 4/89
> *Video:* [live-action, 25 min, also Spanish] Southwest Series, 1988. SLJ 4/89

1976 CALDECOTT AWARDS

Why Mosquitoes Buzz in People's Ears: A West African Tale retold by Verna Aardema. Illustrated by Leo and Diane Dillon. Dial, 1975. Caldecott Medal Book.

> *Audio:* "Why Mosquitoes Buzz in People's Ears and Tales for the Third Ear from Equatorial Africa" [record or cassette, 38 min] Caedmon, 1978. ALSC, ESLC
> *Audio:* [cassette, 10 min] Weston Woods, 1976. ALSC, MMA
> *Braille/print:* [BR5916] NLSBPH. ESLC
> *Film:* [animated, 10 min] Weston Woods, 1984.
> *Filmstrip/sound:* [filmstrip/cassette, 46 fr/11 min] Weston Woods, 1976. ESLC, MMA
> *Kit:* [cassette/poster/book/puppets] Society for Visual Education, 1976. op BKL 5/15/77, CMCE

Read-along: [cassette/book, 11 min] Random, nd.

Read-along: [cassette/book] Weston Woods, nd.

Talking book: [RC22905] NLSBPH. ESLC

Video: "Animal Stories" includes *Why Mosquitoes Buzz in People's Ears* [animated, 30 min] Children's Circle, 1984. BVC, PCGV

Video: [animated, 10 min] Weston Woods, 1984. ESLC

See also Leo and Diane Dillon, "Media about Newbery/Caldecott Authors and Illustrators."

The Desert Is Theirs by Byrd Baylor. Illustrated by Peter Parnall. Scribner, 1975. Caldecott Honor Book.

Audio: [cassette] Southwest Series, nd.

Strega Nona: An Old Tale retold and illustrated by Tomie dePaola. Prentice, 1975. Caldecott Honor Book.

Audio: [cassette, 8 min] Weston Woods, 1977. ALSC, MMA

Doll: "Strega Nona" [13 in] Weston Woods, nd.

Film: [animated, 9 min, also Danish/Swedish] Weston Woods, 1978. AFVF, CINE, MMA

Filmstrip/sound: [filmstrip/cassette, 55 fr/12 min] Weston Woods, 1978. ESLC, MMA

Read-along: [Story hour series, cassette/book, 10 min] Simon & Schuster, 1989.

Read-along: [cassette/book] Weston Woods, nd.

Talking book: [RD8527] NLSBPH. ESLC

Video: "Foolish Frog and Other Stories" includes *Strega Nona* [animated, 36 min] Children's Circle, 1978, released 1985. BVC, PCGV

Video: "Strega Nona and Other Stories" [about 30 min] Children's Circle, 198?. CINE

Video: [animated, 9 min, also Danish/Swedish] Weston Woods, 1978. ESLC

About the Book-into-Film Process:

Filmstrip/sound: "Gene Deitch: Animating Strega Nona" [filmstrip/cassette, 59 fr/13 min] Weston Woods, 1979. MMA

See also Tomie dePaola, "Media about Newbery/Caldecott Authors and Illustrators."

1975 CALDECOTT AWARDS

Arrow to the Sun: A Pueblo Indian Tale adapted and illustrated by Gerald McDermott. Viking, 1974. Caldecott Medal Book.

Audio: "Folktales from the Picture Book Parade" includes *Arrow to the Sun* [record or cassette, 40 min] Weston Woods, 1981. ALSC, ESLC, MMA

Audio: [cassette, 9 min] Weston Woods, 1975.

Film: [animated, 12 min] Films Inc., 1983.

Film: [animated, also 8 mm, 12 min] Texture, 1973. ALSC, CINE, CMCE, MMA

Filmstrip/sound: [filmstrip/cassette, 36 fr/9 min, also Spanish] Weston Woods, 1975. ESLC, MMA

Read-along: [cassette/book] Weston Woods, nd.

Talking book: [Az-BPH(AZCB1074)RC] NLSBPH.

Video: [animated, 12 min] Films Inc, 1983.

Video: [animated, 12 min] Texture, 1973. ALSC

About the Book:

Filmstrip/sound: "Caldecott Medal Winners" includes discussion of *Arrow to the Sun* [4 filmstrips/4 cassettes] Meridian, 1986.

Video: "Caldecott Medal Winners" includes discussion of *Arrow to the Sun* [filmstrip-on-video] Meridian, 1986.

Jambo Means Hello: Swahili Alphabet Book by Muriel Feelings. Illustrated by Tom Feelings. Dial, 1974. Caldecott Honor Book.

none located

See also Muriel and Tom Feelings, "Media about Newbery/Caldecott Authors and illustrators."

1974 CALDECOTT AWARDS

Duffy and the Devil: A Cornish Tale retold by Harve Zemach. Illustrated by Margot Zemach. Farrar, 1973. Caldecott Medal Book.

> *Braille:* [BR6265] NLSBPH. ESLC
> *Filmstrip/sound:* [Famous author/illustrator series, 2 filmstrips/2 records or cassettes, 78 fr/17 min] Miller-Brody, 1975. ESLC, MMA
> *Read-along:* [cassette/book] Random, 1975. MMA
> *Talking book/print:* [RD6868] NLSBPH. ESLC
> *Video:* [filmstrip-on-video, 18 min] Random, 1985.
> *Video:* [Best of cover to cover series, 15 min] WETA-TV, 1974. op

Cathedral: The Story of Its Construction by David Macaulay. Houghton, 1973. Caldecott Honor Book.

> *Kit:* "The Middle Ages School Kit" [videos/student background materials] PBS, 198?.
> *Talking book:* [RD9719] NLSBPH.
> *Video:* [animated with live-action, b&w/color, 58 min] PBS, 1985. AFVF, ALSC, BKL 5/15/90, BVC, CINE
>
> *See also* David Macaulay, "Media about Newbery/Caldecott Authors and Illustrators."

Three Jovial Huntsmen adapted and illustrated by Susan Jeffers. Bradbury, 1973. Caldecott Honor Book.

> none located

1973 CALDECOTT AWARDS

The Funny Little Woman retold by Arlene Mosel. Illustrated by Blair Lent. Dutton, 1972. Caldecott Medal Book.

> *Audio:* [record or cassette, 9 min] Weston Woods, 1973. MMA
> *Braille/print:* [BR5921] NLSBPH. ESLC

> *Filmstrip/sound:* [filmstrip/record or cassette, 38 fr/9 min] Weston Woods, 1973. ESLC, MMA
> *Talking book:* [RC22908] NLSBPH. ESLC

See also Blair Lent, "Media about Newbery/Caldecott Authors and Illustrators."

Anansi the Spider: A Tale from the Ashanti adapted and illustrated by Gerald McDermott. Holt, 1972. Caldecott Honor Book.

> *Audio:* [record or cassette, 10 min] Weston Woods, 1973. MMA
> *Film:* [animated, 10 min] Films Inc, 1983. AFVF, CINE
> *Film:* [animated, also 8mm, 10 min] Texture, 1969. AFVF, BKL 10/1/76, CINE, CMCE, MMA
> *Filmstrip/sound:* [filmstrip/record or cassette, 43 fr/10 min] Weston Woods, 1973. CMCE, ESLC, MMA
> *Read-along:* [cassette/book] Weston Woods, nd.
> *Video:* [animated, 10 min] Films Inc, 1983. AFVF, CINE
> *Video:* [animated, 10 min] Texture, 1969.

Hosie's Alphabet by Hosea, Tobias, and Lisa Baskin. Illustrated by Leonard Baskin. Viking, 1972. Caldecott Honor Book.

> none located
>
> *See also* Leonard Baskin, "Media about Newbery/Caldecott Authors and Illustrators."

Snow-White and the Seven Dwarfs: A Tale from the Brothers Grimm translated from the German by Randall Jarrell. Illustrated by Nancy Ekholm Burkert. Farrar, 1972. Caldecott Honor Book.

> *Braille:* [BR7536] NLSBPH.
>
> *See also* Randall Jarrell, "Media about Newbery/Caldecott Authors and Illustrators."

When Clay Sings by Byrd Baylor. Illustrated by Tom Bahti. Scribner, 1972. Caldecott Honor Book.

> none located

1972 CALDECOTT AWARDS

One Fine Day retold and illustrated by Nonny Hogrogian. Macmillan, 1971. Caldecott Medal Book.

Audio: "Stories from Many Lands from the Picture Book Parade" includes *One Fine Day* [cassette] Weston Woods, 1986.

Audio: [cassette, 5 min] Weston Woods, 1973. MMA

Braille/print: [BR5905] NLSBPH.

Filmstrip/sound: [filmstrip/record or cassette, 27 fr/5 min] Weston Woods, 1973. ESLC

Kit: [cassette/poster/book/puppets] Society for Visual Education, 1976. op ESLC

Read-along: [cassette/book] Weston Woods, nd.

Talking book: [RD20954] NLSBPH. ESLC

Talking book/print: [TB4463] NLSBPH. ESLC

About the Book:

Software: "The Literary Mapper: Level 1" includes discussion of *One Fine Day* Teacher Support Software, 198?.

Hildilid's Night by Cheli Duran Ryan. Illustrated by Arnold Lobel. Macmillan, 1971. Caldecott Medal Book.

Talking book/print: [TB4444] NLSBPH.

See also Arnold Lobel, "Media about Newbery/ Caldecott Authors and Illustrators."

If All the Seas Were One Sea retold and illustrated by Janina Domanska. Macmillan, 1971. Caldecott Honor Book.

none located

Moja Means One: Swahili Counting Book by Muriel Feelings. Illustrated by Tom Feelings. Dial, 1971. Caldecott Honor Book.

none located

See also Muriel and Tom Feelings, "Media about Newbery/Caldecott Authors and Illustrators."

1971 CALDECOTT AWARDS

A Story, A Story retold and illustrated by Gail E. Haley. Atheneum, 1970. Caldecott Medal Book.

Audio: "Folktales from the Picture Book Parade" includes *A Story, A Story* [record or cassette, 40 min] Weston Woods, 1981. ALSC, ESLC, MMA

Audio: [record or cassette, 10 min] Weston Woods, 1972. MMA

Braille/print: [BR6103] NLSBPH. ESLC

Film: [animated, 10 min] Weston Woods, 1973. ALSC, MMA

Filmstrip/sound: [filmstrip/record or cassette, 40 fr/10 min] Weston Woods, 1971. CMCE, ESLC, MMA

Read-along: [cassette/book] Weston Woods, nd.

Talking book: [TB3784] NLSBPH. ESLC

Video: "Strega Nona and Other Stories" includes *A Story, A Story* [about 30 min] Children's Circle, 198?.

Video: "Foolish Frog and Other Stories" includes *A Story, A Story* [animated, 36 min] Children's Circle, 1978, released 1985. BVC, PCGV

Video: [animated, 10 min, also Danish] Weston Woods, 1973. ALSC, ESLC

See also Gail E. Haley, "Media about Newbery/ Caldecott Authors and Illustrators."

The Angry Moon retold by William Sleator. Illustrated by Blair Lent. Atlantic, 1970. Caldecott Honor Book.

Read-along: [cassette/book] Random, nd.

Video: [Sixteen tales series, 15 min] AIT, 1984.

See also Blair Lent, "Media about Newbery/ Caldecott Authors and Illustrators."

Frog and Toad Are Friends by Arnold Lobel. Harper, 1970. Caldecott Honor Book.

Audio: "Frog and Toad" includes *Frog and Toad Are Friends* [Junior cassette library series, 2 cassettes] Listening Library, 1987. Note: read by the author
Film: [animated, 18 min] Churchill, 1985. ALSC
Filmstrip/sound: [5 filmstrips/5 records or cassettes, about 200 fr/30 min] Miller-Brody, 1976. ESLC Note: available as individual filmstrips: "Spring," "The Story," "A Lost Button," "A Swim," and "The Letter"
Poster: [18x24 in] Peaceable Kingdom, nd.
Read-along: [I can read series, cassette/book, 15 min] Caedmon, 1985. ESLC Note: read by the author
Talking book/print: [RD6452] NLSBPH. ESLC
Video: [animated, cc, 18 min] Churchill, 1985. ALSC, BVC
Video: "Arnold Lobel Video Showcase" includes selections from *Frog and Toad Are Friends* [filmstrip-on-video, 60 min] Random, 1985. ESLC, PC
Video: [Tilson's book shop series, 15 min] GPN, 1975.

About the Book-into-Film Process:

Film: "Frog and Toad: Behind the Scenes" [10 min] Churchill, 1988.
Video: "Frog and Toad: Behind the Scenes" [10 min] Churchill, 1988.

See also Arnold Lobel, "Media about Newbery/ Caldecott Authors and Illustrators."

In the Night Kitchen by Maurice Sendak. Harper, 1970. Caldecott Honor Book.

Audio: "Where the Wild Things Are and Other Stories" includes *In the Night Kitchen* [record or cassette, 42 min] Caedmon, 1977. ALSC, ESLC
Audio: [cassette] Weston Woods, nd.
Film: [animated, 6 min] Weston Woods, 1988. ALSC
Filmstrip/sound: [filmstrip/cassette, 48 fr/6 min] Weston Woods, 1986. BKL/E, ESLC

Poster: [18x24 in] Peaceable Kingdom, nd.
Read-along: [cassette/book] Weston Woods, nd.
Talking book: [TB4079] NLSBPH. ESLC
Video: "The Maurice Sendak Library" includes *In the Night Kitchen* [animated, 35 min] Children's Circle, 1989. AFVF, CINE
Video: [animated, 6 min] Weston Woods, 1988. ALSC, BVC, ESLC

See also Maurice Sendak, "Media about Newbery/Caldecott Authors and Illustrators."

1970 CALDECOTT AWARDS

Sylvester and the Magic Pebble by William Steig. Windmill, 1969. Caldecott Medal Book.

Audio: [cassette, 10 min] Weston Woods, 1990.
Braille/print: [BR1267] NLSBPH.
Film: [animated, 10 min] Weston Woods, 1990.
Filmstrip/sound: [filmstrip/cassette, 50 fr/11 min] Weston Woods, 1990.
Kit: [cassette/poster/puppets] Society for Visual Education, 1976. op BKL 10/77, CMCE
Read-along: [Story hour series, cassette/book] Simon & Schuster, 1988.
Read-along: [cassette/book] Weston Woods, nd.
Talking book: [RD13086] NLSBPH.
Video: [animated, 10 min] Weston Woods, 1990.
Video: [Storytime series, 15 min] GPN, 1976.
Video: [Picture book park series, 14 min] AIT, 1974.

Alexander and the Wind-Up Mouse by Leo Lionni. Pantheon, 1969. Caldecott Honor Book.

Audio: "Frederick and Ten Other Stories of Mice, Snails, Fish and Other Beings" includes *Alexander and the Wind-Up Mouse* [record or cassette, 52 min] Caedmon, 1976. ESLC, MMA

Braille: [BRA2850 or BRA4099] NLSBPH. ESLC

Filmstrip/sound: [Sights and sound filmstrips series, filmstrip/record or cassette, 36 fr/7 min] Random, 1978. MMA

Read-along: "Frederick and His Friends" includes *Alexander and the Wind-Up Mouse* [cassette/book, 20 min] Knopf, 1989.

Read-along: [cassette/book, 7 min] Random, nd. MMA

Talking book: [TB3289] NLSBPH. ESLC

Talking book: "Frederick's Fables: A Leo Lionni Treasury of Favorite Stories" includes *Alexander and the Wind-Up Mouse* [RC24444] NLSBPH.

Video: "Leo Lionni's Caldecotts" includes *Alexander and the Wind-Up Mouse* [filmstrip-on-video, 16 min] Random, 1985. ESLC

Video: [Storytime series, 15 min] GPN, 1976.

Goggles! by Ezra Jack Keats. Macmillan, 1969. Caldecott Honor Book.

Audio: [record or cassette, 6 min] Weston Woods, nd. MMA

Braille: [BRA3646] NLSBPH. ESLC

Film: [live-action, 11 min] Coronet/MTI, 1988.

Film: [iconographic, 6 min, also Spanish] Weston Woods, 1974. MMA

Filmstrip/sound: "Stories about Friends" includes *Goggles!* [Literature for children: Introduction to picture books series 7B, filmstrip/cassette, 71 fr/10 min] Pied Piper, 1982.

Filmstrip/sound: [filmstrip/record or cassette, 30 fr/6 min, also Spanish] Weston Woods, 1974. ESLC, MMA

Read-along: [cassette/book] Weston Woods, nd.

Talking book: [TB3288] NLSBPH. ESLC

Video: [live-action, 11 min] Coronet/MTI, 1988. PC

Video: "Stories about Friends" includes *Goggles!* [Literature for children: Introduction to picture books series 7B, about 10 min] Pied Piper, 198?.

Video: [iconographic, 6 min, also Spanish] Weston Woods, 1974. ESLC

See also Ezra Jack Keats, "Media about Newbery/Caldecott Authors and Illustrators."

The Judge: An Untrue Tale by Harve Zemach. Illustrated by Margot Zemach. Farrar, 1969. Caldecott Honor Book.

Braille/print: [BR1434] NLSBPH. ESLC

Film: [Famous author/illustrator series, 7 min] Miller-Brody, 1976. MMA

Filmstrip/sound: [Famous author/illustrator series, filmstrip/record or cassette, 47 fr/5 min] Miller-Brody, 1975. ESLC, MMA

Filmstrip/sound: [Gold media collection, 2 filmstrips/cassette, 29 min] Pied Piper, nd.

Video: [filmstrip-on-video, 29 min] Pied Piper, nd.

Video: [filmstrip-on-video, 5 min] Random, nd.

Pop Corn and Ma Goodness by Edna Mitchell Preston. Illustrated by Robert Andrew Parker. Viking, 1969. Caldecott Honor Book.

Talking book: [TB3298] NLSBPH.

Thy Friend, Obadiah by Brinton Turkle. Viking, 1969. Caldecott Honor Book.

Braille: [BR1433 or BRA2850] NLSBPH. ESLC

Filmstrip/sound: [filmstrip/record or cassette, 28 fr/6 min] Live Oak, 1971. ESLC, MMA
Note: narrated by the author

Filmstrip/sound: [filmstrip/cassette] Miller-Brody, nd. Note: narrated by the author

Talking book: [Nj-B(C1347m)RC or RD14137] NLSBPH.

1969 CALDECOTT AWARDS

The Fool of the World and the Flying Ship: A Russian Tale retold by Arthur Ransome. Illustrated by Uri Shulevitz. Farrar, 1968. Caldecott Medal Book.

Audio: [cassette, 14 min] Weston Woods, nd. MMA

Braille: [BR949] NLSBPH. ESLC

Filmstrip/sound: [filmstrip/cassette, 56 fr/15 min] Weston Woods, 1979. ESLC, MMA

Read-along: [cassette/book] Random, nd.

Talking book: [RC16474] NLSBPH. ESLC

Why the Sun and the Moon Live in the Sky: An African Folktale retold by Elphinstone Dayrell. Illustrated by Blair Lent. Houghton, 1968. Caldecott Honor Book.

> *Film:* [Children's storybook theater series, animated, also 8mm, 11 min] ACI, 1970. MMA
> *Filmstrip/sound:* [filmstrip/cassette, 67 fr/11 min] ACI, 1973. MMA
> *Video:* [Children's storybook theater series, animated, 11 min] AIMS, 1971.

See also Blair Lent, "Media about Newbery/Caldecott Authors and Illustrators."

1968 CALDECOTT AWARDS

Drummer Hoff adapted by Barbara Emberley. Illustrated by Ed Emberley. Prentice-Hall, 1967. Caldecott Medal Book.

> *Audio:* [Anthology of children's literature series, cassette] Troll, nd.
> *Audio:* [record or cassette, 4 min, also Spanish] Weston Woods, nd. MMA
> *Braille/print:* [BR727] NLSBPH.
> *Film:* [animated, also 8 mm, 6 min, also Spanish] Weston Woods, 1969. MMA
> *Filmstrip/sound:* [filmstrip/record or cassette, 34 fr/4 min, also Spanish] Weston Woods, 1968. ESLC, MMA
> *Read-along:* [cassette/book] Weston Woods, nd.
> *Video:* "Five Stories for the Very Young" includes *Drummer Hoff* [animated, 33 min] Children's Circle, 1969, released 1983. BVC, PCGV
> *Video:* [animated, 6 min, also Danish/Dutch/Spanish/Welsh] Weston Woods, 1969. MMA

> *About the Book-into-Film Process:*

> *Film:* "Gene Deitch: The Picture Book Animated" [25 min] Weston Woods, 1976. MMA
> *Video:* "Gene Deitch: The Picture Book Animated" [25 min] Weston Woods, 1976.

See also Ed Emberley, "Media about Newbery/Caldecott Authors and Illustrators."

Frederick by Leo Lionni. Pantheon, 1967. Caldecott Honor Book.

> *Audio:* "Frederick and Ten Other Stories of Mice, Snails, Fish and Other Beings" [record or cassette, 52 min] Caedmon, 1976. ESLC, MMA
> *Braille:* [BR760] NLSBPH. ESLC
> *Film:* [animated, 6 min] Connecticut Films, 1971. op MMA
> *Film:* [6 min] Lucerne, nd.
> *Filmstrip/sound:* [filmstrip/cassette, 47 fr] Miller-Brody, 1974.
> *Read-along:* "Frederick and His Friends" includes *Frederick* [cassette/book, 20 min] Knopf, 1989.
> *Read-along:* [cassette/book, 5 min] Random, 1976. ESLC
> *Talking book:* "Frederick's Fables: A Leo Lionni Treasury of Favorite Stories" includes *Frederick* [RC24444] NLSBPH.
> *Video:* "Five Lionni Classics" includes *Frederick* [animated, 30 min] RH Home Video, 1986. BVC, PCGV
> *Video:* "Leo Lionni's Caldecotts" includes *Frederick* [filmstrip-on-video, 16 min] Random, 1985. ESLC
> *Video:* "Mice Are Nice" includes *Frederick* [Picture book park series, 15 min] AIT, 1974.
> *Video:* [6 min] Lucerne, nd.

The Emperor and the Kite by Jane Yolen. Illustrated by Ed Young. World, 1967. Caldecott Honor Book.

> *Braille:* [BR728] NLSBPH. ESLC
> *Filmstrip/sound:* [Look, listen and read series, filmstrip/cassette, 49 fr/12 min] Listening Library, 1976. CMCE, ESLC, MMA
> *Filmstrip/sound:* [filmstrip/cassette, 38 min] Miller-Brody, nd.
> *Talking book:* [Nj-B(BPH)(C1349m)RC] NLSBPH.

See also Jane Yolen, "Media about Newbery/Caldecott Authors and Illustrators."

Seashore Story by Taro Yashima. Viking, 1967. Caldecott Honor Book.

> none located

1967 CALDECOTT AWARDS

Sam, Bangs, and Moonshine by Evaline Ness. Holt, 1966. Caldecott Medal Book.

> *Braille:* [BR507] NLSBPH.
> *Film:* [live-action, 15 min] Phoenix/BFA, 1976. BKL 5/15/77, CMCE
> *Filmstrip/sound:* [Famous author/illustrator series, filmstrip/record or cassette, 62 fr/ 14 min] Miller-Brody, 1976. MMA
> *Read-along:* [cassette/book] Random, nd. MMA
> *Video:* [filmstrip-on-video, 14 min] Random, 1988.
> *Video:* [live-action, 15 min] Phoenix/BFA, 1976.
> *Video:* "What Mary Jo Shared/Sam, Bangs, and Moonshine" [28 min] Phoenix/BFA, nd.

> *See also* Evaline Ness, "Media about Newbery/ Caldecott Authors and Illustrators."

One Wide River to Cross adapted by Barbara Emberley. Illustrated by Ed Emberley. Prentice-Hall, 1966. Caldecott Honor Book.

> *Filmstrip/sound:* [filmstrip/record, 40 fr/4 min] Educational Enrichment Materials, 1969. op MMA

> *See also* Ed Emberley, "Media about Newbery/ Caldecott Authors and Illustrators."

1966 CALDECOTT AWARDS

Always Room for One More by Sorche Nic Leodhas, pseud. (Leclaire Alger). Illustrated by Nonny Hogrogian. Holt, 1965. Caldecott Medal Book.

> *Braille:* [BR216] NLSBPH. ESLC
> *Talking book:* [RC22447] NLSBPH.

Hide and Seek Fog by Alvin Tresselt. Illustrated by Roger Duvoisin. Lothrop, 1965. Caldecott Honor Book.

> *Audio:* [record or cassette, 7 min] Weston Woods, 1973. MMA
> *Filmstrip/sound:* [filmstrip/record or cassette, 32 fr/7 min] Weston Woods, 1971. CMCE, ESLC, MMA

Just Me by Marie Hall Ets. Viking, 1965. Caldecott Honor Book.

> *Audio:* [record or cassette, 8 min] Weston Woods, nd. MMA
> *Braille/print:* [BR3798] NLSBPH. ESLC
> *Filmstrip/sound:* [filmstrip/record or cassette, 33 fr/8 min] Weston Woods, 1969. ESLC, MMA
> *Read-along:* [cassette/book, 9 min] Live Oak, 1985. ESLC
> *Read-along:* [cassette/book] Random, nd.

Tom Tit Tot: An English Folktale retold and illustrated by Evaline Ness. Scribner, 1965. Caldecott Honor Book.

> none located

> *See also* Evaline Ness, "Media about Newbery/ Caldecott Authors and Illustrators."

1965 CALDECOTT AWARDS

May I Bring a Friend? by Beatrice Schenk de Regniers. Illustrated by Beni Montresor. Atheneum, 1964. Caldecott Medal Book.

> *Audio:* [cassette] Weston Woods, nd.
> *Filmstrip/sound:* [filmstrip/record or cassette, 32 fr/7 min] Weston Woods, 1973. CMCE, ESLC, MMA
> *Poster:* [Study prints set 2, 17x24 in] Horn Book Magazine, 1971-1974. op ESLC
> *Read-along:* [cassette/book] Weston Woods, nd.
> *Video:* [Picture book part series, 15 min] AIT, 1974.

A Pocketful of Cricket by Rebecca Caudill. Illustrated by Evaline Ness. Holt, 1964. Caldecott Honor Book.

> *Audio:* [cassette] Random, nd.
> *Braille:* [BR24] NLSBPH. ESLC
> *Filmstrip/sound:* [Famous author/illustrator series, 2 filmstrips/2 records or cassettes, 100 fr/20 min] Miller-Brody, 1976. ESLC

See also Rebecca Caudill and Evaline Ness, "Media about Newbery/Caldecott Authors and Illustrators."

Rain Makes Applesauce by Julian Scheer. Illustrated by Marvin Bileck. Holiday, 1964. Caldecott Honor Book.

    none located

The Wave by Margaret Hodges. Illustrated by Blair Lent. Houghton, 1964. Caldecott Honor Book.

    Film: [iconographic, also 8 mm, 9 min] Phoenix/BFA, 1968. MMA
    Filmstrip/sound: [filmstrip/record or cassette, 59 fr/6 min, also Spanish] Phoenix/BFA, 1968. ESLC
    Filmstrip/sound: [Folktale series, filmstrip/cassette] Miller-Brody, nd.
    Talking book: [TB4621] NLSBPH.
    Video: [iconographic, 9 min] Phoenix/BFA, 198?

    See also Blair Lent, "Media about Newbery/ Caldecott Authors and Illustrators."

1964 CALDECOTT AWARDS

Where the Wild Things Are by Maurice Sendak. Harper, 1963. Caldecott Medal Book.

    Audio: [cassette, 6 min] Weston Woods, 1989.
    Audio: "Where the Wild Things Are—Outside Over There" [cassette, 60 min] Caedmon, 1988.
    Audio: "Maurice Sendak Soundbook" includes *Where the Wild Things Are* [4 records or cassettes, about 200 min] Caedmon, 1981. MMA
    Audio: "Where the Wild Things Are and Other Stories" [record or cassette, 42 min] Caedmon, 1977. ALSC, ESLC
    Audio: [record or cassette, 5 min] Weston Woods, nd. MMA
    Audio: "Picture Book Parade 119" includes *Where the Wild Things Are* [record or cassette] Weston Woods, nd. ESLC, MMA
    Bookmark: "Your Library: Where the Wild Things Are" ALA, 1988.
    Braille/print: [BR5919] NLSBPH. ESLC

    Doll: "Wild Things Dolls: Bird Lady, Bull, Max, and Monster" [11 in] Weston Woods, nd.
    Film: [animated, 8 min] Weston Woods, 1988. BKL 12/1/89, SLJ 7/90
    Film: [animated, also 8 mm, 8 min, also Dutch/ French/German/Spanish] Weston Woods, 1974. ALSC, BKL 7/15/75, CINE, MMA
    Filmstrip/sound: [filmstrip/record or cassette, 39 fr/5 min, also Spanish] Weston Woods, 1968. ESLC, MMA
    Poster: "Your Library: Where the Wild Things Are" [22x34 in] ALA, 1988.
    Poster: [18x24 in] Peaceable Kingdom, nd.
    Read-along: [cassette/book] Weston Woods, 1989.
    Talking book: [RC22906] NLSBPH. ESLC
    Video: "The Maurice Sendak Library" includes *Where the Wild Things Are* [35 min] Children's Circle, 1989. CINE
    Video: [animated, cc, 8 min] Weston Woods, 1988. BKL 12/1/89, SLJ 7/90
    Video: [live-action operetta, 40 min] Home Vision, 1987.
    Video: [animated, 8 min, also Dutch/French/ German/Spanish] Weston Woods, 1973. ALSC, BKL 7/15/75, BVC, CINE, ESLC, MMA

About the Book:

    Film: "Max Made Mischief: An Approach to Literature" [30 min] Documentaries for Learning, 1977. op
    Film: "Maurice Sendak" includes discussion of *Where the Wild Things Are* [Signature collection, 14 min] Weston Woods, 1965. MMA
    Film: "Gene Deitch: The Picture Book Animated" [25 min] Weston Woods, nd. MMA
    Filmstrip/sound: "Caldecott Medal Winners" includes discussion of *Where the Wild Things Are* [4 filmstrips/4 cassettes] Meridian, 1986.
    Software: "Great Wild Imaginings" includes discussion of *Where the Wild Things Are* [Write On! series] Humanities Software, 198?.
    Video: "Caldecott Medal Winners" includes discussion of *Where the Wild Things Are* [filmstrip-on-video] Meridian, 1986.
    Video: "Maurice Sendak" includes discussion of *Where the Wild Things Are* [Signature collection, 14 min] Weston Woods, 1965.

See also Maurice Sendak, "Media about Newbery/Caldecott Authors and Illustrators."

All in the Morning Early by Sorche Nic Leodhas, pseud. (Leclaire Alger). Illustrated by Evaline Ness. Holt, 1963. Caldecott Honor Book.

    Film: [animated, 10 min] Phoenix/BFA, 1969. MMA

    Filmstrip/sound: [Folktale series, filmstrip/record or cassette, 74 fr, also Spanish] Phoenix/BFA, 197?.

    Talking book: [RD6751] NLSBPH.

    Video: [animated, 10 min] Phoenix/BFA, 1969.

    See also Evaline Ness, "Media about Newbery/Caldecott Authors and Illustrators."

Mother Goose and Nursery Rhymes illustrated by Philip Reed. Atheneum, 1963. Caldecott Honor Book.

    none located

Swimmy by Leo Lionni. Pantheon, 1963. Caldecott Honor Book.

    Audio: "Frederick and Ten Other Stories of Mice, Snails, Fish and Other Beings" includes *Swimmy* [record or cassette, 52 min] Caedmon, 1976. ESLC, MMA

    Film: [animated, 6 min] Connecticut Films, 1969. op MMA

    Film: [6 min] Lucerne, nd.

    Filmstrip/sound: [Sights and sounds series, filmstrip/record or cassette, 30 fr] Random, 1974.

    Read-along: "Frederick and His Friends" includes *Swimmy* [cassette/book, 20 min] Knopf, 1989.

    Read-along: [cassette/book, 3 min] Random, 1976. ESLC

    Talking book: "Frederick's Fables: A Leo Lionni Treasury of Favorite Stories" includes *Swimmy* [RC24444] NLSBPH.

    Video: "Five Lionni Classics" includes *Swimmy* [animated, 30 min] RH Home Video, 1986. BVC, PCGV

    Video: "Leo Lionni's Caldecotts" includes *Swimmy* [filmstrip-on-video, 16 min] Random, 1985. ESLC

    Video: [6 min] Lucerne, nd.

1963 CALDECOTT AWARDS

The Snowy Day by Ezra Jack Keats. Viking, 1962. Caldecott Medal Book.

    Audio: [cassette] Random, nd.

    Audio: [record or cassette, 6 min] Weston Woods, nd. MMA

    Audio: "Bedtime Stories from the Picture Book Parade" includes *The Snowy Day* [cassette] Weston Woods, nd.

    Audio: "Picture Book Parade 115" includes *The Snowy Day* [record or cassette] Weston Woods, nd. ESLC, MMA

    Braille/print: [BR4677] NLSBPH. ESLC

    Film: [animated, also 8 mm, 6 min, also Spanish/Swedish/Turkish] Weston Woods, 1964.

    Film: "The Lively Art of Picture Books" includes *The Snowy Day* [57 min] Weston Woods, 1964. MMA

    Filmstrip: [Picture book parade series 8, 24 fr, script] Weston Woods, 1965. ESLC, MMA

    Filmstrip/sound: [filmstrip/record or cassette, 28 fr/6 min, also Spanish] Weston Woods, 1965. ESLC, MMA

    Poster: [Study prints set 1, 17x24 in] Horn Book Magazine, 1971-1974. op ESLC

    Read-along: [cassette/book, 9 min, also Spanish] Live Oak, 1974. ESLC

    Read-along: [cassette/book] Random, nd.

    Read-along: [cassette/book] Weston Woods, nd.

    Talking book: [RD13067] NLSBPH. ESLC

    Video: "Smile for Auntie and Other Stories" includes *The Snowy Day* [animated, 30 min] Children's Circle, 1964, released 1985. PCGV

    Video: [animated, cc, 6 min, also Dutch/German/Spanish/Swedish/Turkish] Weston Woods, 1964. ESLC

    Video: "The Lively Art of Picture Books" includes *The Snowy Day* [57 min] Weston Woods, 1964. MMA

About the Book:

Filmstrip/sound: "Caldecott Medal Winners" includes discussion of *The Snowy Day* [4 filmstrips/4 cassettes] Meridian, 1986.

Video: "Caldecott Medal Winners" includes discussion of *The Snowy Day* [filmstrip-on-video] Meridian, 1986.

See also Ezra Jack Keats, "Media about Newbery/Caldecott Authors and Illustrators."

Mr. Rabbit and the Lovely Present by Charlotte Zolotow. Illustrated by Maurice Sendak. Harper, 1962. Caldecott Honor Book.

Audio: [record or cassette, 7 min] Weston Woods, nd. MMA
Audio: "Picture Book Parade 119" includes *Mr. Rabbit and the Lovely Present* [record or cassette] Weston Woods, nd. ESLC, MMA
Braille/print: [BR3387] NLSBPH. ESLC
Filmstrip/sound: [filmstrip/record or cassette, 26 fr/7 min] Weston Woods, 1962. ESLC, MMA
Read-along: [cassette/book, 10 min] Live Oak, 1987. ESLC
Read-along: [cassette/book] Random, nd.
Read-along: [cassette/book] Weston Woods, nd.
Video: "Presents" includes *Mr. Rabbit and the Lovely Present* [Picture book park series, 15 min] AIT, 1974.

See also Maurice Sendak and Charlotte Zolotow, "Media about Newbery/Caldecott Authors and Illustrators."

The Sun Is a Golden Earring by Natalia M. Belting. Illustrated by Bernarda Bryson. Holt, 1962.

none located

1962 CALDECOTT AWARDS

Once a Mouse retold and illustrated by Marcia Brown. Scribner, 1961. Caldecott Medal Book.

Audio: [record or cassette, 6 min] Random, nd. MMA
Braille: [BR5912 or BRA4367] NLSBPH. ESLC
Filmstrip/sound: [Famous author/illustrator series, filmstrip/record or cassette, 42 fr/6 min] Miller-Brody, 1977. ALSC, ESLC, MMA
Talking book: [RC22903] NLSBPH. ESLC

Video: [filmstrip-on-video, 6 min] Random, 1987.

See also Marcia Brown, "Media about Newbery/Caldecott Authors and Illustrators."

The Day We Saw the Sun Come Up by Alice E. Goudey. Illustrated by Adrienne Adams. Scribner, 1961. Caldecott Honor Book.

Talking book: [RC11370] NLSBPH.

The Fox Went Out on a Chilly Night: An Old Song illustrated by Peter Spier. Doubleday, 1961. Caldecott Honor Book.

Audio: [record or cassette, 8 min] Weston Woods, nd. MMA
Film: [iconographic, also 8 mm, 8 min] Weston Woods, 1969. MMA
Filmstrip: [24 fr, script] Weston Woods, nd. ESLC, MMA
Filmstrip/sound: [filmstrip/record or cassette, 40 fr/8 min] Weston Woods, 1965. ESLC, MMA
Read-along: [cassette/book] Weston Woods, nd.
Video: [iconographic, 8 min] Weston Woods, 1969. MMA

See also Peter Spier, "Media about Newbery/Caldecott Authors and Illustrators."

Little Bear's Visit by Else Holmelund Minarik. Illustrated by Maurice Sendak. Harper, 1961. Caldecott Honor Book.

Audio: "Little Bear" includes *Little Bear's Visit* [Junior cassette library series, 2 cassettes] Listening Library, 198?.
Audio: [record or cassette, 14 min] Weston Woods, nd. MMA
Audio: "Picture Book Parade 119" includes *Little Bear's Visit* [record or cassette] Weston Woods, nd. ESLC, MMA
Braille: [BRA6820] NLSBPH. ESLC
Filmstrip/sound: [filmstrip/record or cassette, 53 fr/14 min] Weston Woods, 1967. ESLC, MMA
Read-along: [I can read series, cassette/book, 15 min] Caedmon, 1984. ESLC
Read-along: [cassette/book] Weston Woods, nd.

Talking book: [RC7033] NLSBPH. ESLC

See also Else Holmelund Minarik and Maurice Sendak, "Media about Newbery/Caldecott Authors and Illustrators."

1961 CALDECOTT AWARDS

Baboushka and the Three Kings by Ruth Robbins. Illustrated by Nicolas Sidjakov. Parnassus, 1960. Caldecott Medal Book.

Talking book: [RC23548] NLSBPH.

Inch by Inch by Leo Lionni. Ivan Obolensky, 1960. Caldecott Honor Book.

Talking book/print: [TB4690] NLSBPH.

1960 CALDECOTT AWARDS

Nine Days to Christmas by Marie Hall Ets and Aurora Labastida. Illustrated by Marie Hall Ets. Viking, 1959. Caldecott Medal Book.

Braille/print: [BR5922] NLSBPH.
Poster: [Study prints set 2, 17x24 in] Horn Book Magazine, 1971-1974. op ESLC
Talking book: [RC22909] NLSBPH.

Houses from the Sea by Alice E. Goudey. Illustrated by Adrienne Adams. Scribner, 1959. Caldecott Honor Book.

Filmstrip/sound: [filmstrip/cassette, 49 fr/10 min] Miller-Brody, 1974. ESLC

The Moon Jumpers by Janice May Udry. Illustrated by Maurice Sendak. Harper, 1959. Caldecott Honor Book.

none located

See also Maurice Sendak, "Media about Newbery/Caldecott Authors and Illustrators."

1959 CALDECOTT AWARDS

Chanticleer and the Fox adapted from Chaucer's *The Canterbury Tales* and illustrated by Barbara Cooney. Crowell, 1958. Caldecott Medal Book.

Audio: [record or cassette, 10 min] Weston Woods, nd. MMA
Audio: "Picture Book Parade: Beloved Stories in Words and Music 107" includes *Chanticleer and the Fox* [record or cassette] Weston Woods, nd. ESLC, MMA
Braille: [BRA6856] NLSBPH. ESLC
Filmstrip: [Picture book parade series, 44 fr, script] Weston Woods, nd. ESLC, MMA
Filmstrip/sound: [filmstrip/record or cassette, 48 fr/10 min] Weston Woods, 1965. ESLC, MMA
Poster: [Study prints set 3, 17x24 in] Horn Book Magazine, 1971-1974. op ESLC
Read-along: [cassette/book] Weston Woods, nd.

The House That Jack Built: La Maison que Jacques a Bâtie by Antonio Frasconi. Harcourt, 1958. Caldecott Honor Book.

none located

See also Antonio Frasconi, "Media about Newbery/Caldecott Authors and Illustrators."

Umbrella by Taro Yashima. Viking, 1958. Caldecott Honor Book.

Audio: [record or cassette, 5 min] Weston Woods, nd. MMA
Filmstrip/sound: "Just Like Me" includes *Umbrella* [Literature for children: Introduction to picture books series 7A, filmstrip/cassette, 72 fr/11 min] Pied Piper, 1982.
Filmstrip/sound: [filmstrip/record or cassette, 23 fr/5 min] Weston Woods, 1969. ESLC, MMA
Read-along: [cassette/book, 9 min] Live Oak, 1985. ESLC
Read-along: [cassette/book] Weston Woods, nd.
Talking book: [TB4451] NLSBPH. ESLC

Video: "Just Like Me" includes *Umbrella* [Literature for children: Introduction to picture books series 7A, about 11 min] Pied Piper, 198?.

What Do You Say, Dear? by Sesyle Joslin. Illustrated by Maurice Sendak. W.R. Scott, 1958. Caldecott Honor Book.

> *Audio:* [cassette] Weston Woods, nd.
> *Braille/print:* [BR5068] NLSBPH.
> *Filmstrip:* [Picture book parade series, 27 fr, script] Weston Woods, 1964. ESLC, MMA
> *Filmstrip/sound:* [filmstrip/record or cassette, 27 fr/5 min, also Spanish] Weston Woods, 1964. ESLC
> *Read-along:* [cassette/book] Spoken Arts, nd.
> *Read-along:* [cassette/book] Weston Woods, nd.
> *Talking book:* [RD13042] NLSBPH.

> *See also* Maurice Sendak, "Media about Newbery/Caldecott Authors and Illustrators."

1958 CALDECOTT AWARDS

Time of Wonder by Robert McCloskey. Viking, 1957. Caldecott Medal Book.

> *Audio:* [record or cassette, 13 min] Weston Woods, nd. MMA
> *Audio:* "Picture Book Parade: Beloved Stories in Words and Music 107" includes *Time of Wonder* [record or cassette] Weston Woods, nd. ESLC, MMA
> *Braille/print:* [BR5624 or BRA2372] NLSBPH. ESLC
> *Film:* "The Lively Art of Picture Books" includes *Time of Wonder* [57 min] Weston Woods, 1964. MMA
> *Film:* [Picture book parade series, iconographic, 13 min] Weston Woods, 1961. MMA
> *Filmstrip:* [Picture book parade series, 55 fr, script] Weston Woods, nd. ESLC, MMA
> *Filmstrip/sound:* [filmstrip/record or cassette, 59 fr/13 min] Weston Woods, 1965. ESLC, MMA
> *Read-along:* [cassette/book] Weston Woods, nd.
> *Talking book:* [RD6292] NLSBPH. ESLC

Video: "Owl Moon and Other Stories" includes *Time of Wonder* [35 min] Children's Circle, 1990.
Video: "The Robert McCloskey Library" includes *Time of Wonder* [55 min] Children's Circle, 1990.
Video: "The Lively Art of Picture Books" includes *Time of Wonder* [57 min] Weston Woods, 1964. MMA
Video: [iconographic, 13 min] Weston Woods, 1961. ESLC, MMA

> *See also* Robert McCloskey, "Media about Newbery/Caldecott Authors and Illustrators."

Anatole and the Cat by Eve Titus. Illustrated by Paul Galdone. McGraw-Hill, 1957. Caldecott Honor Book.

> *Talking book:* [RD13072] NLSBPH.

Fly High, Fly Low by Don Freeman. Viking, 1957. Caldecott Honor Book.

> *Braille:* [BRA6947] NLSBPH.
> *Talking book:* [RD11426] NLSBPH.

> *See also* Don Freeman, "Media about Newbery/Caldecott Authors and Illustrators."

1957 CALDECOTT AWARDS

A Tree Is Nice by Janice May Udry. Illustrated by Marc Simont. Harper, 1956. Caldecott Medal Book.

> *Audio:* [record or cassette, 4 min] Weston Woods, nd. MMA
> *Audio:* "Picture Book Parade: Beloved Stories in Words and Music 107" includes *A Tree Is Nice* [record or cassette] Weston Woods, nd. ESLC, MMA
> *Braille/print:* [BR6122] NLSBPH. ESLC
> *Filmstrip:* [Picture book parade series, 27 fr, script] Weston Woods, nd. ESLC, MMA
> *Filmstrip/sound:* [filmstrip/record or cassette, 31 fr/4 min] Weston Woods, 1965. ESLC, MMA
> *Read-along:* [cassette/book] Weston Woods, nd.

Anatole by Eve Titus. Illustrated by Paul Galdone. McGraw-Hill, 1956. Caldecott Honor Book.

> *Braille:* [BRA1600] NLSBPH.
> *Film:* [animated, 9 min] Texture, 1960. MMA
> *Filmstrip/sound:* [Picture book showcase: Just for fun series, filmstrip/cassette, 52 fr/10 min] Encyclopedia Britannica, 1979. ESLC
> *Talking book:* [Mi-BPH(MSL3029)RM] NLSBPH.

Gillespie and the Guards by Benjamin Elkin. Illustrated by James Daugherty. Viking, 1956. Caldecott Honor Book.

> *Talking book:* [Mi-BPH(MSL3354)RM] NLSBPH.

> *See also* James Daugherty, "Media about Newbery/Caldecott Authors and Illustrators."

Lion by William Pène du Bois. Viking, 1956. Caldecott Honor Book.

> none located

Mr. Penny's Race Horse by Marie Hall Ets. Viking, 1956. Caldecott Honor Book.

> none located

1 Is One by Tasha Tudor. Walck, 1956. Caldecott Honor Book.

> none located

1956 CALDECOTT AWARDS

Frog Went A-Courtin' retold by John Langstaff. Illustrated by Feodor Rojankovsky. Harcourt, 1955. Caldecott Medal Book.

> *Audio:* [record or cassette, 13 min] Weston Woods, nd. MMA
> *Audio:* "Picture Book Parade: Beloved Stories in Words and Music 108" includes *Frog Went A-Courtin'* [record or cassette] Weston Woods, nd. ESLC, MMA
> *Film:* [Picture book parade series, iconographic, 12 min] Weston Woods, 1961. MMA
> *Filmstrip:* [Picture book parade series, 31 fr, script] Weston Woods, nd. ESLC, MMA

> *Filmstrip/sound:* [filmstrip/record or cassette, 35 fr/13 min] Weston Woods, 1965. ESLC, MMA
> *Poster:* [Study prints set 3, 17x24 in] Horn Book Magazine, 1971-1974. op ESLC
> *Read-along:* [cassette/book] Weston Woods, nd.
> *Video:* [iconographic, 12 min] Weston Woods, 1961. MMA

Crow Boy by Taro Yashima. Viking, 1955. Caldecott Honor Book.

> *Audio:* [record or cassette, 7 min] Weston Woods, nd. MMA
> *Audio:* "Picture Book Parade: Beloved Stories in Words and Music 111" includes *Crow Boy* [record or cassette] Weston Woods, nd. ESLC, MMA
> *Braille/print:* [BR3880 or BRA1599] NLSBPH. ESLC
> *Film:* [iconographic, 13 min] Weston Woods, 1971. MMA
> *Filmstrip:* [Picture book parade series, 53 fr, script] Weston Woods, nd. ESLC, MMA
> *Filmstrip/sound:* [filmstrip/record or cassette, 53 fr/7 min] Weston Woods, 1968. ESLC, MMA
> *Read-along:* [cassette/book, 10 min] Live Oak, 1985. ESLC
> *Read-along:* [cassette/book] Random, nd.
> *Read-along:* [cassette/book] Weston Woods, nd.
> *Video:* [iconographic, 13 min] Weston Woods, 1971.

Play with Me by Marie Hall Ets. Viking, 1955. Caldecott Honor Book.

> *Audio:* [record or cassette, 6 min] Weston Woods, nd. MMA
> *Audio:* "Picture Book Parade: Beloved Stories in Words and Music 112" includes *Play with Me* [record or cassette] Weston Woods, nd. ESLC, MMA
> *Braille/print:* [BR4681] NLSBPH.
> *Filmstrip:* [Picture book parade series, 30 fr, script] Weston Woods, nd. ESLC, MMA
> *Filmstrip/sound:* [filmstrip/record or cassette, 30 fr/6 min] Weston Woods, 1965. ESLC, MMA

Read-along: [cassette/book, 6 min] Live Oak, 1975. ESLC
Read-along: [cassette/book] Random, nd.
Read-along: [cassette/book] Weston Woods, nd.

1955 CALDECOTT AWARDS

Cinderella, or the Little Glass Slipper illustrated and translated from the French of Charles Perrault by Marcia Brown. Scribner, 1954. Caldecott Medal Book.

> *Audio:* [2 cassettes] Miller-Brody, 1974.
> *Braille/print:* [BR6111 or BRA4738] NLSBPH. ESLC
> *Filmstrip/sound:* [2 filmstrips/2 records or cassettes, 61 fr/12 min] Miller-Brody, 1974. ESLC
> *Poster:* [Study prints set 2, 17x24 in] Horn Book Magazine, 1971-1974. op ESLC
> *Read-along:* [cassette/book] Random, nd.
> *Talking book:* [RC22320] NLSBPH.
>
> *See also* Marcia Brown, "Media about Newbery/Caldecott Authors and Illustrators."

Book of Nursery and Mother Goose Rhymes illustrated by Marguerite de Angeli. Doubleday, 1954. Caldecott Honor Book.

> *Braille:* [BR1316] NLSBPH.
> *Talking book:* [RD15679] NLSBPH.
>
> *See also* Marguerite de Angeli, "Media about Newbery/Caldecott Authors and illustrators."

The Thanksgiving Story by Alice Dalgliesh. Illustrated by Helen Sewell. Scribner, 1954. Caldecott Honor Book.

> *Braille:* [BR2187] NLSBPH. ESLC
> *Talking book:* [RC26489] NLSBPH.

Wheel on the Chimney by Margaret Wise Brown. Illustrated by Tibor Gergely. Lippincott, 1954. Caldecott Honor Book.

> *Audio:* [record or cassette, 7 min] Weston Woods, nd. MMA

Audio: "Picture Book Parade 116" includes *Wheel on the Chimney* [record or cassette] Weston Woods, nd. ESLC, MMA
Braille/print: [BR3635] NLSBPH. ESLC
Film: [iconographic, also 8 mm, 7 min] Weston Woods, 1969.
Filmstrip: [Picture book parade series, 38 fr, script] Weston Woods, 1966. ESLC, MMA
Filmstrip/sound: [filmstrip/record or cassette, 38 fr/7 min] Weston Woods, 1966. ESLC, MMA
Read-along: [cassette/book] Weston Woods, nd.
Talking book: [RC23195] NLSBPH. ESLC
Video: [iconographic, 7 min] Weston Woods, 1969. ESLC

1954 CALDECOTT AWARDS

Madeline's Rescue by Ludwig Bemelmans. Viking, 1953. Caldecott Medal Book.

> *Audio:* [cassette, 6 min] Weston Woods, 1989.
> *Audio:* "Madeline and Other Bemelmans" includes *Madeline's Rescue* [record or cassette] Caedmon, nd. ESLC, MMA
> *Audio:* [cassette] Miller-Brody, nd.
> *Audio:* "Madeline and Other Children's Stories, Set 1" includes *Madeline's Rescue* [6 cassettes] Random, nd.
> *Audio:* [record or cassette, 6 min] Weston Woods, nd. MMA
> *Audio:* "Picture Book Parade: Beloved Stories in Words and Music 108" includes *Madeline's Rescue* [record or cassette] Weston Woods, nd. ESLC, MMA
> *Braille/print:* [BR5901 or BRA4718] NLSBPH. ESLC
> *Doll:* "Madeline" [14 in] Weston Woods, nd.
> *Film:* [animated, cc, 7 min] Texture, 1966. MMA
> *Film:* [animated, 7 min] Weston Woods, 1959, released 1990. BKL 12/15/90, SLJ 6/91
> *Filmstrip:* [Picture book parade series, 50 fr, script] Weston Woods, nd. ESLC, MMA
> *Filmstrip/sound:* [filmstrip/record or cassette, 54 fr/6 min] Weston Woods, 1965. ESLC, MMA
> *Poster:* [Study prints set 2, 17x24 in] Horn Book Magazine, 1971-1974. op ESLC

Read-along: [StoryTapes series, cassette/book, 10 min] Puffin, 1989.

Read-along: [cassette/book, 10 min] Live Oak, 1978. ESLC

Read-along: [cassette/book] Weston Woods, nd.

Talking book: [RC7034] NLSBPH. ESLC

Video: "Madeline's Rescue and Other Stories about Madeline" [animated, 23 min] Children's Circle, 1990.

Video: [animated, 7 min] Weston Woods, 1959, released 1990. BKL 12/15/90, SLJ 6/91

Green Eyes by A. Birnbaum. Capitol, 1953. Caldecott Honor Book.

Film: [About real animals series, animated, 6 min] Screenscope, 1971. op

Film: [Reading incentive series, 7 min] Bank Street College of Education, 1967. op

Filmstrip/sound: [Educational experiences: About real animals series, filmstrip/record or cassette, 41 fr/6 min] Western Publishing Co, 1972. op

Video: [About real animals series, animated, 6 min] Screenscope, 1977. op

Journey Cake, Ho! by Ruth Sawyer. Illustrated by Robert McCloskey. Viking, 1953. Caldecott Honor Book.

Audio: [record or cassette, 11 min] Weston Woods, nd. MMA

Audio: "Classic Tales from the Picture Book Parade" includes *Journey Cake, Ho!* [cassette] Weston Woods, nd.

Audio: "Picture Book Parade 118" includes *Journey Cake, Ho!* [record or cassette] Weston Woods, nd. ESLC, MMA

Filmstrip/sound: [filmstrip/record or cassette, 37 fr/11 min] Weston Woods, 1967. ESLC, MMA

Read-along: [cassette/book] Weston Woods, nd.

Talking book/print: [RD7327] NLSBPH. ESLC

Video: "Classic Tales from the Picture Book Parade" includes *Journey Cake, Ho!* Weston Woods, 1986.

See also Robert McCloskey and Ruth Sawyer, "Media about Newbery/Caldecott Authors and Illustrators."

The Steadfast Tin Soldier translated by M. R. James from the story by Hans Christian Andersen. Illustrated by Marcia Brown. Scribner, 1953. Caldecott Honor Book.

none located

See also Marcia Brown, "Media about Newbery/Caldecott Authors and Illustrators."

A Very Special House by Ruth Krauss. Illustrated by Maurice Sendak. Harper, 1953. Caldecott Honor Book.

Audio: [Anthology of children's literature series, cassette] Troll, nd.

See also Maurice Sendak, "Media about Newbery/Caldecott Authors and Illustrators."

When Will the World Be Mine? by Miriam Schlein. Illustrated by Jean Charlot. W.R. Scott, 1953. Caldecott Honor Book.

none located

1953 CALDECOTT AWARDS

The Biggest Bear by Lynd Ward. Houghton, 1952. Caldecott Medal Book.

Audio: [Anthology of children's literature series, cassette] Troll, nd.

Audio: [record or cassette, 7 min] Weston Woods, nd. MMA

Audio: "Picture Book Parade: Beloved Stories in Words and Music 104" includes *The Biggest Bear* [record or cassette] Weston Woods, nd. ESLC, MMA

Braille/print: [BR5917 or BRA2347] NLSBPH. ESLC

Filmstrip: [Picture book parade series, 47 fr, script] Weston Woods, nd. ESLC, MMA

Filmstrip/sound: [filmstrip/record or cassette, 48 fr/7 min] Weston Woods, 1968. ESLC, MMA

Read-along: [cassette/book] Houghton, 1989.

Read-along: [cassette/book] Weston Woods, nd.

Talking book: [TB2166] NLSBPH. ESLC

See also Lynd Ward, "Media about Newbery/Caldecott Authors and Illustrators."

Ape in a Cape: An Alphabet of Odd Animals by Fritz Eichenberg. Harcourt, 1952. Caldecott Honor Book.

none located

Five Little Monkeys by Juliet Kepes. Houghton, 1952. Caldecott Honor Book.

none located

One Morning in Maine by Robert McCloskey. Viking, 1952. Caldecott Honor Book.

Braille/print: [BR4300] NLSBPH. ESLC
Filmstrip/sound: [filmstrip/cassette, 65 fr/19 min] Live Oak, 1978. ESLC, MMA
Filmstrip/sound: [filmstrip/cassette] Miller-Brody, nd.
Talking book: [RD6292] NLSBPH. ESLC

See also Robert McCloskey, "Media about Newbery/Caldecott Authors and Illustrators."

Puss In Boots illustrated and translated from the French of Charles Perrault by Marcia Brown. Scribner, 1952. Caldecott Honor Book.

Audio: [cassette, 13 min] Random, 1979. ESLC, MMA
Filmstrip/sound: [filmstrip/cassette, 93 fr/13 min] Miller-Brody, 1979. ESLC, MMA

See also Marcia Brown, "Media about Newbery/Caldecott Authors and Illustrators."

The Storm Book by Charlotte Zolotow. Illustrated by Margaret Bloy Graham. Harper, 1952. Caldecott Honor Book.

none located

See also Charlotte Zolotow, "Media about Newbery/Caldecott Authors and Illustrators."

1952 CALDECOTT AWARDS

Finders Keepers by Will, pseud. (William Lipkind). Illustrated by Nicolas, pseud. (Nicolas Mordvinoff). Harcourt, 1951. Caldecott Medal Book.

Audio: [record or cassette, 7 min] Weston Woods, nd. MMA
Audio: "Picture Book Parade: Beloved Stories in Words and Music 107" includes *Finders Keepers* [record or cassette] Weston Woods, nd. ESLC, MMA
Braille/print: [BR4659] NLSBPH.
Filmstrip: [Picture book parade series, 37 fr, script] Weston Woods, nd. ESLC, MMA
Filmstrip/sound: [filmstrip/record or cassette, 40 fr/7 min] Weston Woods, 1952. ESLC, MMA
Talking book: [TB406] NLSBPH.

All Falling Down by Gene Zion. Illustrated by Margaret Bloy Graham. Harper, 1951. Caldecott Honor Book.

none located

Bear Party by William Pène du Bois. Viking, 1951. Caldecott Honor Book.

Filmstrip/sound: [filmstrip/record or cassette, 46 fr/5 min] Live Oak, 1970. ESLC, MMA
Filmstrip/sound: [filmstrip/cassette] Miller-Brody, nd.
Read-along: [cassette/book, 7 min] Live Oak, 1991.

Feather Mountain by Elizabeth Olds. Houghton, 1951. Caldecott Honor Book.

none located

Mr. T.W. Anthony Woo by Marie Hall Ets. Viking, 1951. Caldecott Honor Book.

none located

Skipper John's Cook by Marcia Brown. Scribner, 1951. Caldecott Honor Book.

none located

See also Marcia Brown, "Media about New-bery/Caldecott Authors and Illustrators."

1951 CALDECOTT AWARDS

The Egg Tree by Katherine Milhous. Scribner, 1950. Caldecott Medal Book.

> *Braille/print:* [BR6109 or BRA11145] NLSBPH.
> *Poster:* [Study prints set 1, 17x24 in] Horn Book Magazine, 1971-1974. op ESLC
> *Talking book:* [RD10971] NLSBPH.

Dick Whittington and His Cat told and illustrated by Marcia Brown. Scribner, 1950. Caldecott Honor Book.

> *Braille:* [BR4673 or BRA4720] NLSBPH. ESLC
> *Talking book:* [RD13678] NLSBPH.

> See also Marcia Brown, "Media about New-bery/Caldecott Authors and Illustrators."

If I Ran the Zoo by Dr. Seuss, pseud. (Theodor Seuss Geisel). Random, 1950. Caldecott Honor Book.

> *Audio:* "Nine Best-Loved Dr. Seuss Stories" includes *If I Ran the Zoo* [cassette] RCA, nd. op
> *Braille/print:* [BR4661] NLSBPH. ESLC
> *Filmstrip/sound:* "If I Ran the Circus/If I Ran the Zoo" [2 filmstrips/2 records or cassettes, 322 fr] Random, 1977. ESLC
> *Read-along:* [cassette/book] Random, nd.
> *Talking book:* [Nj-B(C958m)RC or RD13030] NLSBPH. ESLC
> *Video:* [filmstrip-on-video, 18 min] Random, 1985.
> *Video:* "Dr. Seuss' Caldecotts" includes *If I Ran the Zoo* [filmstrip-on-video, 52 min] Random, 1985. ESLC

> *About the Book:*

> *Software:* "If I Ran the World I" includes discussion of *If I Ran the Zoo* [Write On! series] Humanities Software, 198?.
> *Software:* "If I Ran the World II" includes discussion of *If I Ran the Zoo* [Write On! series] Humanities Software, 198?.

See also Theodor Seuss Geisel, "Media about Newbery/Caldecott Authors and illustrators."

The Most Wonderful Doll in the World by Phyllis McGinley. Illustrated by Helen Stone. Lippincott, 1950. Caldecott Honor Book.

> none located

T-Bone, the Baby Sitter by Clare Turlay Newberry. Harper, 1950. Caldecott Honor Book.

> none located

The Two Reds by Will, pseud. (William Lipkind). Illustrated by Nicolas, pseud. (Nicolas Mordvinoff). Harcourt, 1950. Caldecott Honor Book.

> none located

1950 CALDECOTT AWARDS

Song of the Swallows by Leo Politi. Scribner, 1949. Caldecott Medal Book.

> *Braille/print:* [BR6101] NLSBPH. ESLC
> *Filmstrip/sound:* [filmstrip/record or cassette, 51 fr/9 min] Miller-Brody, 1974. ESLC
> *Poster:* [Study prints set 1, 17x24 in] Horn Book Magazine, 1971-1974. op ESLC
> *Read-along:* [cassette/book] Random, nd.
> *Talking book:* [RD13663] NLSBPH. ESLC

> See also Leo Politi, "Media about Newbery/ Caldecott Authors and Illustrators."

America's Ethan Allen by Stewart Holbrook. Illustrated by Lynd Ward. Houghton, 1949. Caldecott Honor Book.

> none located

> See also Lynd Ward, "Media about Newbery/ Caldecott Authors and Illustrators."

Bartholomew and the Oobleck by Dr. Seuss, pseud. (Theodor Seuss Geisel). Random, 1949. Caldecott Honor Book.

> *Audio:* "Nine Best-Loved Dr. Seuss Stories" includes *Bartholomew and the Oobleck* [cassette] RCA, nd. op

Filmstrip/sound: [filmstrip/cassette, 126 fr/25 min] Miller-Brody, 1981. ESLC, MMA
Read-along: [cassette/book] Random, nd.
Talking book: [RD13028] NLSBPH. ESLC
Video: [filmstrip-on-video, 25 min] Random, 1985.
Video: "Dr. Seuss' Caldecotts" includes *Bartholomew and the Oobleck* [filmstrip-on-video, 52 min] Random, 1985. ESLC

See also Theodor Seuss Geisel, "Media about Newbery/Caldecott Authors and illustrators."

The Happy Day by Ruth Krauss. Illustrated by Marc Simont. Harper, 1949. Caldecott Honor Book.

Audio: [record or cassette, 3 min] Weston Woods, nd. MMA
Braille: [BR7530] NLSBPH.
Filmstrip/sound: "The Happy Day, and Where Does the Butterfly Go When It Rains" [2 filmstrips/record or cassette, 37 fr/5 min] Weston Woods, 1962. ESLC, MMA
Read-along: [cassette/book] Weston Woods, nd.

Henry Fisherman by Marcia Brown. Scribner, 1949. Caldecott Honor Book.

none located

See also Marcia Brown, "Media about Newbery/Caldecott Authors and Illustrators."

The Wild Birthday Cake by Lavinia R. Davis. Illustrated by Hildegard Woodward. Doubleday, 1949. Caldecott Honor Book.

Braille: [BRA6823] NLSBPH.

1949 CALDECOTT AWARDS

The Big Snow by Berta and Elmer Hader. Macmillan, 1948. Caldecott Medal Book.

Audio: [record or cassette, 11 min] Weston Woods, nd. MMA
Audio: "Picture Book Parade: Beloved Stories in Words and Music 108" includes *The Big Snow* [record or cassette] Weston Woods, nd. ESLC, MMA
Braille: [BR2128] NLSBPH. ESLC

Filmstrip: [Picture book parade series, 50 fr, script] Weston Woods, nd. ESLC, MMA
Filmstrip/sound: [filmstrip/record or cassette, 53 fr/11 min] Weston Woods, 1965. ESLC, MMA
Read-along: [cassette/book] Weston Woods, nd.
Talking book: [RC29072] NLSBPH.

All Around the Town by Phyllis McGinley. Illustrated by Helen Stone. Lippincott, 1948. Caldecott Honor Book.

none located

Blueberries for Sal by Robert McCloskey. Viking, 1948. Caldecott Honor Book.

Audio: [record or cassette, 9 min] Weston Woods, nd. MMA
Audio: "Picture Book Parade: Beloved Stories in Words and Music 112" includes *Blueberries for Sal* [record or cassette] Weston Woods, nd. ESLC, MMA
Braille: [BRA6793] NLSBPH. ESLC
Film: [iconographic, also 8 mm, 9 min] Weston Woods, 1967. MMA
Filmstrip: [Picture book parade series, 47 fr, script] Weston Woods, nd. ESLC, MMA
Filmstrip/sound: [filmstrip/record or cassette, 47 fr/9 min] Weston Woods, nd. ESLC, MMA
Read-along: [StoryTapes series, cassette/book, 10 min] Puffin, 1989.
Read-along: [cassette/book, 10 min] Live Oak, 1978.
Read-along: [cassette/book] Random, nd.
Read-along: [cassette/book] Weston Woods, nd.
Talking book: [RC10774] NLSBPH. ESLC
Video: "The Robert McCloskey Library" includes *Blueberries for Sal* [55 min] Children's Circle, 1990.
Video: "Corduroy and Other Bear Stories" includes *Blueberries for Sal* [16 min] Children's Circle, 1984. BVC
Video: [iconographic, 9 min] Weston Woods, 1967. ESLC, MMA

See also Robert McCloskey, "Media about Newbery/Caldecott Authors and Illustrators."

Fish in the Air by Kurt Wiese. Viking, 1948. Caldecott Honor Book.

> *Audio:* [record or cassette, 7 min] Weston Woods, nd. MMA
> *Audio:* "Picture Book Parade 118" includes *Fish in the Air* [record or cassette] Weston Woods, nd. ESLC, MMA
> *Filmstrip/sound:* [filmstrip/record or cassette, 34 fr/7 min] Weston Woods, 1967. ESLC, MMA

Juanita by Leo Politi. Scribner, 1948. Caldecott Honor Book.

> *Braille:* [BR2657] NLSBPH.

> *See also* Leo Politi, "Media about Newbery/Caldecott Authors and Illustrators."

1948 CALDECOTT AWARDS

White Snow, Bright Snow by Alvin Tresselt. Illustrated by Roger Duvoisin. Lothrop, 1947. Caldecott Medal Book.

> *Audio:* [record or cassette, 7 min] Weston Woods, nd. MMA
> *Audio:* "Picture Book Parade: Beloved Stories in Words and Music 106" includes *White Snow, Bright Snow* [record or cassette] Weston Woods, nd. ESLC, MMA
> *Braille:* [BRA6614] NLSBPH.
> *Filmstrip:* [Picture book parade series, 35 fr, script] Weston Woods, nd. ESLC, MMA
> *Filmstrip/sound:* [filmstrip/record or cassette, 37 fr/7 min] Weston Woods, 1965. ESLC, MMA
> *Read-along:* [cassette/book] Weston Woods, nd.
> *Talking book:* [RD15563] NLSBPH.

Bambino the Clown by Georges Schreiber. Viking, 1947. Caldecott Honor Book.

> none located

McElligot's Pool by Dr. Seuss, pseud. (Theodor Seuss Geisel). Random, 1947. Caldecott Honor Book.

> *Braille/print:* [BR2367] NLSBPH. ESLC
> *Filmstrip/sound:* [filmstrip/cassette, 79 fr/10 min] Miller-Brody, 1981. ESLC, MMA
> *Read-along:* [cassette/book] Random, nd. MMA
> *Talking book:* [Mi-BPH(MSL3063)RM or Nj-B(C1385m)RC or RD13003] NLSBPH. ESLC
> *Video:* [filmstrip-on-video, 13 min] Random, 1988.
> *Video:* "Dr. Seuss' Caldecotts" includes *McElligot's Pool* [filmstrip-on-video, 52 min] Random, 1985. ESLC

> *See also* Theodor Seuss Geisel, "Media about Newbery/Caldecott Authors and illustrators."

Roger and the Fox by Lavinia R. Davis. Illustrated by Hildegard Woodward. Doubleday, 1947. Caldecott Honor Book.

> *Braille:* [BRA6826] NLSBPH.

Song of Robin Hood selected and edited by Anne Malcolmson. Designed and illustrated by Virginia Lee Burton. Houghton, 1947. Caldecott Honor Book.

> none located

Stone Soup: An Old Tale told and illustrated by Marcia Brown. Scribner, 1947. Caldecott Honor Book.

> *Audio:* "Folktales from the Picture Book Parade" includes *Stone Soup* [record or cassette, 40 min] Weston Woods, 1981. ALSC, ESLC, MMA
> *Audio:* [record or cassette, 11 min, also Spanish] Weston Woods, nd. MMA
> *Audio:* "Picture Book Parade: Beloved Stories in Words and Music 102" includes *Stone Soup* [record or cassette] Weston Woods, nd. ESLC, MMA
> *Braille:* [BRA6859 or BRA13948] NLSBPH. ESLC
> *Film:* [iconographic, color/b&w, 11 min, also French/Spanish] Weston Woods, 1955.

Filmstrip: [Picture book parade series, 46 fr, script] Weston Woods, 1957. ESLC, MMA

Filmstrip/sound: [filmstrip/record or cassette, 47 fr/11 min, also Italian/Spanish] Weston Woods, 1965. ESLC, MMA

Read-along: [cassette/book] Live Oak, nd.

Read-along: [cassette/book] Random, nd.

Read-along: [cassette/book] Weston Woods, nd.

Video: [iconographic, 11 min, also French/Italian/Spanish] Weston Woods, 1955.

See also Marcia Brown, "Media about Newbery/Caldecott Authors and Illustrators."

1947 CALDECOTT AWARDS

The Little Island by Golden MacDonald, pseud. (Margaret Wise Brown). Illustrated by Leonard Weisgard. Doubleday, 1946. Caldecott Medal Book.

Audio: [record or cassette, 6 min] Weston Woods, nd. MMA

Audio: "Picture Book Parade: Beloved Stories in Words and Music 108" includes *The Little Island* [record or cassette] Weston Woods, nd. ESLC, MMA

Braille/print: [BR3888] NLSBPH.

Filmstrip: [Picture book parade series, 36 fr, script] Weston Woods, nd. ESLC, MMA

Filmstrip/sound: [filmstrip/record or cassette, 39 fr/6 min] Weston Woods, 1965. ESLC, MMA

Read-along: [Blue ribbon series, cassette/book] Scholastic, nd.

Boats on the River by Marjorie Flack. Illustrated by Jay Hyde Barnum. Viking, 1946. Caldecott Honor Book.

Braille: [BRA6914] NLSBPH.

Talking book: [Nj-B(C1378m)RC] NLSBPH.

Pedro, the Angel of Olvera Street by Leo Politi. Scribner, 1946. Caldecott Honor Book.

Talking book: [RD8096] NLSBPH.

See also Leo Politi, "Media about Newbery/Caldecott Authors and Illustrators."

Rain Drop Splash by Alvin Tresselt. Illustrated by Leonard Weisgard. Lothrop, 1946. Caldecott Honor Book.

Audio: [record or cassette, 4 min] Weston Woods, nd. MMA

Braille: [BRA6604] NLSBPH. ESLC

Film: [Friendly giant series, b&w, 15 min] Indiana University National Educational Television, 1955. op

Filmstrip/sound: [filmstrip/record or cassette, 32 fr/4 min] Weston Woods, 1968. ESLC, MMA

Sing in Praise: A Collection of the Best Loved Hymns by Opal Wheeler. Illustrated by Marjorie Torrey. Dutton, 1946. Caldecott Honor Book.

none located

Timothy Turtle by Al Graham. Illustrated by Tony Palazzo. Welch, 1946. Caldecott Honor Book.

Talking book: [RC11664] NLSBPH.

1946 CALDECOTT AWARDS

The Rooster Crows: A Book of American Rhymes and Jingles by Maud and Miska Petersham. Macmillan, 1945. Caldecott Medal Book.

Audio: "More Americana" includes *The Rooster Crows* [Books and around series, 3-3/4 ips tape, 30 min] KUOM Radio-University of Minnesota, nd. op

Braille: [BRA4368] NLSBPH. ESLC

Talking book: [RC21585] NLSBPH. ESLC

Little Lost Lamb by Golden MacDonald, pseud. (Margaret Wise Brown). Illustrated by Leonard Weisgard. Doubleday, 1945. Caldecott Honor Book.

Audio: [Stories are for fun series, 3-3/4 ips tape, 13 min] National Center for Audio Tapes, nd. op

Braille: [BRA6685] NLSBPH.

My Mother Is the Most Beautiful Woman in the World by Becky Reyher. Illustrated by Ruth Gannett. Lothrop, 1945. Caldecott Honor Book.

> *Braille:* [BRA1413] NLSBPH.
> *Film:* [animated, also 8 mm, 9 min] Phoenix/ BFA, 1968. MMA
> *Filmstrip/sound:* [Children's literature series, filmstrip/record or cassette, 38 fr/15 min] McGraw-Hill, 1972. MMA
> *Filmstrip/sound:* [Folk tale series, filmstrip/ record or cassette, 74 fr/8 min, also Spanish] Phoenix/BFA, 1968. ESLC
> *Talking book:* [TB1117] NLSBPH.
> *Video:* [animated, 9 min] Phoenix/BFA, 1968. MMA

Sing Mother Goose by Opal Wheeler. Illustrated by Marjorie Torrey. Dutton, 1945. Caldecott Honor Book.

> none located

You Can Write Chinese by Kurt Wiese. Viking, 1945. Caldecott Honor Book.

> none located

1945 CALDECOTT AWARDS

Prayer for a Child by Rachel Field. Illustrated by Elizabeth Orton Jones. Macmillan, 1944. Caldecott Medal Book.

> *Braille/print:* [BR1800] NLSBPH.
> *Talking book:* [RD20898] NLSBPH.

> *See also* Elizabeth Orton Jones, "Media about Newbery/Caldecott Authors and illustrators."

The Christmas Anna Angel by Ruth Sawyer. Illustrated by Kate Seredy. Viking, 1944. Caldecott Honor Book.

> *Audio:* [Book fair series, cassette, 15 min] National Center for Audio Tapes, nd. op
> *Braille:* [BRA16020] NLSBPH.

> *See also* Ruth Sawyer and Kate Seredy, "Media about Newbery/Caldecott Authors and Illustrators."

In the Forest by Marie Hall Ets. Viking, 1944. Caldecott Honor Book.

> *Audio:* [cassette] Random, nd.
> *Audio:* [record or cassette, 4 min] Weston Woods, nd. MMA
> *Audio:* "Picture Book Parade: Beloved Stories in Words and Music 105" includes *In the Forest* [record or cassette] Weston Woods, nd. ESLC, MMA
> *Braille:* [BRA1577] NLSBPH. ESLC
> *Film:* [Picture book parade series, iconographic, b&w, 5 min] Weston Woods, 1960. MMA
> *Filmstrip:* [Picture book parade series, b&w, 39 fr, script] Weston Woods, nd. ESLC, MMA
> *Filmstrip/sound:* [filmstrip/record or cassette, 40 fr/5 min] Weston Woods, 1965. ESLC, MMA
> *Read-along:* [cassette/book, 7 min] Live Oak, 1978.
> *Read-along:* [cassette/book] Random, nd.

Mother Goose: Seventy-Seven Verses with Pictures illustrated by Tasha Tudor. Walck, 1944. Caldecott Honor Book.

> *Talking book/print:* [TB4436] NLSBPH.

Yonie Wondernose by Marguerite de Angeli. Doubleday, 1944. Caldecott Honor Book.

> *Audio:* [Stories are for fun series, cassette, 15 min] National Center for Audio Tapes, 1961. op
> *Braille:* [BRA6936] NLSBPH.

> *See also* Marguerite de Angeli, "Media about Newbery/Caldecott Authors and illustrators."

1944 CALDECOTT AWARDS

Many Moons by James Thurber. Illustrated by Louis Slobodkin. Harcourt, 1943. Caldecott Medal Book.

> *Audio:* [record or cassette] Caedmon, 1971. ESLC, MMA

Audio: [Books to remember series, 3-3/4 ips tape, 15 min] National Center for Audio Tapes, 1961. op

Audio: [World of stories series, 3-3/4 ips tape, 15 min] National Center for Audio Tapes, 1961. op

Audio: "James Thurber" includes *Many Moons* [Books and around series, 3-3/4 ips tape, 30 min] KUOM Radio-University of Minnesota, nd. op

Audio: [I open the door series, 3-3/4 ips tape, 15 min] National Center for Audio Tapes, nd. op

Braille: [BRA6594] NLSBPH.

Film: [animated, 10 min] Films Inc, 1983.

Film: [animated, 13 min] CRM, 1975. MMA

Film: [animated, 10 min] Texture, 1964. MMA

Filmstrip/sound: [Magic of storytelling series, filmstrip/cassette, 45 fr/9 min] Clearvue, 1979.

Poster: [Study prints set 3, 17x24 in] Horn Book Magazine, 1971-1974. op ESLC

Talking book/print: [TB4446] NLSBPH.

See also James Thurber and Louis Slobodkin, "Media about Newbery/Caldecott Authors and Illustrators."

A Child's Good Night Book by Margaret Wise Brown. Illustrated by Jean Charlot. W.R. Scott, 1943. Caldecott Honor Book.

none located

Good-Luck Horse by Chih-Yi Chan. Illustrated by Plato Chan. Whittlesey, 1943. Caldecott Honor Book.

none located

The Mighty Hunter by Berta and Elmer Hader. Macmillan, 1943. Caldecott Honor Book.

Audio: [Stories are for fun series, cassette, 12 min] National Center for Audio Tapes, nd. op

Braille: [BRA5513] NLSBPH.

Video: "Mighty Hunters" includes *The Mighty Hunter* [Picture book park series, 14 min] AIT, 1974.

Pierre Pidgeon by Lee Kingman. Illustrated by Arnold E. Bare. Houghton, 1943. Caldecott Honor Book.

none located

Small Rain: Verses from the Bible selected by Jessie Orton Jones. Illustrated by Elizabeth Orton Jones. Viking, 1943. Caldecott Honor Book.

none located

See also Elizabeth Orton Jones, "Media about Newbery/Caldecott Authors and illustrators."

1943 CALDECOTT AWARDS

The Little House by Virginia Lee Burton. Houghton, 1942. Caldecott Medal Book.

Audio: "The Summer People and The Little House" [cassette, 60 min] Caedmon, nd.

Audio: [cassette] Weston Woods, nd.

Braille/print: [BR5903 or BRA6831] NLSBPH. ESLC

Film: [8 min] Disney, 1988.

Film: "Deluxe Cartoon Parade Set E" includes *The Little House* [31 min] Macmillan, nd. op

Filmstrip/sound: [Fantasy classics series, filmstrip/cassette, 59 fr] Disney, 1973.

Filmstrip/sound: [filmstrip/record or cassette, 55 fr/13 min] Weston Woods, 1973. CMCE, ESLC

Read-along: [cassette/book] Houghton, 1989.

Read-along: [cassette/book] Disney, nd.

Read-along: [cassette/book] Weston Woods, nd.

Talking book: [RD20955] NLSBPH.

Video: [8 min] Disney, 1988.

Dash and Dart by Mary and Conrad Buff. Viking, 1942. Caldecott Honor Book.

Braille: [BRA6927] NLSBPH.

Marshmallow by Clare Turlay Newberry. Harper, 1942. Caldecott Honor Book.

Braille: [BRA4730] NLSBPH.

1942 CALDECOTT AWARDS

Make Way for Ducklings by Robert McCloskey. Viking, 1941. Caldecott Medal Book.

> *Audio:* [cassette, 12 min] Weston Woods, 1989.
> *Audio:* [cassette] Random, nd.
> *Audio:* [record or cassette, 11 min, also Spanish] Weston Woods, nd. MMA
> *Audio:* "Picture Book Parade: Beloved Stories in Words and Music 101" includes *Make Way for Ducklings* [record or cassette] Weston Woods, nd. ESLC, MMA
> *Braille/print:* [BR1739] NLSBPH. ESLC
> *Film:* [Picture book parade series, iconographic, also 8 mm, b&w, 11 min, also Italian/Spanish] Weston Woods, 1955. MMA
> *Filmstrip:* [Picture book parade series, 47 fr, script] Weston Woods, nd. ESLC, MMA
> *Filmstrip/sound:* [filmstrip/record or cassette, 47 fr/11 min, also Italian/Spanish] Weston Woods, 1968. ESLC, MMA
> *Poster:* "Make Way for Reading" [22x34 in] ALA, 1990.
> *Read-along:* [StoryTapes series, cassette/book] Puffin, 1988.
> *Read-along:* [cassette/book, 11 min] Live Oak, 1975. ESLC
> *Read-along:* [cassette/book] Random, nd.
> *Read-along:* [cassette/book] Weston Woods, nd.
> *Talking book:* [TB2166] NLSBPH. ESLC
> *Video:* "The Robert McCloskey Library" includes *Make Way for Ducklings* [55 min] Children's Circle, 1990.
> *Video:* "Smile for Auntie and Other Stories" includes *Make Way for Ducklings* [animated, 30 min] Children's Circle, 1955, released 1985. PCGV
> *Video:* [iconographic, cc, 11 min, also Italian/Spanish] Weston Woods, 1955, released 1980. ESLC, MMA

> *About the Book:*

> *Video:* [Imagine that series, b&w, 15 min] Twenty-One Inch Classroom, nd. op

See also Robert McCloskey, "Media about Newbery/Caldecott Authors and Illustrators."

An American ABC by Maud and Miska Petersham. Macmillan, 1941. Caldecott Honor Book.

none located

In My Mother's House by Ann Nolan Clark. Illustrated by Velino Herrera. Viking, 1941. Caldecott Honor Book.

> *Braille:* [BRA5822] NLSBPH.
> *Talking book:* [Az-BPH(AZCB1182)RC] NLSBPH.

Nothing at All by Wanda Gág. Coward, 1941. Caldecott Honor Book.

> *Talking book:* [RD7271] NLSBPH.

> *See also* Wanda Gág, "Media about Newbery/Caldecott Authors and Illustrators."

Paddle-to-the-Sea by Holling C. Holling. Houghton, 1941. Caldecott Honor Book.

> *Braille:* [BR1684] NLSBPH.
> *Film:* [live-action, 28 min] National Film Board of Canada, 1966. MMA
> *Film:* "Children's Film Festival" includes *Paddle-to-the-Sea* [85 min] National Film Board of Canada, nd.
> *Filmstrip/sound:* [filmstrip/cassette, 106 fr/25 min] National Film Board of Canada, nd. ESLC
> *Talking book:* [RC22676] NLSBPH
> *Video:* [Magic pages series, 14 min] AIT, 1976.
> *Video:* [live-action, 28 min] National Film Board of Canada, 1966.

See also Holling C. Holling, "Media about Newbery/Caldecott Authors and Illustrators."

1941 CALDECOTT AWARDS

They Were Strong and Good by Robert Lawson. Viking, 1940. Caldecott Medal Book.

> *Audio:* [record or cassette, 13 min] Weston Woods, nd. MMA

Audio: "Picture Book Parade 119" includes *They Were Strong and Good* [record or cassette] Weston Woods, nd. ESLC, MMA

Filmstrip/sound: [Our American heritage series, filmstrip/record or cassette] Weston Woods, 1975.

Filmstrip/sound: [filmstrip/record or cassette, 39 fr/13 min] Weston Woods, 1967. ESLC, MMA

Read-along: [cassette/book] Weston Woods, nd.

See also Robert Lawson, "Media about Newbery/Caldecott Authors and Illustrators."

April's Kittens by Clare Turlay Newberry. Harper, 1940. Caldecott Honor Book.

none located

1940 CALDECOTT AWARDS

Abraham Lincoln by Ingri and Edgar Parin d'Aulaire. Doubleday, 1939. Caldecott Medal Book.

Braille: [BR5871] NLSBPH. ESLC

Filmstrip/sound: [filmstrip/cassette, 71 fr/12 min] Spoken Arts, 1982. ESLC

Poster: [Study prints set 3, 17x24 in] Horn Book Magazine, 1971-1974. op ESLC

Read-along: [cassette/book, 12 min] Spoken Arts, 1986.

Talking book: [RC21812] NLSBPH. ESLC

Video: [filmstrip-on-video] American School, nd.

Video: [filmstrip-on-video, 41 min] Spoken Arts, nd.

See also Edgar Parin D'Aulaire and Ingri D'Aulaire, "Media about Newbery/Caldecott Authors and Illustrators."

The Ageless Story illustrated by Lauren Ford. Dodd, 1939. Caldecott Honor Book.

none located

Cock-a-Doodle Doo: The Story of a Little Red Rooster by Berta and Elmer Hader. Macmillan, 1939. Caldecott Honor Book.

none located

Madeline by Ludwig Bemelmans. Viking, 1939. Caldecott Honor Book.

Audio: "Madeline and Other Bemelmans" [record or cassette] Caedmon, nd. ESLC, MMA

Audio: "Madeline and Other Stories" [cassette] Listening Library, nd.

Audio: [cassette] Random, nd.

Audio: "Madeline and Other Children's Stories, Set 1" [6 cassettes] Random, nd.

Braille/print: [BR3644 or BRA4718] NLSBPH. ESLC

Doll: "Madeline" [14 in] Weston Woods, nd.

Film: [animated, 7 min] Churchill, 1988.

Film: [7 min] Learning Corp, 1969.

Film: [animated, 7 min] Learning Corp, 1952. MMA

Filmstrip/sound: [filmstrip/cassette, 80 fr/7 min] Miller-Brody, 1985. ESLC

Filmstrip/sound: "Exploring New Places" includes *Madeline* [Literature for children: Introduction to picture books series 7B, filmstrip/cassette, 70 fr/10 min] Pied Piper, 1982.

Poster: [21x15 in] Peaceable Kingdom, nd.

Read-along: [StoryTapes series, cassette/book] Puffin, 1988.

Read-along: [cassette/book, 8 min] Live Oak, 1975. ESLC

Read-along: [cassette/book] Listening Library, nd.

Talking book: [RD7034] NLSBPH. ESLC

Video: [HBO project knowledge series, animated musical, cc, 30 min] Ambrose, 1989. BKL 2/15/89, BVC, PC, SLJ 8/89, VRG Winter 1990 Note: home-use version available from Lightyear Entertainment

Video: [filmstrip-on-video, 7 min] Random, 1989. ESLC

Video: [animated, 7 min] Churchill, 1988.

Video: "Exploring New Places" includes *Madeline* [Literature for children: Introduction to picture books series 7B, about 10 min] Pied Piper, 198?.

Video: [7 min] Learning Corp, 1969.

1939 CALDECOTT AWARDS

Mei Li by Thomas Handforth. Doubleday, 1938. Caldecott Medal Book.

> *Braille/print:* [BR6104] NLSBPH.
> *Poster:* [Study prints set 1, 17x24 in] Horn Book Magazine, 1971-1974. op ESLC
> *Talking book:* [RC13619] NLSBPH.

Andy and the Lion by James Daugherty. Viking, 1938. Caldecott Honor Book.

> *Audio:* [Stories are for fun series, 3-3/4 ips tape, 15 min] National Center for Audio Tapes, nd. op
> *Audio:* [Anthology of children's literature series, cassette] Troll, nd.
> *Audio:* [record or cassette, 7 min, also Spanish] Weston Woods, nd. MMA
> *Audio:* "Picture Book Parade: Beloved Stories in Words and Music 104" includes *Andy and the Lion* [record or cassette] Weston Woods, nd. ESLC, MMA
> *Braille/print:* [BR4293 or BRA6094] NLSBPH. ESLC
> *Film:* [Picture book parade series, iconographic, 10 min, also Spanish] Weston Woods, 1955. MMA
> *Filmstrip:* [Picture book parade series, 42 fr, script] Weston Woods, nd. ESLC, MMA
> *Filmstrip/sound:* [filmstrip/record or cassette, 42 fr/7 min, also Italian/Spanish] Weston Woods, 1968. ESLC, MMA
> *Read-along:* [cassette/book] Weston Woods, nd.
> *Talking book:* [Mi-BPH(MSL3353)RM or Mi-BPH(MSL4869)RM] NLSBPH.
> *Video:* "Animal Stories" includes *Andy and the Lion* [animated, 30 min] Children's Circle, 1955, released 1986. BVC, PCGV
> *Video:* [iconographic, 10 min, also Spanish] Weston Woods, 1955. ESLC, MMA

> *See also* James Daugherty, "Media about Newbery/Caldecott Authors and Illustrators."

Barkis by Clare Turlay Newberry. Harper, 1938. Caldecott Honor Book.

> none located

The Forest Pool by Laura Adams Armer. Longmans, 1938. Caldecott Honor Book.

> none located

Snow White and the Seven Dwarfs translated from the German of the Brothers Grimm and illustrated by Wanda Gág. Coward, 1938. Caldecott Honor Book.

> *Talking book:* [RC18633] NLSBPH.

> *See also* Wanda Gág, "Media about Newbery/Caldecott Authors and Illustrators."

Wee Gillis by Munro Leaf. Illustrated by Robert Lawson. Viking, 1938. Caldecott Honor Book.

> *Audio:* "The Story of Ferdinand and Other Stories" includes *Wee Gillis* [record or cassette] Caedmon, 1959. ESLC
> *Film:* [live-action, 19 min] Churchill, 1985. ALSC
> *Video:* [live-action, 19 min] Churchill, 1985. ALSC, BVC

> *See also* Robert Lawson, "Media about Newbery/Caldecott Authors and Illustrators."

1938 CALDECOTT AWARDS

Animals of the Bible selected by Helen Dean Fish. Illustrated by Dorothy P. Lathrop. Stokes, 1937. Caldecott Medal Book.

> none located

Four and Twenty Blackbirds: Nursery Rhymes of Yesterday Recalled for Children of To-Day compiled by Helen Dean Fish. Illustrated by Robert Lawson. Stokes, 1937. Caldecott Honor Book.

> none located

> *See also* Robert Lawson, "Media about Newbery/Caldecott Authors and Illustrators."

Seven Simeons: A Russian Tale retold and illustrated by Boris Artzybasheff. Viking, 1937. Caldecott Honor Book.

> *Braille:* [BR681] NLSBPH.
> *Talking book:* [Tx-BPH(CBT2021)RC] NLSBPH.

MEDIA ABOUT NEWBERY/CALDECOTT
AUTHORS AND ILLUSTRATORS

Alexander, Lloyd

Audio: "Lloyd Alexander: Born Storyteller" [cassette, 41 min] Center for Cassette Studies, nd. op

Audio: "Lloyd Alexander" [Meet the author series, cassette, 20 min] Imperial, nd. op

Filmstrip/sound: "Lloyd Alexander" [Meet the Newbery author series, filmstrip/record or cassette, 94 fr/13 min] Miller-Brody, 1974. CMCE, ESLC, L, MMA

Video: "Lloyd Alexander, Evaline Ness and Ann Durrell" Profiles in Literature, 1972. op

Armstrong, William

Audio: "William Armstrong" [cassette] Pathways Educational Programs, nd. op

Filmstrip/sound: "William Armstrong" [Meet the Newbery author series, filmstrip/record or cassette, 87 fr/10 min] Miller-Brody, 1977. BKL 1/1/78, CMCE, ESLC, MMA

Babbitt, Natalie

Audio: "Natalie Babbitt" [Authors on tape series, cassette] Trumpet, 198?.

Filmstrip/sound: "Natalie Babbitt" [Meet the Newbery author series, filmstrip/record or cassette, 104 fr/15 min] Miller-Brody, 1978. ESLC, MMA

Baskin, Leonard

Audio: "Leonard Baskin" [cassette, 28 min] Center for Cassette Studies, nd. op

Audio: "A Sculptor's Philosophy of Art" [cassette] Center for Cassette Studies, 197?. op

Film: "Images of Leonard Baskin" [Artist at work series, 28 min] Contemporary Films, 1965. op

Blos, Joan W.

Audio: "Newbery Medal Acceptance Speech" [cassette] Weston Woods, 1980. op

Bontemps, Arna

Audio: "Arna Bontemps" [Meet the author series, cassette, 20 min] Imperial, nd. op

Filmstrip/sound: "Arna Bontemps and Aaron Douglas" [Profiles of black achievement series, 2 filmstrips/2 cassettes, 166 fr] Guidance Assoc, nd.

Video: "Arna Bontemps" Profiles in Liteature, 1971. op

Brink, Carol Ryrie

Filmstrip/sound: "Carol Ryrie Brink" [Meet the Newbery author series, filmstrip/record or cassette, 86 fr/15 min] Miller-Brody, 1976. CMCE, ESLC, MMA

Brown, Marcia

Audio: "Caldecott Medal Acceptance Speech" [cassette] Weston Woods, 1983. op

Byars, Betsy

Audio: "Betsy Byars" [Authors on tape series, cassette] Trumpet, 198?.

Filmstrip/sound: "Betsy Byars" [Meet the Newbery author series, filmstrip/record or cassette, 95 fr/12 min] Miller-Brody, 1978. ESLC, MMA

Kit: "Betsy Byars" [Author kits series, cassette/poster/teaching aids] Trumpet, 198?.

Poster: "Readers as Writers I" [3 mini-posters 8-1/2x11 in, with packet including letters and photos] ALA, 1988.

Caudill, Rebecca

Audio: "Rebecca Caudill" [Meet the author series, cassette, 20 min] Imperial, nd. op

Film: "Child of Appalachia" [18 min] Northern Illinois University, 1978.

Cleary, Beverly

Audio: "Beverly Cleary" [Authors on tape series, cassette] Trumpet, 198?.

Filmstrip/sound: "Beverly Cleary" [Meet the Newbery author series, filmstrip/cassette, 112 fr/13 min] Miller-Brody, 1979. ESLC, MMA

Kit: "Beverly Cleary" [Author kits series, cassette/poster/teaching aids] Trumpet, 198?.

Poster: "Readers as Writers II" [3 mini-posters 8-1/2x11 in, with packet including letters and photos] ALA, 1990.

Collier, Christopher and James Lincoln Collier

Filmstrip/sound: "James Lincoln Collier and Christopher Collier" [Meet the Newbery author series, filmstrip/cassette, 113 fr/11 min] Miller-Brody, 1981. ESLC, MMA

Cooney, Barbara

Film: "The Lively Art of Picture Books" [57 min] Weston Woods, 1965. MMA

Video: "The Lively Art of Picture Books" [57 min] Weston Woods, 1965. MMA

Cooper, Susan

Audio: "Newbery Medal Acceptance" [cassette], Weston Woods, 1976. op

Filmstrip/sound: "Susan Cooper" [Meet the Newbery author series, filmstrip/record or cassette, 97 fr/13 min] Miller-Brody, 1977. ESLC, MMA

Daugherty, James

Film: "James Daugherty" [Signature collection, 19 min] Weston Woods, 1972.

Video: "James Daugherty" [Signature collection, 19 min] Weston Woods, 1972.

d'Aulaire, Edgar Parin and Ingri

Film: "Children of the Northlights" [Signature collection, 20 min] Weston Woods, 1977. CINE, CMCS

Video: "Children of the Northlights" [Signature collection, 20 min] Weston Woods, 1977. CINE, CMCS

de Angeli, Marguerite

Audio: "Marguerite de Angeli" [Authors for children series, 3-3/4 ips tape, 25 min] National Center for Audio Tapes, nd. op

Video: "Marguerite de Angeli" Profiles in Literature, 1976. op

de Treviño, Elizabeth Borton de see Treviño, Elizabeth Borton de

dePaola, Tomie

Kit: "Tomie dePaola" [Author kits series, cassette/poster/teaching aids] Trumpet, 198?.

Dillon, Leo and Diane

Audio: "Leo and Diane Dillon" [cassette], Scholastic, 1992.

Audio: "Caldecott Medal Acceptance" [cassette], Weston Woods, 1977. op

Audio: "Caldecott Medal Acceptance" [cassette], Weston Woods, 1976.

Dr. Seuss see Geisel, Theodor Seuss

Edmonds, Walter

> *Film:* "Walter D. Edmonds: The Presence of the Past" [Writers on writing series, 18 min] Davidson, 1972.

Egielski, Richard

> *Audio:* "Caldecott Medal Acceptance Speech" [cassette] Weston Woods, 1987. op

Emberley, Ed

> *Film:* "Making Picture Books with Ed Emberley" [30 min] University of Michigan Television Center, nd. op

Enright, Elizabeth

> *Audio:* "Elizabeth Enright" [Authors for children series, 3-3/4 ips tape, 15 min] National Center for Audio Tapes, nd. op

Estes, Eleanor

> *Filmstrip/sound:* "Eleanor Estes" [Meet the Newbery author series, filmstrip/record or cassette, 95 fr/14 min] Miller-Brody, 1974. CMCE, ESLC, L, MMA
> *Video:* "Eleanor Estes" Profiles in Literature, 1975. op

Feelings, Tom and Muriel

> *Video:* "Tom and Muriel Feelings" Profiles in Literature, 1971. op.

Fleischman, Sid

> *Audio:* "Newbery Medal Acceptance Speech" [cassette] Weston Woods, 1987. op
> *Audio:* "Sid Fleischman: Mr. Mysterious" [cassette, 41 min] Center for Cassette Studies, nd. op
> *Filmstrip/sound:* "Meet the Newbery Author: Sid Fleischman" [First choice: Authors and books series, 2 filmstrips/cassette, 20 min] Pied Piper, 198?.
> *Video:* "Meet the Newbery Author: Sid Fleischman" [First choice: Authors and books series, 20 min] Pied Piper, 1987. ESLC

Foster, Genevieve

> *Film:* "Genevieve Foster's World" [13 min] Connecticut films, 1970. op

Fox, Paula

> *Audio:* "Paula Fox" [Authors on tape series, cassette] Trumpet, 198?.

Frasconi, Antonio

> *Film:* "Antonio Frasconi, Graphic Artist" [also Spanish, 20 min] Pablo Frasconi, 1975. op

Freedman, Russell

> *Audio:* "Newbery Medal Acceptance Speech" [cassette] Weston Woods, 1988. op
> *Video:* "Meet the Newbery Author: Russell Freedman" [20 min] American School, 1991. BKL 6/1/91
> *Video:* "Russell Freedman" [cassette] Scholastic, 1991.
> *Video:* "A Visit with Russell Freedman" [18 min] Houghton, 1990. BKL 1/1/91, SLJ 4/91

Freeman, Don

> *Film:* "Storymaker" [14 min] Churchill, 1972.
> *Video:* "Storymaker" [14 min] Churchill, 1972.

Fritz, Jean

> *Audio:* "Jean Fritz" [Authors on tape series, cassette] Trumpet, 198?.
> *Poster:* "Readers as Writers I" [3 mini-posters 8-1/2x11 in, with packet including letters and photos] ALA, 1988.
> *Video:* "Visit with Jean Fritz" [20 min] Putnam, 1987. ESLC

Gág, Wanda

> *Filmstrip/sound:* "Wanda Gág, 1893-1946" [filmstrip/cassette, 86 fr/16 min] Heritage, 1984. ESLC
> *Video:* "Wanda Gág, 1893-1946: A Minnesota Childhood" [10 min] Heritage, 1984.

Geisel, Theodor Seuss

Filmstrip/sound: "Who's Dr. Seuss? Meet Ted Geisel" [filmstrip/cassette, 122 fr/13 min] Miller-Brody, 1980. ESLC, L, MMA

Filmstrip/sound: "Best of Dr. Seuss" includes "Who's Dr. Seuss? Meet Ted Geisel" [filmstrip/cassette] Random, 198?.

George, Jean Craighead

Audio: "Jean Craighead George" [Authors on tape series, cassette] Trumpet, 198?.

Audio: "Newbery Medal Acceptance Speech" [cassette] Weston Woods, 1973. op

Filmstrip/sound: "Jean Craighead George" [Meet the Newbery author series, filmstrip/record or cassette, 99 fr/16 min] Miller-Brody, 1974. CMCE, ELSC, L, MMA

Video: "Her Side of the Mountain: A Conversation with Jean Craighead George" [27 min] Podell, 1989. SLJ 5/90

Video: "Jean George, Writing" [Pass it along series, 15 min] GPN, 1984.

Video: "Jean George" Profiles in Literature, 1974. op

Gipson, Fred

Audio: "Fred Gipson" [Authors for children series, 3-3/4 ips tape, 15 min] National Center for Audio Tapes, nd. op

Goble, Paul

Audio: "Caldecott Medal Acceptance Speech" [cassette] Weston Woods, 1979. op

Poster: "Readers as Writers II" [3 mini-posters 8-1/2x11 in, with packet including letters and photos] ALA, 1990.

Gray, Elizabeth Janet

Video: "Elizabeth Gray Vining" Profiles in Literature, 1969. op

Greene, Bette

Filmstrip/sound: "Bette Greene" [Meet the Newbery author series, 2 Filmstrips/record or cassette, 100 fr/13 min] Miller-Brody, 1978. MMA

Haley, Gail E.

Filmstrip/sound: "Gail E. Haley: Wood and Linoleum Illustration" [filmstrip/cassette, 72 fr/17 min] Weston Woods, 1978. CMCS, MMA

Hall, Donald

Audio: "Donald Hall: Interview" [cassette, 29 min] New Letters, 1987.

Video: "Donald Hall" [Poets talking series, 29 min] University of Michigan Television Center, 1975. op

Hamilton, Virginia

Audio: "Virginia Hamilton" [cassette] Scholastic, 1991.

Audio: "Virginia Hamilton" [Authors on tape series, cassette] Trumpet, 198?.

Filmstrip/sound: "Virginia Hamilton" [Meet the Newbery author series, filmstrip/record or cassette, 101 fr/15 min] Miller-Brody, 1976. ALSC, BKL 12/1/76, CMCE, ESLC, L, MMA

Henry, Marguerite

Audio: "Marguerite Henry" [Authors for children series, 3-3/4 ips tape, 15 min] National Center for Audio Tapes, nd. op

Film: "Story of a Book (2nd ed)" [16 min] Pied Piper, 1980.

Filmstrip/sound: "Story of a Book (2nd ed)" [First choice: Author and books series, filmstrip/cassette, 124 fr/16 min] Pied Piper, 1982. ALSC, MMA

Filmstrip/sound: "Marguerite Henry" [Meet the Newbery author series, filmstrip/record or cassette, 85 fr/18 min] Miller-Brody, 1974. ESLC

Poster: "Readers as writers I" [3 mini-posters 8-1/2x11 in, with packet including letters and photos] ALA, 1988.

Video: "Story of a Book (2nd ed)" [16 min] Pied Piper, 1980.

Highwater, Jamake

Filmstrip/sound: "Jamake Highwater" [Meet the Newbery author series, filmstrip/cassette, 118 fr/18 min] Miller-Brody, 1980. MMA

Holling, Holling C.

Filmstrip/sound: "Enjoying Illustrations (rev ed)" [Literature for children series 3, filmstrip/cassette] Pied Piper, 1983.
Filmstrip/sound: "Story of a Book" [Literature for children series 1, filmstrip/cassette, about 12 min] Pied Piper, 198?.
Video: "Story of a Book" [Literature for children series 1, 11 min] Pied Piper, 198?.

Hunt, Irene

Audio: "Irene Hunt" [cassette, 15 min] Pathways Educational Programs, 196?. op MMA
Video: "Writing for Children with Irene Hunt" [b&w, 30 min] University of Michigan Television Center, 1967. op

Hyman, Trina Schart

Audio: "Caldecott Medal Acceptance Speech" [cassette] Weston Woods, 1985. op

James, Will

Audio: "Lone Cowboy: My Life Story" [9 cassettes, 810 min] Books on Tape, nd.
Film: "The Man They Call Will James" [30 min] Direct Cinema, 1991. BKL 9/1/91
Video: "The Man They Call Will James" [30 min] Direct Cinema, 1991. BKL 9/1/91
Video: "Alias Will James" National Film Board of Canada, 1989.

Jarrell, Randall

Audio: "American Prose, Part 3" [Audio sketches of American writers series, cassette] NPR, 1981.
Film: "Books and Children in Today's World" [b&w, 45 min] University of North Carolina
Audio: visual Bureau, nd. op

Jones, Elizabeth Orton

Audio: "Caldecott Medal Acceptance Speech" [cassette] Weston Woods, 1980. op
Audio: "Elizabeth Orton Jones" [Meet the author series, cassette, 20 min] Imperial, nd. op

Jukes, Mavis

Film: "The Writing Process: A Conversation with Mavis Jukes" [20 min] Coronet/MTI, 1989. SLJ 8/90
Video: "The Writing Process: A Conversation with Mavis Jukes" [20 min] Coronet/MTI, 1989. SLJ 8/90

Keats, Ezra Jack

Audio: "Our Favorite Mr. Keats" [cassette, 33 min] Center for Cassette Studies, nd. op
Film: "Ezra Jack Keats" [Signature collection, 17 min] Weston Woods, 1970. BKL 6/15/71, CMCS, MMA
Video: "Ezra Jack Keats" [Signature collection, 17 min] Weston Woods, 1970.
Video: "Ezra Jack Keats" Profiles in Literature, 1980. op

Konigsburg, E.L.

Audio: "Focus on Elaine Konigsburg" [cassette, 37 min] Center for Cassette Studies, nd. op
Filmstrip/sound: "From the Mixed-Up Files of Mrs. Basil E. Frankweiler" includes author interview [First choice: Authors and books series, 2 filmstrips/cassette, 154 fr/34 min] Pied Piper, 1980. MMA

Krumgold, Joseph

Video: "Joseph Krumgold" Profiles in Literature, 1971. op

Latham, Jean Lee

Audio: "Jean Lee Latham" [Authors for children series, 3-3/4 ips tape, 15 min] National Center for Audio Tapes, nd. op

Lawson, Robert

Audio: "Newbery Medal Acceptance Speech" [cassette] Weston Woods, 1980. op

Le Guin, Ursula

Audio: "Ursula Le Guin" [cassette, 54 min] Center for Cassette Studies, 1973. op

L'Engle, Madeleine

Audio: "A Conversation with Madeleine L'Engle" [cassette, 60 min] Center for Cassette Studies, nd. op

Film: "Madeleine L'Engle: Star Gazer" [29 min] Ishtar, 1989. BKL 5/1/90, SLJ 5/90, YASD

Filmstrip/sound: "Madeleine L'Engle" [Meet the Newbery author series, 102 fr/16 min] Miller-Brody, 1974. ESLC, MMA

Video: "Madeleine L'Engle" Profiles in Literature, 1970. op

Video: "Madeleine L'Engle: Star Gazer" [29 min] Ishtar, 1989. ALSC, BKL 5/1/90, BVC, SLJ 5/90

Lenski, Lois

Audio: "Lois Lenski: Children's Storywriter" [Once upon a time in Ohio series, 3-3/4 ips tape, 15 min] Ohio State Museum, 1961. op

Lent, Blair

Audio: "Caldecott Medal Acceptance Speech" [cassette] Weston Woods, 1973. op

Lobel, Arnold

Audio: "Caldecott Medal Acceptance Speech" [cassette] Weston Woods, 1981. op

Filmstrip/sound: "Arnold Lobel (rev ed)" [Meet the Newbery author series, filmstrip/cassette, 104 fr/12 min] Random, 1986. ESLC

Filmstrip/sound: "Arnold Lobel" [Meet the Newbery author series, filmstrip/record or cassette, 97 fr/11 min] Miller-Brody, 1978. ALSC, ESLC, MMA

Poster: "Readers as Writers II" [3 mini-posters 8-1/2x11 in, with packet including letters and photos] ALA, 1990.

Video: "Arnold Lobel" Profiles in Literature, 1973. op

Video: "Arnold Lobel Showcase" includes "Arnold Lobel: Meet the Newbery Author" [filmstrip-on-video, 60 min] Random, 1985. ESLC, PC

Lowry, Lois

Video: "A Visit with Lois Lowry" [19 min] Houghton, 1985. ESLC

Macaulay, David

Audio: "David Macaulay" [Authors on tape series, cassette] Trumpet, 198?.

Video: "David Macaulay in His Studio" [25 min] Houghton, 1983. ESLC

Video: "A Visit with David Macaulay" [25 min] Houghton, 1983.

MacLachlan, Patricia

Audio: "Author Talks" includes Patricia MacLachlan [cassette, 35 min] Children's Book Council, 1990.

Audio: "Newbery Medal Acceptance Speech" [cassette] Weston Woods, 1986. op; also ALA, 199?

Audio: "Patricia MacLachlan" [Authors on tape series, cassette] Trumpet, 198?.

Marshall, James

Kit: "James Marshall" [Author kits series, cassette/poster/teaching aids] Trumpet, 198?.

Video: "James Marshall in His Studio" Houghton, 1990?

Mazer, Norma Fox

Audio: "Author Talks" includes Norma Fox Mazer [cassette, 35 min] Children's Book Council, 1990.

McCloskey, Robert

Film: "Robert McCloskey" [Signature collection, 18 min] Weston Woods, 1965. MMA

Film: "The Lively Art of Picture Books" [57 min] Weston Woods, 1964. MMA

Filmstrip/sound: "Enjoying Illustrations (rev ed)" [Literature for children series 3, filmstrip/cassette, about 12 min] Pied Piper, 1983.

Kit: "Robert McCloskey" [Author kits series, cassette/poster/teaching aids] Trumpet, 198?.

Video: "The Robert McCloskey Library" includes "Getting to Know Robert McCloskey" [55 min] Children's Circle, 1990.

Video: "Enjoying Illustrations" [Literature for children series 3, about 12 min] Pied Piper, 198?.

Video: "Robert McCloskey" Profiles in Literature, 1977. op

Video: "Robert McCloskey" [Signature collection, 18 min] Weston Woods, 1965.

Video: "The Lively Art of Picture Books" [57 min] Weston Woods, 1964. MMA

McKinley, Robin

Audio: "Newbery Medal Acceptance Speech" [cassette] Weston Woods, 1985. op

Minarik, Else Holmelund

Audio: "Else Holmelund Minarik" [Authors on tape series, cassette] Trumpet, 198?.

Myers, Walter Dean

Audio: "Author Talks" includes Walter Dean Myers [cassette, 35 min] Children's Book Council, 1990.

Audio: "Walter Dean Myers" [Authors on tape series, cassette] Trumpet, 198?.

Naylor, Phyllis Reynolds

Audio: "Phyllis Naylor" [cassette, 59 min] American Audio, 1989.

Ness, Evaline

Poster: "Readers as Writers I" [3 mini-posters 8-1/2x11 in, with packet including letters and photos] ALA, 1988.

Video: "Lloyd Alexander, Evaline Ness and Ann Durrell" Profiles in Literature, 1972. op

O'Dell, Scott

Filmstrip/sound: "Scott O'Dell" [Meet the Newbery author series, filmstrip/record or cassette, 85 fr/13 min] Miller-Brody, 1974. ESLC, MMA

Kit: "Scott O'Dell" [Author kits series, cassette/poster/teaching aids] Trumpet, 198?.

Video: "Scott O'Dell" Profiles in Literature, 1976. op

Video: "A Visit with Scott O'Dell" [Author and artist series, 13 min] Houghton, 1983. ESLC

Paterson, Katherine

Audio: "Katherine Paterson" [cassette] Scholastic, 1992.

Audio: "Katherine Paterson: An Interview" [cassette, 45 min] Miller-Brody, 1983. MMA

Audio: "Newbery Medal Acceptance Speech" [cassette] Weston Woods, 1981. op

Audio: "Newbery Medal Acceptance Speech" [cassette] Weston Woods, 1978. op

Filmstrip/sound: "Katherine Paterson" [Meet the Newbery author series, filmstrip/cassette, 145 fr/20 min] Miller-Brody, 1983. ESLC, L

Video: "The Author's Eye: Katherine Paterson" [25 min] American School, 1989.

Paulsen, Gary

Audio: "Gary Paulsen" [cassette] Scholastic, 1991.

Audio: "Gary Paulsen" [Authors on tape series, cassette] Trumpet, 198?.

Video: "Share the Excitement" includes Gary Paulsen [60 min] Bantam, 1991.

Peet, Bill

Audio: "Picture Book World of Bill Peet" [cassette, 59 min] Center for Cassette Studies, nd. op

Video: "Bill Peet in His Studio" [14 min] Houghton, 1983. ESLC

Pinkney, Jerry

Video: "Meet the Caldecott Illustrator: Jerry Pinkney" [21 min] American School, 1991. BKL 6/15/91

Politi, Leo

Film: "Learning about People through Books" [Living in the west television series, b&w, 15 min] Los Angeles County Schools, 1962. op

Raskin, Ellen

Audio: "Newbery Medal Acceptance Speech" [cassette] Weston Woods, 1979. op

Rawlings, Marjorie Kinnan

Braille: "Cross Creek" [BRA6228] NLSBPH.

Talking book: "Cross Creek" [RC14299] NLSBPH.

Video: "Cross Creek" [live-action, 120 min] HBO, 1983.

Rylant, Cynthia

Filmstrip/sound: "Meet the Newbery Author: Cynthia Rylant" [filmstrip/cassette, 17 min] American School, 1990. BKL 9/1/90, SLJ 1/91

Video: "Meet the Newbery Author: Cynthia Rylant" [17 min] American School, 1990. ALSC, BKL 9/1/90, SLJ 1/91

Video: "Meet the Picture Book Author: Cynthia Rylant" [10 min] American School, 1990.

Sandoz, Mari

Audio: "Mari Sandoz" [Western American writers series, cassette, 35 min] Everett/Edwards, nd. op

Video: "Past, Present, Future: Mari Sandoz" [30 min] GPN, nd.

Video: "Song of the Plains: The Story of Mari Sandoz" [60 min] GPN, nd.

Sawyer, Ruth

Audio: "Ruth Sawyer, Storyteller" [2 records or cassette] Weston Woods, 1968. ESLC

Schoenherr, John

Audio: "Caldecott Medal Acceptance Speech" [cassette] Weston Woods, 1988. op

Selden, George *see* Thompson, George

Sendak, Maurice

Audio: "Maurice Sendak: An Interview" [cassette, 25 min] Tapes for Readers, nd.

Film: "Sendak" [Signature collection, 27 min] Weston Woods, 1987. CINE

Film: "Max Made Mischief: An Approach to Literature" [30 min] Documentaries for Learning, 1977. op

Film: "Maurice Sendak" [Signature collection, 14 min] Weston Woods, 1965. MMA

Film: "The Lively Art of Picture Books" [57 min] Weston Woods, 1964. MMA

Kit: "Maurice Sendak" [Author kits series, cassette/poster/teaching aids] Trumpet, 198?.

Video: "Maurice Sendak" Profiles in Literature, 1977. op

Video: "The Maurice Sendak Library" includes "Getting to Know Maurice Sendak" [35 min] Children's Circle, 1989.

Video: "Sendak" [Signature collection, 27 min] Weston Woods, 1987.

Video: "Maurice Sendak" [Signature collection, 14 min] Weston Woods, 1965.

Video: "The Lively Art of Picture Books" [57 min] Weston Woods, 1964. MMA

Seredy, Kate

Audio: "Kate Seredy" [Meet the author series, cassette, 20 min] Imperial, nd. op

Seuss, Dr. *see* Geisel, Theodor Seuss

Singer, Isaac Bashevis

Audio: "Isaac Bashevis Singer: An Interview" [cassette, 45 min] Tapes for Readers, 1968.

Audio: "Conversations with Creative People over 70" [cassette, 59 min] NPR, nd.

Film: "Isaac in America: A Journey with Isaac Bashevis Singer" [58 min] Direct Cinema, 1986.

Film: "A Conversation with Isaac Bashevis Singer" [Eternal light series, b&w, 30 min] National Academy for Adult Jewish Studies, 1967. op

Filmstrip/sound: "Isaac Bashevis Singer" [Meet the Newbery author series, filmstrip/ record or cassette, 88 fr/18 min] Miller-Brody, 1976. BKL 10/15/76, CMCE, ESLC, L, MMA

Video: "Isaac in America: A Journey with Issac Bashevis Singer" [58 min] Direct Cinema, 1986.

Slobodkin, Louis

Audio: "Louis Slobodkin" [Authors for children series, 3-3/4 ips tape, 30 min] National Center for

Audio: Tapes, nd. op

Speare, Elizabeth George

Kit: "Elizabeth George Speare" [Author kits series, cassette/poster/teaching aids] Trumpet, 198?.

Video: "Elizabeth George Speare" Profiles in Literature, 1975. op

Video: "A Visit with Elizabeth George Speare" [Author and artist series, 15 min] Houghton, 1986. ESLC

Spier, Peter

Audio: "Caldecott Medal Acceptance Speech" [cassette] Weston Woods, 1978. op

Film: "American Songfest" includes Peter Spier [Signature collection, 42 min] Weston Woods, 1976.

Kit: "Peter Spier" [Author kits series, cassette/poster/teaching aids] Trumpet, 198?.

Video: "American Songfest" includes Peter Spier [Signature collection, 42 min] Weston Woods, 1976.

Spinelli, Jerry

Audio: "Jerry Spinelli" [cassette] Scholastic, 1991.

Audio: "Author Talks" includes Jerry Spinelli [cassette, 35 min] Children's Book Council, 1990.

Audio: "Newbery Medal Acceptance" [cassette] Weston Woods, 1990. op

Steele, William O.

Audio: "William O. Steele" [Meet the author series, cassette, 20 min] Imperial, 1969. op

Stolz, Mary

Audio: "Mary Stolz" [Meet the author series, cassette, 20 min] Imperial, nd. op

Taylor, Mildred D.

Audio: "Author Talks" includes Mildred D. Taylor [cassette, 35 min] Children's Book Council, 1990.

Audio: "Newbery Medal Acceptance" [cassette] Weston Woods, 1977. op

Kit: "Mildred Taylor" [Author kits series, cassette/poster/teaching aids] Trumpet, 198?.

Video: "Meet the Newbery Author: Mildred D. Taylor" [21 min] American School, 1991. BKL 6/1/91

Video: "Mildred D. Taylor: Roll of Thunder, Hear My Cry" [26 min] Films for the Humanities, 1988, released 1991. LJ 11/1/91, SLJ 11/91

Thompson, George

Audio: "George Selden" [Authors on tape series, cassette] Trumpet, 198?.

Thurber, James

Audio: "The Round Table Crowd" [cassette, 27 min] Center for Cassette Studies, nd. op

Film: "James Thurber: Reflections on His Boyhood" [b&w, 21 min] IQ Films, 1966. op

Treviño, Elizabeth Borton de

Video: "Elizabeth Borton de Treviño" [also Spanish] Profiles in Literature, 1977. op

Tunis, Edwin

Audio: "Mr. Edwin Tunis" [Authors for children series, 3-3/4 ips tape, 21 min] National Center for Audio Tapes, nd. op

Van Allsburg, Chris

Audio: "Caldecott Medal Acceptance Speech" [cassette] Weston Woods, 1986. op

Audio: "Caldecott Medal Acceptance Speech" [cassette] Weston Woods, 1982. op

Filmstrip/sound: "Book Review/Fantasy" discusses work of Chris Van Allsburg [Literature to enjoy and write about series 2, filmstrip/cassette, about 20 min] Pied Piper, 1989. SLJ 5/90

Video: "Book Review/Fantasy" discusses work of Chris Van Allsburg [Literature to enjoy and write about series 2, about 20 min] Pied Piper, 1989. SLJ 5/90

Vining, Elizabeth see Gray, Elizabeth Janet

Voigt, Cynthia

Audio: "Newbery Medal Acceptance Speech" [cassette] Weston Woods, 1983. op

Ward, Lynd

Video: "Lynd Ward and May McNeer" Profiles in Literature, 1974. op

White, E.B.

Filmstrip/sound: "E.B. White" [Meet the Newbery author series, filmstrip/cassette] Miller-Brody, 1988.

Wier, Ester

Audio: "Ester Wier" [Authors for children series, 3-3/4 ips tape, 13 min] National Center for Audio Tapes, nd. op

Wilder, Laura Ingalls

Audio: "Laura Ingalls Wilder" [Books and around series, 3-3/4 ips tape, 30 min] KUOM Radio-University of Minnesota, nd. op

Filmstrip/sound: "Laura Ingalls Wilder" [Meet the Newbery author series, filmstrip/cassette, 122 fr/17 min] Miller-Brody, 1980. ESLC, MMA

Filmstrip/sound: "The Will and the Way of Laura Ingalls Wilder" [Filmstrip/cassette] Miller-Brody, 1979.

Filmstrip/sound: "Laura: Little House, Big Prairie" [filmstrip/record or cassette, 140 fr/18 min] Perfection Form, 1975. BKL 6/1/77, CMCE

Talking book: "Laura Ingalls Wilder: Growing up in the Little House" [RC27852] NLSBPH.

Willard, Nancy

Audio: "Newbery Medal Acceptance Speech" [cassette] Weston Woods, 1982. op

Filmstrip/sound: "Nancy Willard" [Meet the Newbery author series, filmstrip/cassette, 155 fr/19 min] Miller-Brody, 1983. ESLC, L

Williams, Vera B.

Audio: "Vera B. Williams" [cassette] Scholastic, 1991.

Wojciechowska, Maia

Audio: "Maia Wojciechowska" [Authors for children series, 3-3/4 ips tape, 15 min] National Center for Audio Tapes, nd. op

Video: "An Author's View of Children's Literature" [English for elementary teachers literature series, b&w, 30 min] National Council of Teachers of English, nd. op

Yates, Elizabeth

Audio: "Elizabeth Yates" [Meet the author series, cassette, 20 min] Imperial, nd. op

Filmstrip/sound: "Elizabeth Yates" [Meet the Newbery author series, filmstrip/record or cassette, 113 fr/19 min] Miller-Brody, 1976. BKL 12/15/76, CMCE, ESLC

Yep, Laurence

Filmstrip/sound: "Laurence Yep" [Meet the Newbery author series, filmstrip/cassette, 84 fr/12 min] Miller-Brody, 1981. ESLC, MMA

Yolen, Jane

Poster: "Readers as Writers II" [3 mini-posters 8-1/2x11 in, with packet including letters and photos] ALA, 1990.

Zolotow, Charlotte

Filmstrip/sound: "The Best of Charlotte Zolotow" includes "Charlotte Zolotow: The Grower" [filmstrip/cassette] Random, 1988.

Filmstrip/sound: "Charlotte Zolotow: The Grower" [filmstrip/cassette, 147 fr/18 min] Miller-Brody, 1982. ESLC, L

APPENDIX A:
NEWBERY MEDAL AND HONOR BOOKS
1922-1992

Note: Honor Book listings are in alphabetical order within the award year. "No record" indicates that Honor Books for that year, if any, are not known and records do not exist to indicate which books received the designation for that year.

1922

Medal Book

Story of Mankind by Hendrik Van Loon

Honor Books

Cedric the Forester by Bernard Marshall
Golden Fleece and the Heroes Who Lived Before Achilles by Padraic Colum
Great Quest by Charles B. Hawes
Old Tobacco Shop by William Bowen
Windy Hill by Cornelia Meigs

1923

Medal Book

Voyages of Dr. Dolittle by Hugh Lofting

Honor Books

No record

1924

Medal Book

Dark Frigate by Charles B. Hawes

Honor Books

No record

1925

Medal Book

Tales from Silver Lands by Charles Finger

Honor Books

Dream Coach by Anne Parrish
Nicholas by Anne Moore

1926

Medal Book

Shen of the Sea by Arthur Chrisman

Honor Book

Voyagers by Padraic Colum

1927

Medal Book

Smoky, the Cowhorse by Will James

Honor Books

No record

1928

Medal Book

Gayneck: The Story of a Pigeon by Dhan Mukerji

Honor Books

Downright Dencey by Caroline Snedeker
Wonder Smith and His Son by Ella Young

1929

Medal Book

Trumpeter of Krakow by Eric Kelly

Honor Books

Boy Who Was by Grace Hallock
Clearing Weather by Cornelia Meigs
Millions of Cats by Wanda Gág
Pigtail of Ah Lee Ben Loo by John Bennett
Runaway Papoose by Grace Moon
Tod of the Fens by Elinor Whitney

1930

Medal Book

Hitty by Rachel Field

Honor Books

Daughter of the Seine by Jeanette Eaton
Jumping-Off Place by Marian McNeely
Little Blacknose by Hildegarde Swift
Pran of Albania by Elizabeth Miller

Tangle-Coated Horse and Other Tales by Ella Young
Vaino by Julia Adams

1931

Medal Book

Cat Who Went to Heaven by Elizabeth Coatsworth

Honor Books

Dark Star of Itza by Alida Malkus
Floating Island by Anne Parrish
Garram the Hunter by Herbert Best
Meggy Macintosh by Elizabeth Gray
Mountains Are Free by Julia Adams
Ood-Le-Uk the Wanderer by Alison Lide and Margaret Johansen
Queer Person by Ralph Hubbard
Spice and the Devil's Cave by Agnes Hewes

1932

Medal Book

Waterless Mountain by Laura Armer

Honor Books

Boy of the South Seas by Eunice Tietjens
Calico Bush by Rachel Field
Fairy Circus by Dorothy Lathrop
Jane's Island by Marjorie Allee
Out of the Flame by Eloise Lownsbery
Truce of the Wolf and Other Tales of Old Italy by Mary Davis

1933

Medal Book

Young Fu of the Upper Yangtze by Elizabeth Lewis

Honor Books

Children of the Soil by Nora Burglon
Railroad to Freedom by Hildegarde Swift
Swift Rivers by Cornelia Meigs

1934

Medal Book

Invicible Louisa by Cornelia Meigs

Honor Books

ABC Bunny by Wanda Gág
Apprentice of Florence by Anne Kyle
Big Tree of Bunlahy by Padraic Colum
Forgotten Daughter by Caroline Snedeker
Glory of the Seas by Agnes Hewes
New Land by Sarah Schmidt
Swords of Steel by Elsie Singmaster
Winged Girl of Knossos by Erick Berry

1935

Medal Book

Dobry by Monica Shannon

Honor Books

Davy Crockett by Constance Rourke
Day on Skates by Hilda Van Stockum
Pageant of Chinese History by Elizabeth Seeger

1936

Medal Book

Caddie Woodlawn by Carol Brink

Honor Books

All Sail Set by Amrstrong Sperry
Good Master by Kate Seredy
Honk, the Moose by Phil Stong
Young Walter Scott by Elizabeth Gray

1937

Medal Book

Roller Skates by Ruth Sawyer

Honor Books

Audubon by Constance Rourke
Codfish Market by Agnes Hewes
Golden Basket by Ludwig Bemelmans
Phebe Fairchild, Her Book by Lois Lenski
Whistler's Van by Idwal Jones
Winterbound by Margery Bianco

1938

Medal Book

White Stag by Kate Seredy

Honor Books

Bright Island by Mabel Robinson
On the Banks of Plum Creek by Laura Wilder
Pecos Bill by James Bowman

1939

Medal Book

Thimble Summer by Elizabeth Enright

Honor Books

"Hello the Boat" by Phyllis Crawford
Leader by Destiny by Jeanette Eaton
Mr. Popper's Penguins by Richard and Florence
  Atwater
Nino by Valenti Angelo
Penn by Elizabeth Gray

1940

Medal Book

Daniel Boone by James Daugherty

Honor Books

Boy with a Pack by Stephen Meader
By the Shores of Silver Lake by Laura Wilder
Runner of the Mountain Tops by Mabel Robinson
Singing Tree by Kate Seredy

1941

Medal Book

Call It Courage by Armstrong Sperry

Honor Books

Blue Willow by Doris Gates
Long Winter by Laura Wilder
Nansen by Anna Hall
Young Mac of Fort Vancouver by Mary Jane Carr

1942

Medal Book

Matchlock Gun by Walter Edmonds

Honor Books

Down Ryton Water by Eva Gaggin
George Washington's World by Genevieve Foster
Indian Captive by Lois Lenski
Little Town on the Prairie by Laura Wilder

1943

Medal Book

Adam of the Road by Elizabeth Gray

Honor Books

"Have You Seen Tom Thumb?" by Mabel Hunt
Middle Moffat by Eleanor Estes

1944

Medal Book

Johnny Tremain by Esther Forbes

Honor Books

Fog Magic by Julia Sauer
Mountain Born by Elizabeth Yates
Rufus M. by Eleanor Estes

These Happy Golden Years by Laura Wilder

1945

Medal Book

Rabbit Hill by Robert Lawson

Honor Books

Abraham Lincoln's World by Genevieve Foster
Hundred Dresses by Eleanor Estes
Lone Journey by Jeanette Eaton
Silver Pencil by Alice Dalgliesh

1946

Medal Book

Strawberry Girl by Lois Lenski

Honor Books

Bhimsa, the Dancing Bear by Christine Weston
Justin Morgan Had a Horse by Marguerite Henry
Moved-Outers by Florence Means
New Found World by Katherine Shippen

1947

Medal Book

Miss Hickory by Carolyn Bailey

Honor Books

Avion My Uncle Flew by Cyrus Fisher
Big Tree by Mary and Conrad Buff
Heavenly Tenants by William Maxwell
Hidden Treasures of Glaston by Eleanore Jewett
Wonderful Year by Nancy Barnes

1948

Medal Book

Twenty-One Balloons by William du Bois

Honor Books

Cow-Tail Switch, and Other West African Stories by
   Harold Courlander
Li Lun by Carolyn Treffinger
Misty of Chincoteague by Marguerite Henry
Pancakes—Paris by Claire Bishop
Quaint and Curious Education of Johnny Longfoot by
   Catherine Besterman

1949

Medal Book

King of the Wind by Marguerite Henry

Honor Books

Daughter of the Mountain by Louise Rankin
My Father's Dragon by Ruth Gannett
Seabird by Holling Holling
Story of the Negro by Arna Bontemps

1950

Medal Book

Door In the Wall by Marguerite de Angeli

Honor Books

Blue Cat of Castle Town by Catherine Coblentz
George Washington by Genevieve Foster
Kildee House by Rutherford Montgomery
Song of the Pines by Walter and Marion Havighurst
Tree of Freedom by Rebecca Caudill

1951

Medal Book

Amos Fortune: Free Man by Elizabeth Yates

Honor Books

Abraham Lincoln: Friend of the People by Clara
   Judson
Better Known as Johnny Appleseed by Mabel Hunt

Gandhi: Fighter without a Sword by Jeanette Eaton
Story of Appleby Capple by Anne Parrish

1952

Medal Book

Ginger Pye by Eleanor Estes

Honor Books

Americans Before Columbus by Elizabeth Baity
Apple and the Arrow by Mary and Conrad Buff
Defender by Nicholas Kalashnikoff
Light at Tern Rock by Julia Sauer
Minn of the Mississippi by Holling Holling

1953

Medal Book

Secret of the Andes by Ann Clark

Honor Books

Bears on Hemlock Mountain by Alice Dalgliesh
Birthdays of Freedom, Volume 1 by Genevieve Foster
Charlotte's Web by E. B. White
Moccasin Trail by Eloise McGraw
Red Sails to Capri by Ann Weil

1954

Medal Book

. . . And Now Miguel by Joseph Krumgold

Honor Books

All Alone by Claire Bishop
Hurry Home, Candy by Meindert DeJong
Magic Maize by Mary and Conrad Buff
Shadrach by Meidert DeJong
Theodore Roosevelt by Clara Judson

1955

Medal Book

Wheel on the School by Meindert DeJong

Honor Books

Banner In the Sky by James Ullman
Courage of Sarah Noble by Alice Dalgliesh

1956

Medal Book

Carry On, Mr. Bowditch by Jean Latham

Honor Books

Golden Name Day by Jennie Lindquist
Men, Microscopes and Living Things by Katherine Shippen
Secret River by Marjorie Rawlings

1957

Medal Book

Miracles on Maple Hill by Virginia Sorensen

Honor Books

Black Fox of Lorne by Marguerite de Angeli
Corn Grows Ripe by Dorothy Rhoads
House of Sixty Fathers by Meindert DeJong
Mr. Justice Holmes by Clara Judson
Old Yeller by Fred Gipson

1958

Medal Book

Rifles for Watie by Harold Keith

Honor Books

Gone-Away Lake by Elizabeth Enright
Great Wheel by Robert Lawson

Horsecatcher by Mari Sandoz
Tom Paine by Leo Gurko

1959

Medal Book

Witch of Blackbird Pond by Elizabeth Speare

Honor Books

Along Came a Dog by Meindert DeJong
Chúcaro by Frances Kalnay
Family Under the Bridge by Natalie Carlson
Perilous Road by William Steele

1960

Medal Book

Onion John by Joseph Krumgold

Honor Books

America Is Born by Gerald Johnson
Gammage Cup by Carol Kendall
My Side of the Mountain by Jean George

1961

Medal Book

Island of the Blue Dolphins by Scott O'Dell

Honor Books

America Moves Forward by Gerald Johnson
Cricket In Times Square by George Selden
Old Ramon by Jack Schaefer

1962

Medal Book

Bronze Bow by Elizabeth Speare

Honor Books

Belling the Tiger by Mary Stolz
Frontier Living by Edwin Tunis
Golden Goblet by Eloise McGraw

1963

Medal Book

Wrinkle In Time by Madeleine L'Engle

Honor Books

Men of Athens by Olivia Coolidge
Thistle and Thyme by Sorche Nic Leodhas

1964

Medal Book

It's Like This, Cat by Emily Neville

Honor Books

Loner by Ester Weir
Rascal by Sterling North

1965

Medal Book

Shadow of a Bull by Maia Wojciechowska

Honor Book

Across Five Aprils by Irene Hunt

1966

Medal Book

I, Juan de Pareja by Elizabeth de Treviño

Honor Books

Animal Family by Randall Jarrell

Black Cauldron by Lloyd Alexander
Noonday Friends by Mary Stolz

1967

Medal Book

Up a Road Slowly by Irene Hunt

Honor Books

Jazz Man by Mary Weik
King's Fifth by Scott O'Dell
Zlateh the Goat by Isaac Singer

1968

Medal Book

From the Mixed-Up Files of Mrs. Basil E. Frankweiler
   by E. L. Konigsburg

Honor Books

Black Pearl by Scott O'Dell
Egypt Game by Zilpha Snyder
Fearsome Inn by Isaac Singer
Jennifer, Hecate, Macbeth, William McKinley, and Me,
   Elizabeth by E. L. Konigsburg

1969

Medal Book

High King by Lloyd Alexander

Honor Books

To Be a Slave by Julius Lester
When Shlemiel Went to Warsaw by Isaac Singer

1970

Medal Book

Sounder by William Armstrong

Honor Books

Journey Outside by Mary Steele
Many Ways of Seeing by Janet Moore
Our Eddie by Sulmith Ish-Kishor

1971

Medal Book

Summer of the Swans by Betsy Byars

Honor Books

Enchantress from the Stars by Sylvia Engdahl
Knee-Knock Rise by Natalie Babbit
Sing Down the Moon by Scott O'Dell

1972

Medal Book

Mrs. Frisby and the Rats of NIMH by Robert O'Brien

Honor Books

Annie and the Old One by Miska Miles
Headless Cupid by Zilpha Snyder
Incident at Hawk's Hill by Allan Eckert
Planet of Junior Brown by Virginia Hamilton
Tombs of Atuan by Ursula Le Guin

1973

Medal Book

Julie of the Wolves by Jean George

Honor Books

Frog and Toad Together by Arnold Lobel
Upstairs Room by Johanna Reiss
Witches of Worm by Zilpha Snyder

1974

Medal Book

Slave Dancer by Paula Fox

Honor Book

Dark Is Rising by Susan Cooper

1975

Medal Book

M. C. Higgins, the Great by Virginia Hamilton

Honor Books

Figgs & Phantoms by Ellen Raskin
My Brother Sam Is Dead by James Collier and Christopher Collier
Perilous Gard by Elizabeth Pope
Philip Hall Likes Me by Bette Greene

1976

Medal Book

Grey King by Susan Cooper

Honor Books

Dragonwings by Laurence Yep
Hundred Penny Box by Sharon Mathis

1977

Medal Book

Roll of Thunder, Hear My Cry by Mildred Taylor

Honor Books

Abel's Island by William Steig
String in the Harp by Nancy Bond

1978

Medal Book

Bridge to Terabithia by Katherine Paterson

Honor Books

Anpao by Jamake Highwater
Ramona and Her Father by Beverly Cleary

1979

Medal Book

Westing Game by Ellen Raskin

Honor Book

Great Gilly Hopkins by Katherine Paterson

1980

Medal Book

Gathering of Days by Joan Blos

Honor Book

Road from Home by David Kheridan

1981

Medal Book

Jacob Have I Loved by Katherine Paterson

Honor Books

Fledgling by Jane Langton
Ring of Endless Light by Madeleine L'Engle

1982

Medal Book

Visit to William Blake's Inn by Nancy Willard

Honor Books

Ramona Quimby, Age 8 by Beverly Cleary
Upon the Head of a Goat by Aranka Siegel

1983

Medal Book

Dicey's Song by Cythia Voigt

Honor Books

Blue Sword by Robin McKinley
Doctor De Soto by William Steig
Graven Images by Paul Fleischman
Homesick by Jean Fritz
Sweet Whispers, Brother Rush by Virginia Hamilton

1984

Medal Book

Dear Mr. Henshaw by Beverly Cleary

Honor Books

Sign of the Beaver by Elizabeth Speare
Solitary Blue by Cynthia Voigt
Sugaring Time by Kathryn Lasky
Wish Giver by Bill Brittain

1985

Medal Book

Hero and the Crown by Robin McKinley

Honor Books

Like Jake and Me by Mavis Jukes
Moves Make the Man by Bruce Brooks
One-Eyed Cat by Paula Fox

1986

Medal Book

Sarah, Plain and Tall by Patricia MacLachlan

Honor Books

Commodore Perry in the Land of Shogun by Rhoda Blumberg
Dogsong by Gary Paulsen

1987

Medal Book

Whipping Boy by Sid Fleischman

Honor Books

Fine White Dust by Cynthia Rylant
Volcano by Patricia Lauber
On My Honor by Marion Bauer

1988

Medal Book

Lincoln by Russell Freedman

Honor Books

After the Rain by Norma Fox Mazer
Hatchet by Gary Paulsen

1989

Medal Book

Joyful Noise by Paul Fleischman

Honor Books

In the Beginning by Virginia Hamilton
Scorpions by Walter Myers

1990

Medal Book

Number the Stars by Lois Lowry

Honor Books

Afternoon of the Elves by Janet Taylor Lisle
Shabanu by Suzanne Staples
Winter Room by Gary Paulsen

1991

Medal Book

Maniac Magee by Jerry Spinelli

Honor Book

True Confessions of Charlotte Doyle by Avi

1992

Medal Book

Shiloh by Phyllis Reynolds Naylor

Honor Books

Nothing But the Truth by Avi
Wright Brothers by Russell Freedman

APPENDIX B:
CALDECOTT MEDAL AND HONOR BOOKS
1938-1992

Note: Honor Book listings are in alphabetical order within the award year. The code "il." designates an illustrated book only; "by" designates a written and illustrated book by the awardee.

1938

Medal Book

Animals of the Bible il. Dorothy Lathrop

Honor Books

Four and Twenty Blackbirds il. Robert Lawson
Seven Simeons il. Boris Artzybasheff

1939

Medal Book

Mei Li by Thomas Handforth

Honor Books

Andy and the Lion by James Daugherty
Barkis by Clare Newberry
Forest Pool by Laura Armer
Snow White and the Seven Dwarfs by Wanda Gág
Wee Gillis il. Robert Lawson

1940

Medal Book

Abraham Lincoln by Ingri and Edgar D'Aulaire

Honor Books

Ageless Story il. Lauren Ford
Cock-a-Doodle-Doo by Berta and Elmer Hader
Madeline by Ludwig Bemelmans

1941

Medal Book

They Were Strong and Good by Robert Lawson

Honor Book

April's Kittens by Clare Newberry

1942

Medal Book

Make Way for Ducklings by Robert McCloskey

Honor Books

American ABC by Maud and Miska Petersham

In My Mother's House il. Velino Herrera
Nothing At All by Wanda Gág
Paddle-to-the-Sea by Holling Holling

1943

Medal Book

Little House by Virginia Burton

Honor Books

Dash and Dart il. Conrad Buff
Marshmallow by Clare Newberry

1944

Medal Book

Many Moons il. Louis Slobodkin

Honor Books

Child's Good Night Book il. Jean Charlot
Good Luck Horse il. Plato Chan
Mighty Hunter by Berta and Elmer Hader
Pierre Pigeon il. Arnold Bare
Small Rain il. Elizabeth Jones

1945

Medal Book

Prayer for a Child il. Elizabeth Jones

Honor Books

Christmas Anna Angel il. Kate Seredy
In the Forest by Marie Ets
Mother Goose il. Tasha Tudor
Yonie Wondernose by Marguerite de Angeli

1946

Medal Book

Rooster Crows by Maud and Miska Petersham

Honor Books

Little Lost Lamb il. Leonard Weisgard
My Mother Is the Most Beautiful Woman in the World
    il. Ruth Gannett
Sing Mother Goose il. Marjorie Torrey
You Can Write Chinese by Kurt Wiese

1947

Medal Book

Little Island il. Leonard Weisgard

Honor Books

Boats on the River il. Jay Barnum
Pedro by Leo Politi
Rain Drop Splash il. Leonard Weisgard
Sing In Praise il. Marjorie Torrey
Timothy Turtle il. Tony Palazzo

1948

Medal Book

White Snow, Bright Snow il. Roger Duvoisin

Honor Books

Bambino, the Clown by Georges Schreiber
McElligot's Pool by Dr. Seuss
Roger and the Fox il. Hildegard Woodward
Song of Robin Hood il. Virginia Burton
Stone Soup by Marcia Brown

1949

Medal Book

Big Snow by Berta and Elmer Hader

Honor Books

All Around the Town il. Helen Stone
Blueberries for Sal by Robert McCloskey
Fish In the Air by Kurt Wiese
Juanita by Leo Politi

1950

Medal Book

Song of the Swallows by Leo Politi

Honor Books

America's Ethan Allen il. Lynd Ward
Bartholomew and the Oobleck by Dr. Seuss
Happy Day il. Marc Simont
Henry—Fisherman by Marcia Brown
Wild Birthday Cake il. Hildegard Woodward

1951

Medal Book

Egg Tree by Katherine Milhous

Honor Books

Dick Whittington and His Cat by Marcia Brown
If I Ran the Zoo by Dr. Seuss
Most Wonderful Doll in the World il. Helen Stone
T-Bone, the Baby Sitter by Clare Newberry
Two Reds il. Nicolas

1952

Medal Book

Finders Keepers il. Nicolas

Honor Books

All Falling Down il. Margaret Graham
Bear Party by William du Bois
Feather Mountain by Elizabeth Olds
Mr. T. W. Anthony Woo by Marie Ets
Skipper John's Cook by Marcia Brown

1953

Medal Book

Biggest Bear by Lynd Ward

Honor Books

Ape in a Cape by Fritz Eichenberg
Five Little Monkeys by Juliet Kepes
One Morning in Maine by Robert McCloskey
Puss In Boots by Marcia Brown
Storm Book il. Margaret Graham

1954

Medal Book

Madeline's Rescue by Ludwig Bemelmans

Honor Books

Green Eyes il. Abe Birnbaum
Journey Cake, Ho! il. Robert McCloskey
Steadfast Tin Soldier by Marcia Brown
Very Special House il. Maurice Sendak
When Will the World Be Mine? il. Jean Charlot

1955

Medal Book

Cinderella il. Marcia Brown

Honor Books

Book of Nursery and Mother Goose Rhymes il. Marguerite
   de Angeli
Thanksgiving Story il. Helen Sewell
Wheel on the Chimney il. Tibor Gergely

1956

Medal Book

Frog Went A-Courtin' il. Feodor Rojankovsky

Honor Books

Crow Boy by Taro Yashima
Play With Me by Marie Ets

1957

Medal Book

Tree Is Nice il. Marc Simont

Honor Books

Anatole il. Paul Galdone
Gillespie and the Guards il. James Daugherty
Lion il. William du Bois
Mr. Penny's Race Horse by Marie Ets
1 Is One by Tasha Tudor

1958

Medal Book

Time of Wonder by Robert McCloskey

Honor Books

Anatole and the Cat il. Paul Galdone
Fly High, Fly Low by Don Freeman

1959

Medal Book

Chanticleer and the Fox by Barbara Cooney

Honor Books

House That Jack Built by Antonio Frasconi
Umbrella by Taro Yashima
What Do You Say, Dear? il. Maurice Sendak

1960

Medal Book

Nine Days to Christmas by Marie Ets

Honor Books

Houses from the Sea il. Adrienne Adams
Moon Jumpers il. Maurice Sendak

1961

Medal Book

Baboushka and the Three Kings il. Nicholas Sidjakov

Honor Book

Inch by Inch by Leo Lionni

1962

Medal Book

Once a Mouse il. Marcia Brown

Honor Books

Day We Saw the Sun Come Up il. Adrienne Adams
Fox Went Out on a Chilly Night il. Peter Spier
Little Bear's Visit il. Maurice Sendak

1963

Medal Book

Snowy Day by Ezra Keats

Honor Books

Mr. Rabbit and the Lovely Present il. Maurice Sendak
Sun Is a Golden Earring il. Bernarda Bryson

1964

Medal Book

Where the Wild Things Are by Maurice Sendak

Honor Books

All In the Morning Early il. Evaline Ness
Mother Goose and Nursery Rhymes il. Philip Reed
Swimmy by Leo Lionni

1965

Medal Book

May I Bring a Friend? il. Beni Montresor

Honor Books

Pocketful of Cricket il. Evaline Ness
Rain Makes Applesauce il. Marvin Bileck
Wave il. Blair Lent

1966

Medal Book

Always Room for One More il. Nonny Hogrogian

Honor Books

Hide and Seek Fog il. Roger Duvoisin
Just Me by Marie Ets
Tom Tit Tot il. Evaline Ness

1967

Medal Book

Sam, Bangs and Moonshine by Evaline Ness

Honor Book

One Wide River to Cross il. Ed Emberley

1968

Medal Book

Drummer Hoff il. Ed Emberley

Honor Books

Emperor and the Kite il. Ed Young
Frederick by Leo Lionni
Seashore Story by Taro Yashima

1969

Medal Book

Fool of the World and His Flying Ship il. Uri Shulevitz

Honor Book

Why the Sun and the Moon Live in the Sky il. Blair Lent

1970

Medal Book

Sylvester and the Magic Pebble by William Steig

Honor Books

Alexander and the Wind-Up Mouse by Leo Lionnni
Goggles il. Ezra Jack Keats
Judge il. Margot Zemach
Pop Corn & Ma Goodness il. Robert Parker
Thy Friend, Obadiah by Brinton Turkle

1971

Medal Book

Story, a Story by Gail Haley

Honor Books

Angry Moon il. Blair Lent
Frog and Toad Are Friends by Arnold Lobel
In the Night Kitchen by Maurice Sendak

1972

Medal Book

One Fine Day by Nonny Hogrogian

Honor Books

Hildilid's Night il. Arnold Lobel
If All the Seas Were One Sea il. Janina Domanska
Moja Means One il. Tom Feelings

1973

Medal Book

Funny Little Woman il. Blair Lent

Honor Books

Anansi the Spider by Gerald McDermott
Hosie's Alphabet il. Leonard Baskin
Snow-White and the Seven Dwarfs il. Nancy Burkert
When Clay Sings il. Tom Bahti

1974

Medal Book

Duffy and the Devil il. Margot Zemach

Honor Books

Cathedral by David Macaulay
Three Jovial Huntsmen il. Susan Jeffers

1975

Medal Book

Arrow to the Sun by Gerald McDermott

Honor Book

Jambo Means Hello il. Tom Feelings

1976

Medal Book

Why Mosquitoes Buzz In People's Ears il. Leo and Diane Dillon

Honor Books

Desert Is Theirs il. Peter Parnall
Strega Nona by Tomie dePaola

1977

Medal Book

Ashanti to Zulu il. Leo and Diane Dillon

Honor Books

Amazing Bone by William Steig
Contest by Nonny Hogrogian
Fish for Supper by M. B. Goffstein
Golem by Beverly McDermott
Hawk, I'm Your Brother il. Peter Parnall

1978

Medal Book

Noah's Ark il. Peter Spier

Honor Books

Castle by David Macaulay
It Could Always Be Worse by Margot Zemach

1979

Medal Book

Girl Who Loved Wild Horses by Paul Goble

Honor Books

Freight Train by Donald Crews
Way to Start a Day il. Peter Parnall

1980

Medal Book

Ox-Cart Man il. Barbara Cooney

Honor Books

Ben's Trumpet by Rachel Isadora
Garden of Abdul Gasazi by Chris Van Allsburg
Treasure by Uri Shulevitz

1981

Medal Book

Fables by Arnold Lobel

Honor Books

Bremen-Town Musicians il. Ilse Plume
Grey Lady and the Strawberry Snatcher by Molly Bang
Mice Twice by Joseph Low
Truck by Donald Crews

1982

Medal Book

Jumanji by Chris Van Allsburg

Honor Books

On Market Street il. Anita Lobel
Outside Over There by Maurice Sendak
Visit to William Blake's Inn il. Alice and Martin
    Provensen
Where the Buffaloes Begin il. Stephen Gammell

1983

Medal Book

Shadow il. Marcia Brown

Honor Books

Chair for My Mother by Vera Williams
When I Was Young in the Mountains il. Diane Goode

1984

Medal Book

Glorious Flight by Alice and Martin Provensen

Honor Books

Little Red Riding Hood il. Trina Hyman
Ten, Nine, Eight by Molly Bang

1985

Medal Book

Saint George and the Dragon il. Trina Hyman

Honor Books

Hansel and Gretel il. Paul Zelinsky
Have You See My Duckling? by Nancy Tafuri
Story of Jumping Mouse by John Steptoe

1986

Medal Book

Polar Express by Chris Van Allsburg

Honor Books

King Bidgood's In the Bathtub il. Don Wood
Relatives Came il. Stephen Gammell

1987

Medal Book

Hey, Al! il. Richard Egielski

Honor Books

Alphabatics il. Suse MacDonald
Rumpelstiltskin il. Paul Zelinsky
Village of Round and Square Houses il. Ann
    Grifalconi

1988

Medal Book

Owl Moon il. John Schoenherr

Honor Book

Mufaro's Beautiful Daughters by John Steptoe

1989

Medal Book

Song and Dance Man il. Stephen Gammell

Honor Books

Boy of the Three-Year Nap il. Allen Say
Free Fall by David Weisner
Goldilocks and the Three Bears by James Marshall
Mirandy and Brother Wind il. Jerry Pinkney

1990

Medal Book

Lon Po Po by Ed Young

Honor Books

Bill Peet by Bill Peet
Color Zoo by Lois Ehlert

Hershel and the Hanukkah Goblins il. Trina Hyman
Talking Eggs il. Jerry Pinkney

1991

Medal Book

Black and White by David Macaulay

Honor Books

"More, More, More," Said the Baby by Vera Williams
Puss in Boots by Fred Marcellino

1992

Medal Book

Tuesday by David Wiesner

Honor Book

Tar Beach by Faith Ringgold

APPENDIX C:
BIBLIOGRAPHY OF RESOURCES

REFERENCE BOOKS

AV Market Place 1991. New York: Bowker, 1991.

Audiovisual Materials. Washington, DC: Library of Congress, 1979-1982.

Books in Print 1990-1991: Authors, Titles. 6 vols. New York: Bowker, 1990.

Bowker's Complete Video Directory. 2 vols. New York: Bowker, 1990.

Brown, Lucy Gregor. *Core Media Collection for Elementary Schools.* New York: Bowker, 1978.

———. *Core Media Collection for Secondary Schools.* 2nd ed. New York. Bowker, 1979.

Cascardi, Andrea E. *A Parent's Guide to Video and Audio Cassettes for Children.* New York: Warner, 1987.

Educational Film & Video Locator. 4th ed. 2 vols. New York: Bowker, 1990.

The Elementary School Library Collection: A Guide to Books and Other Media. biennial. Williamsport, PA: Brodart, 1965-.

Films and Other Materials for Projection. Washington, DC: Library of Congress, 1973-1978.

Gaffney, Maureen and Gerry Bond Laybourne. *What to Do When the Lights Go On: A Comprehensive Guide to 16mm Films and Related Activities for Children.* Phoenix, AZ: Oryx, 1981.

——— and Kay Weidemann Scott, comps. and eds. *More Films Kids Like: A Catalog of Short Films for Children.* Chicago: American Library Association, 1977.

Gallant, Jennifer Jung. *Best Videos for Children and Young Adults: A Core Collection for Libraries.* Santa Barbara, CA: ABC-CLIO, 1990.

Goldstein, Ruth M. and Edith Zornow. *Movies for Kids: A Guide for Parents and Teachers on the Entertainment Film for Children.* rev. ed. New York: Frederick Ungar, 1980.

Green, Diana Huss, *et al. Parents' Choice Guide to Videocassettes for Children.* Mount Vernon, NY: Consumers Union, 1989.

Greene, Ellin and Madalynne Schoenfeld, comps. and eds. *A Multimedia Approach to Children's Literature: A Selective List of Films, Filmstrips, and Recordings Based on Children's Books.* Chicago, American Library Association, 1972.

———. ———. 2nd ed. Chicago: American Library Association, 1977.

HBO's Guide to Movies on Videocassette and Cable TV 1991. 2nd ed. New York: HarperCollins, 1990.

Hunt, Mary Alice, ed. *A Multimedia Approach to Children's Literature: A Selective List of Films, Filmstrips, and Recordings Based on Children's Books.* 3rd ed. Chicago: American Library Association, 1983.

Johnson, Ferne, ed. *Opening Doors for Preschool Children and Their Parents.* Chicago: American Library Association, 1976.

Maltin, Leonard. *Leonard Maltin's TV Movies and Video Guide: 1991.* New York: New American Library, 1990.

Martin, Mick and Marsha Porter. *Video Movie Guide 1990.* New York: Ballantine, 1989.

Mason, Sally and James Scholtz, eds. *Video for Libraries: Special Interest Video for Small and Medium-Sized Public Libraries.* Chicago: American Library Association, 1988.

May, Jill P. *Films and Filmstrips for Language Arts: An Annotated Bibliography.* Urbana, IL: National Council of Teachers of English, 1981.

Motion Pictures and Filmstrips. Washington, DC: Library of Congress, 1953-1972.

National Information Center for Educational Media (NICEM). *Audiocassette Finder.* 2nd ed. Medford, NJ: Plexus, 1989. [included in *A-V Online,* see under DATABASES.]

——. *Film & Video Finder.* 3rd ed. 3 vols. Medford, NJ: Plexus, 1991. [included in *A-V Online,* see under DATABASES.]

——. *Filmstrip & Slide Set Finder.* 3 vols. Medford, NJ: Plexus, 1990. [included in *A-V Online,* see under DATABASES.]

——. *Index to AV Producers & Distributors.* 8th ed. Medford, NJ: Plexus, 1991.

National Library Service for the Blind and Physically Handicapped. *Discoveries: Fiction for Elementary School Readers.* Washington, DC: Library of Congress, 1986.

——. *Discoveries: Fiction for Intermediate School Years.* Washington, DC: Library of Congress, 1986.

——. *Discoveries: Fiction for the Youngest Reader.* Washington, DC: Library of Congress, 1986.

——. *Discoveries: Fiction for Young Teens.* Washington, DC: Library of Congress, 1986.

——. *For Younger Readers: Braille and Talking Books.* Washington, DC: Library of Congress, biennial, 1972/73-

——. *Union Catalog.* Washington, DC: Library of Congress, 1990.

——. *Young Adult Fiction.* Washington, DC: Library of Congress, 1981.

National Union Catalog: Audiovisual Materials. Washington, DC: Library of Congress, 1983-.

On Cassette 1990: A Comprehensive Bibliography of Spoken Word Audiocassettes. New York: Bowker, 1990.

Parlato, Salvatore J. *Films Ex Libris: Literature in 16mm and Video.* Jefferson, NC: McFarland, 1980.

——. *SuperFilms: An International Guide to Award-Winning Educational Films.* Metuchen, NJ: Scarecrow, 1976.

Pitman, Randy and Elliott Swanson. *Video Movies: A Core Collection for Libraries.* Santa Barbara, CA: ABC-CLIO, 1990.

Rice, Susan and Barbara Ludlom, comps. and eds. *Films Kids Like: A Catalog of Short Films for Children.* Chicago: American Library Association, 1973.

Rohrlick, Paula. *Exploring the Arts: Films and Video Programs for Young Viewers.* New York: Bowker, 1982.

Scheuer, Steven H. *Movies on TV and Videocassette 1989-1990*. New York: Bantam, 1989.

Street, Douglas, ed. *Children's Novels and the Movies*. New York: Frederick Ungar, 1983.

Thomas, Elaine E. and others. *Recordings for Children: A Selected List of Records and Cassettes*. 4th ed. New York: New York Library Association, 1980.

Voegelin-Carleton, Ardis, ed. *Words on Tape 1990: A Guide to the Audio Cassette Market*. Westport, CT: Meckler, 1990.

Weiner, David J., ed. *The Video Source Book*. 12th ed. 2 vols. Detroit: Gale Research, 1990.

DATABASES

KIDSNET—A computerized clearinghouse for children's television and radio (6856 Eastern Ave NW, Suite 208, Washington DC 20012, 202-291-1400).

A-V Online—The entire contents of the NICEM database, available online through DIALOG (3460 Hillview Ave., Palo Alto, CA 94304, 800-334-2564) and on CD-ROM from SilverPlatter (1 Newton Executive Park, Newton Lower Falls, MA 02162, 800-343-0064).

JOURNALS AND REVIEW SERVICES

Audio Video Review Digest (Gale Research, Book Tower, Detroit, MI 48277), May 1989-.

Booklist (American Library Association, 50 E. Huron St., Chicago, IL 60611), January 1905-.

Children's Video Report (PO Box 3228, Princeton, NJ 08543), May 1985-.

Children's Video Review (E.P. Carsman, 110 Lena Court, Grass Valley, CA 95949), April/May 1987-.

Librarian's Video Resource (formerly Clearview Media Corp, Route 1, Box 25, Bowling Green, VA 22427), 1986/87-.

Media & Methods (American Society of Media Specialists & Librarians, 1429 Walnut St, Philadelphia, PA 19102), Sept 1964-.

Media Review Digest (Pierian Press, Box 1898, Ann Arbor, MI 48106), 1970-.

School Library Journal (Cahners Publishing, 249 W. 17th St., New York, NY 10011), Sept. 1954-.

Sightlines (American Film & Video Association, 920 Barnsdale Rd, Suite 152, LaGrange Park, IL 60525), Sept/Oct 1987-.

Video Librarian (Randy Pitman, PO Box 2725, Bremerton, WA 98310), March 1986-.

Video Rating Guide for Libraries (ABC-CLIO, 130 Cremona Dr, PO Box 1911, Santa Barbara, CA 93116), Jan 1990-.

APPENDIX D:
DIRECTORY OF MEDIA PRODUCERS AND DISTRIBUTORS

This list includes all producers and distributors mentioned in this volume, *except* those for which only "out of print" materials have been listed. Toll-free numbers for requesting current catalogs are listed. Generally, assume catalogs are free of charge unless otherwise is noted; it is prudent to ask when requesting, since company policies do change from time to time.

ACI [Films] *see* AIMS Media

AIMS [Media]
6901 Woodley Avenue
Van Nuys, CA 91406
1-800-367-2467

AIT [Agency for Instructional Technology]
Box A, 1111 West 17th Street
Bloomington, IN 47402
1-800-457-4509

ALA [American Library Association]
50 East Huron Street
Chicago, IL 60611
1-800–545-2433

Ambrose [Video Publishing]
1290 Avenue of the Americas, Suite 2245
New York, NY 10104
1-800-526-4663

American Audio [Prose Library]
PO Box 842
Columbia, MO 65205
1-800-447-2275

American School [Publishers]
PO Box 4520, 155 North Wacker Drive
Chicago, IL 60680
1-800-843-8855

Bantam [Doubleday Dell] and Bantam [Audio]
666 Fifth Avenue
New York, NY 10103
1-800-223-6834

Books on Tape
PO Box 7900
Newport Beach, CA 92658
1-800-626-3333

Caedmon [An Imprint of Harper Audio]
10 East 53rd Street
New York, NY 10022
1-800-242-7737

CBS/FOX [Video]
1211 Avenue of the Americas
New York, NY 10036
212-819-3200
(no catalog available)

Cheshire [Corporation]
PO Box 61109
Denver, CO 80206
303-333-9729

Children's Book Council
568 Broadway
New York, NY 10012
212-966-1990

Children's Circle [CC Studios]
389 Newton Turnpike
Weston, CT 06883
1-800-243-5020

Churchill [Films]
12210 Nebraska Avenue
Los Angeles, CA 90025
1-800-334-7830

Clearvue[/eav]
6465 North Avondale
Chicago, IL 60631
1-800-253-2788

Cornerstone [Books]
Bantam Doubleday Dell , Dept. CNS
100 Pine Avenue
Holmes, PA 19043
1-800-345-8112

Coronet/MTI [Film & Video]
(Distributors of Disney Educational Productions
and Learning Corporation of America)
108 Wilmot Road
Deerfield, IL 60015
1-800-621-2131

CRM [Films]
2233 Faraday Avenue
Carlsbad, CA 92008
1-800-421-0833
(no catalog available)

Davidson [Films]
231 "E" Street
Davis, CA 95616
916-753-9604

Direct Cinema
PO Box 10003
Santa Monica, CA 90410
1-800-345-6748

Disney [Educational Productions] *see* Coronet/MTI
Film & Video

[E. P.] Dutton
Penguin USA
375 Hudson Street
New York, NY 10014
1-800-526-0275

Encyclopedia Britannica [Educational
Corporation]
310 South Michigan Avenue
Chicago, IL 60604
1-800-554-9862

Family Home [Entertainment]
PO Box 10124, 15400 Sherman Way
Van Nuys, CA 91410
1-800-288-5483

Films for the Humanities [& Sciences]
PO Box 2053
Princeton, NJ 08543
1-800-257-5126

Films Inc.
5547 North Ravenswood Avenue
Chicago, IL 60640
1-800-323-4222

G. K. Hall
70 Lincoln Street
Boston, MA 02111
1-800-257-5755

GPN [Great Plains National]
PO Box 80669
Lincoln, NE 68501
1-800-228-4630

Guidance Assoc[iates]
The Center for Humanities
Communications Park, Box 3000
Mount Kisco, NY 10549
1-800-431-1242

Harcourt [Brace Jovanovich]
1259 Sixth Avenue
San Diego, CA 92101
1-800-543-1918

HBO [Video]
1100 Sixth Avenue
New York, NY 10036
212-512-7400
(no catalog available)

Heritage [Media Productions]
105 Par Del Rio
Clifton Park, NY 12065
518-371-9337

Home Vision
PO Box 800
Concord, MA 01742
1-800-262-8600

Houghton [Mifflin]
One Beacon Street
Boston, MA 02108
1-800-272-3362

Humanities Software
PO Box 950, 408 Columbia, Suite 209
Hood River, OR 97031
1-800-245-6737

International Video [Entertainment]
PO Box 10124, 15400 Sherman Way
Van Nuys, CA 91410
1-800-288-5483

Ishtar [Films]
PO Box 51
Patterson, NY 12563
(no catalog available)

[Alfred A.] Knopf
201 East 50th Street
New York, NY 10022
1-800-733-3000

Learning Corp[oration of America] see Coronet/
MTI Film & Video

Lightyear [Entertainment]
350 Fifth Avenue, Suite 5101
New York, NY 10118
1-800-229-STORY

Listening Library
One Park Avenue
Old Greenwich, CT 06870
1-800-243-4504

Live Oak [Media]
PO Box AL
Pine Plains, NY 12567
518-398-1010

Lucerne [Media]
37 Ground Pine Road
Morris Plains, NJ 07950
1-800-341-2293

MCA/Universal Home Video
70 Universal City Plaza
Universal City, CA 91608
818-777-4300
(no catalog available)

McGraw-Hill see American School Publishers

MGM/UA Home Video
10000 West Washington Boulevard
Culver City, CA 90232
213-280-6000
(no catalog available)

Meridian [Educational Corporation]
236 East Front Street
Bloomington, IL 61701
1-800-727-5507

Miller-Brody see American School Publishers

[William] Morrow [and Co.]
105 Madison Avenue
New York, NY 10016
1-800-237-0657

National Film Board of Canada
1251 Avenue of the Americas, 16th floor
New York, NY 10020
1-800-542-2164

New Letters [on the Air]
5100 Rockhill
Kansas City, MO 64110
816-276-1159

NLSBPH [National Library Service for the Blind
and Physically Handicapped]
Library of Congress
Washington, DC 20542
202-707-5100

Northern Ill[inois] Univ[ersity]
Media Distribution Department
DeKalb, IL 60115

NPR [National Public Radio]
2025 "M" Street, Northwest
Washington, DC 20036
202-822-2000

Paramount Home Video
5555 Melrose Avenue
Los Angeles, CA 90038
213-468-5000
(no catalog available)

Pathways of Sound
6 Craigie Circle
Cambridge, MA 02138
617-354-6190

PBS [Video]
1320 Braddock Place
Alexandria, VA 22314
1-800-424-7963

Peaceable Kingdom [Press]
2980 College Avenue, Suite 2
Berkeley, CA 94705
415-644-9801

Perfection Form [Company]
1000 North Second Street
Logan, IA 51546
1-800-831-4190

Phoenix [Films & Video]/BFA [Educational
Media]
468 Park Avenue South
New York, NY 10016
1-800-221-1274

Pied Piper [Media]
1645 Monrovia Avenue
Costa Mesa, CA 92627
1-800-247-8308

Podell [Productions]
Box 244
Scarborough, NY 10510
(no catalog available)

Public Media [Inc.] *see* Films Inc.

Puffin [Books]
Penguin USA
375 Hudson Street
New York, NY 10014
212-366-2000

Putnam [Publishing Group]
200 Madison Avenue
New York, NY 10016
1-800-631-8571

Random [House] *see* American School Publishers

RH Home Video
400 Hahn Road
Westminster, MD 21157
1-800-726-0600

Scholastic [Inc.]
730 Broadway
New York, NY 10003
1-800-392-2179

Simon & Schuster [Audio]
200 Old Tappan Road
Old Tappan, NJ 07675
1-800-223-2348

Southwest Series
743 North Fourth Avenue
Tucson, AZ 85705
602-623-2255

Spoken Arts
1011 SBF Drive
Pinellas Park, FL 34666
1-800-326-4090

Tapes for Readers
5078 Fulton Street, Northwest
Washington, DC 20016
202-362-4585

Teacher Support Software
1035 Northwest 57th Street
Gainesville, FL 32605
1-800-228-2871

Texture [Films] *see* Films Inc.

Troll [Associates]
100 Corporate Drive
Mahwah, NJ 07430
1-800-526-5289

Trumpet [Club]
PO Box 604
Holmes, PA 19043
1-800-826-0110

Weston Woods [Studios]
389 Newton Turnpike
Weston CT 06883
1-800-243-5020

Xerox [Films] *see* Guidance Associates

APPENDIX E:
LIST OF TITLES BY MEDIA FORMATS

A book title under a format heading indicates that the "Newbery Media" or "Caldecott Media" list for that book includes one or more items in the specified format. Names refer to listings in the "Media about Newbery/Caldecott Authors and Illustrators" section. Entries in quotation marks are titles of materials found in the "Media Related to Newbery and Caldecott Books in General" list.

AUDIO

Across Five Aprils
Adam of the Road
After the Rain
Alexander and the Wind-Up Mouse
Alexander, Lloyd
All Sail Set
Amos Fortune, Free Man
Anansi the Spider
And Now Miguel
Andy and the Lion
Annie and the Old One
Anpao
Armstrong, William
Arrow to the Sun
Ashanti to Zulu
Babbitt, Natalie
Banner in the Sky
Bartholomew and the Oobleck
Baskin, Leonard
Big Snow
Biggest Bear

Black Pearl
Blos, Joan W.
Blue Sword
Blue Willow
Blueberries for Sal
Bontemps, Arna
Bremen-Town Musicians
Bridge to Terabithia
Bronze Bow
Brown, Marcia
By the Shores of Silver Lake
Byars, Betsy
Caddie Woodlawn
Call It Courage
Carry On, Mr. Bowditch
Cat Who Went to Heaven
Caudill, Rebecca
Chanticleer and the Fox
Charlotte's Web
Christmas Anna Angel
Chúcaro
Cinderella
Cleary, Beverly
Commodore Perry in the Land of the Shogun
Cooper, Susan
Courage of Sarah Noble
Cow-Tail Switch
Cricket in Times Square
Crow Boy
Daniel Boone
Dark Frigate
Dark is Rising
de Angeli, Marguerite

117

Dear Mr. Henshaw
Desert is Theirs
Dillon, Diane and Leo
Doctor De Soto
Dogsong
Door in the Wall
Dragonwings
Drummer Hoff
Egielski, Richard
Egypt Game
Enright, Elizabeth
Family under the Bridge
Finders Keepers
Fine White Dust
Fish in the Air
Fledgling
Fleischman, Sid
Floating Island
Fool of the World and the Flying Ship
Fox, Paula
Fox Went Out on a Chilly Night
Frederick
Freedman, Russell
Fritz, Jean
Frog and Toad Are Friends
Frog and Toad Together
Frog Went A-Courtin'
From the Mixed-Up Files of Mrs. Basil E. Frankweiler
Funny Little Woman
Gammage Cup
Gandhi, Fighter without a Sword
Gathering of Days
Gay-Neck
George, Jean Craighead
Ginger Pye
Gipson, Fred
Goble, Paul
Goggles!
Golden Fleece
Golden Goblet
Golem
Good Master
Graven Images
Great Gilly Hopkins
Grey King
Hall, Donald
Hamilton, Virginia
Hansel and Gretel
Happy Day
Hatchet
Hawk, I'm Your Brother

Headless Cupid
Henry, Marguerite
Hero and the Crown
Hide and Seek Frog
High King
Homesick
Horsecatcher
House of Sixty Fathers
Hundred Dresses
Hundred Penny Box
Hunt, Irene
Hurry Home, Candy
Hyman, Trina Schart
I, Juan de Pareja
If I Ran the Zoo
In the Forest
In the Night Kitchen
Incident at Hawk's Hill
Invincible Louisa
It's Like This, Cat
Jacob Have I Loved
James, Will
Jarrell, Randall
Johnny Tremain
Jones, Elizabeth Orton
Journey Cake, Ho!
Journey Outside
Joyful Noise
Julie of the Wolves
Just Me
Justin Morgan Had a Horse
Keats, Ezra Jack
King Bidgood's in the Bathtub
King of the Wind
King's Fifth
Knee Knock Rise
Konigsburg, E. L.
Latham, Jean Lee
Lawson, Robert
Le Guin, Ursula
L'Engle, Madeleine
Lenski, Lois
Lent, Blair
Little Bear's Visit
Little House
Little Island
Little Lost Lamb
Lobel, Arnold
Loner
Long Winter
M. C. Higgins the Great

Macaulay, David

MacLachlan, Patricia

Madeline

Madeline's Rescue

Make Way for Ducklings

Many Moons

Matchlock Gun

May I Bring a Friend?

Mazer, Norma Fox

McKinley, Robin

Men of Athens

Mighty Hunter

Millions of Cats

Minarik, Else Holmelund

Miracles on Maple Hill

Miss Hickory

Misty of Chincoteague

Moccasin Trail

Mountain Born

Moves Make the Man

Mr. Popper's Penguins

Mr. Rabbit and the Lovely Present

Mrs. Frisby and the Rats of NIMH

Mufaro's Beautiful Daughters

My Brother Sam Is Dead

My Father's Dragon

Myers, Walter Dean

Naylor, Phyllis Reynolds

Noah's Ark

Noonday Friends

Old Ramon

Old Yeller

On My Honor

On the Banks of Plum Creek

Once a Mouse

One-Eyed Cat

One Fine Day

Onion John

Outside Over There

Owl Moon

Paterson, Katherine

Paulsen, Gary

Pecos Bill

Peet, Bill

Perilous Road

Philip Hall Likes Me, I Reckon Maybe

Planet of Junior Brown

Play with Me

Pocketful of Cricket

Puss in Boots (Marcia Brown, ill.)

Rabbit Hill

Rain Drop Splash

Ramona and Her Father

Ramona Quimby, Age 8

Rascal

Raskin, Ellen

Rifles for Watie

Ring of Endless Light

Road from Home

Roll of Thunder, Hear My Cry

Rooster Crows

Sandoz, Mari

Sarah, Plain and Tall

Sawyer, Ruth

Schoenherr, John

Scorpions

Sendak, Maurice

Seredy, Kate

Shadow

Shadow of a Bull

Shen of the Sea

Sign of the Beaver

Sing Down the Moon

Singer, Isaac Bashevis

Slobodkin, Louis

Smoky, the Cowhorse

Snowy Day

Song and Dance Man

Sounder

Spier, Peter

Spinelli, Jerry

Steele, William O.

Stolz, Mary

Stone Soup

Story, A Story

Story of Mankind

Strawberry Girl

Strega Nona

Sugaring Time

Summer of the Swans

Sweet Whispers, Brother Rush

Swimmy

Sylvester and the Magic Pebble

Tales from Silver Lands

Taylor, Mildred D.

Ten, Nine, Eight

They Were Strong and Good

Thimble Summer

Thompson, George

Thurber, James

Time of Wonder

To Be a Slave

Tombs of Atuan
Treasure
Tree Is Nice
Trumpeter of Krakow
Tunis, Edwin
Twenty-One Balloons
Umbrella
Up a Road Slowly
Upon the Head of the Goat
Upstairs Room
Van Allsburg, Chris
Very Special House
Village of Round and Square Houses
Voigt, Cynthia
Voyages of Doctor Dolittle
Way to Start a Day
Wee Gillis
What Do You Say, Dear?
Wheel on the Chimney
Wheel on the School
When Shlemiel Went to Warsaw
Where the Wild Things Are
Whipping Boy
White Snow, Bright Snow
Why Mosquitoes Buzz in People's Ears
Wier, Ester
Wilder, Laura Ingalls
Willard, Nancy
Williams, Vera B.
Wish Giver
Witch of Blackbird Pond
Witches of Worm
Wojciechowska, Maia
Wonder-Smith and His Son
Wrinkle in Time
Yates, Elizabeth
Yonie Wondernose
Young Fu of the Upper Yangtze
Zlateh the Goat

BOOKMARK

Ramona and Her Father
Ramona Quimby, Age 8
Where the Wild Things Are

BRAILLE

Abraham Lincoln

Abraham Lincoln, Friend of the People
Across Five Aprils
Adam of the Road
Alexander and the Wind-Up Mouse
All Alone
Along Came a Dog
Always Room for One More
America Is Born
America Moves Forward
Amos Fortune, Free Man
Anatole
And Now Miguel
Animal Family
Annie and the Old One
Apple and the Arrow
Audubon
Banner in the Sky
Bears on Hemlock Mountain
Better Known as Johnny Appleseed
Big Snow
Black Cauldron
Black Fox of Lorne
Black Pearl
Blue Willow
Blueberries for Sal
Boats on the River
Book of Nursery and Mother Goose Rhymes
Boy with a Pack
Bronze Bow
By the Shores of Silver Lake
Caddie Woodlawn
Calico Bush
Call It Courage
Carry On, Mr. Bowditch
Cat Who Went to Heaven
Chanticleer and the Fox
Charlotte's Web
Christmas Anna Angel
Commodore Perry in the Land of the Shogun
Courage of Sarah Noble
Cricket in Times Square
Daniel Boone
Dark Frigate
Dark Is Rising
Dash and Dart
Daughter of the Mountains
Dear Mr. Henshaw
Defender
Dicey's Song
Dick Whittington and His Cat
Dobry

Dogsong
Door in the Wall
Downright Dencey
Duffy and the Devil
Egypt Game
Emperor and the Kite
Family under the Bridge
Figgs & Phantoms
Fine White Dust
Fledgling
Fly High, Fly Low
Fool of the World and the Flying Ship
Frederick
From the Mixed-Up Files of Mrs. Basil E. Frankweiler
Frontier Living
Gammage Cup
Gandhi, Fighter without a Sword
Gathering of Days
Ginger Pye
Goggles!
Golden Name Day
Good Master
Great Wheel
Grey King
Happy Day
Headless Cupid
High King
Hitty
Honk, the Moose
Horsecatcher
Hundred Dresses
Hurry Home, Candy
I, Juan de Pareja
In My Mother's House
In the Beginning
In the Forest
Incident at Hawk's Hill
Indian Captive
Invincible Louisa
Island of the Blue Dolphins
It's Like This, Cat
Jacob Have I Loved
Johnny Tremain
Joyful Noise
Juanita
Julie of the Wolves
Jumanji
Kildee House
King of the Wind
King's Fifth
Li Lun

Light at Tern Rock
Lincoln
Little Bear's Visit
Little Lost Lamb
Little Red Riding Hood
Little Town on the Prairie
Loner
Long Winter
M. C. Higgins the Great
Many Moons
Marshmallow
Matchlock Gun
Men, Microscopes, and Living Things
Men of Athens
Middle Moffat
Mighty Hunter
Minn of the Mississippi
Miracles on Maple Hill
Miss Hickory
Misty of Chincoteague
Moccasin Trail
Mr. Popper's Penguins
Mrs. Frisby and the Rats of NIMH
My Father's Dragon
My Mother Is the Most Beautiful Woman in the World
My Side of the Mountain
Noonday Friends
Number the Stars
Old Ramon
Old Yeller
On My Honor
On the Banks of Plum Creek
Once A Mouse
Onion John
Ox-Cart Man
Paddle-to-the-Sea
Pancakes-Paris
Pecos Bill
Pocketful of Cricket
Polar Express
Rabbit Hill
Rain Drop Splash
Ramona and Her Father
Ramona Quimby, Age 8
Rascal
Rawlings, Marjorie Kinnan
Ring of Endless Light
Roger and the Fox
Roll of Thunder, Hear My Cry
Rooster Crows
Rufus M.

Sam, Bangs, and Moonshine
Seabird
Secret of the Andes
Seven Simeons
Shabanu
Shen of the Sea
Sign of the Beaver
Slave Dancer
Smoky, the Cowhorse
Snow White and the Seven Dwarfs (Nancy Ekholm
    Burkert, ill.)
Solitary Blue
Song and Dance Man
Sounder
Stone Soup
Story of Mankind
Story of the Negro
Strawberry Girl
String in the Harp
Tales from Silver Lands
Thanksgiving Story
These Happy Golden Years
Thimble Summer
Thistle and Thyme
Thy Friend, Obadiah
To Be a Slave
Tom Paine
Tombs of Atuan
Twenty-One Balloons
Up a Road Slowly
Upon the Head of the Goat
Volcano
Voyages of Doctor Dolittle
Waterless Mountain
Westing Game
Wheel on the School
When Shlemiel Went to Warsaw
White Snow, Bright Snow
White Stag
Wild Birthday Cake
Winter Room
Witch of Blackbird Pond
Wonder-Smith and His Son
Wrinkle in Time
Yonie Wondernose
Young Fu of the Upper Yangtze
Zlateh the Goat

BRAILLE/PRINT

Alphabatics
Andy and the Lion
Biggest Bear
Boy of the Three-Year Nap
Cinderella
Crow Boy
Doctor De Soto
Drummer Hoff
Egg Tree
Fables
Finders Keepers
Funny Little Woman
Hey, Al
If I Ran the Zoo
Judge
Just Me
Little House
Little Island
Madeline
Madeline's Rescue
Make Way for Ducklings
McElligot's Pool
Mei Li
Millions of Cats
Mirandy and Brother Wind
Mr. Rabbit and the Lovely Present
Nine Days to Christmas
One Fine Day
One Morning in Maine
Play with Me
Prayer for a Child
Relatives Came
Rumpelstiltskin
Snowy Day
Song of the Swallows
Story, A Story
Sylvester and the Magic Pebble
Time of Wonder
Tree Is Nice
Visit to William Blake's Inn
What Do You Say, Dear?
Wheel on the Chimney
Where the Wild Things Are
Why Mosquitoes Buzz in People's Ears

CALENDAR

"Caldecott Calendar"

DOLL

Madeline
Madeline's Rescue
Strega Nona
Where the Wild Things Are

FILM

Abel's Island
Across Five Aprils
All in the Morning Early
Amazing Bone
Anansi the Spider
Anatole
And Now Miguel
Andy and the Lion
Annie and the Old One
Arrow to the Sun
Banner in the Sky
Baskin, Leonard
Blueberries for Sal
Caddie Woodlawn
Call It Courage
Castle
Caudill, Rebecca
Charlotte's Web
Cooney, Barbara
Cow-Tail Switch
Cricket in Times Square
Crow Boy
Daugherty, James
d'Aulaire, Edgar Parin and Ingri
Doctor De Soto
Drummer Hoff
Edmonds, Walter
Emberley, Ed
Foster, Genevieve
Fox Went Out on a Chilly Night
Frasconi, Antonio
Frederick
Freeman, Don
Frog and Toad Are Friends
Frog and Toad Together
Frog Went A-Courtin'
From the Mixed-Up Files of Mrs. Basil E. Frankweiler
Goggles!
Goldilocks and the Three Bears
Green Eyes
Henry, Marguerite

Hundred Penny Box
In the Forest
In the Night Kitchen
Incident at Hawk's Hill
Island of the Blue Dolphins
James, Will
Jarrell, Randall
Johnny Tremain
Judge
Jukes, Mavis
Justin Morgan Had a Horse
Keats, Ezra Jack
L'Engle, Madeleine
Like Jake and Me
Little House
Madeline
Madeline's Rescue
Make Way for Ducklings
Many Moons
McCloskey, Robert
Millions of Cats
Misty of Chincoteague
Mrs. Frisby and the Rats of NIMH
Mufaro's Beautiful Daughters
My Mother Is the Most Beautiful Woman in the World
My Side of the Mountain
Old Yeller
Onion John
Owl Moon
Paddle-to-the-Sea
Politi, Leo
Rabbit Hill
Rain Drop Splash
Ramona Quimby, Age 8
Rascal
Roll of Thunder, Hear My Cry
Rufus M.
Sam, Bangs, and Moonshine
Sendak, Maurice
Singer, Isaac Bashevis
Smoky, the Cowhorse
Snowy Day
Sounder
Spier, Peter
Stone Soup
Story, A Story
Strega Nona
Summer of the Swans
Swimmy
Sylvester and the Magic Pebble
Thurber, James

Time of Wonder
Village of Round and Square Houses
Voyages of Doctor Dolittle
Wave
Wee Gillis
Wheel on the Chimney
Where the Wild Things Are
Why Mosquitoes Buzz in People's Ears
Why the Sun and the Moon Live in the Sky
Zlateh the Goat

FILMSTRIP

Andy and the Lion
Banner in the Sky
Big Snow
Biggest Bear
Blueberries for Sal
Call It Courage
Chanticleer and the Fox
Crow Boy
Finders Keepers
Fox Went Out on a Chilly Night
Frog Went A-Courtin'
In the Forest
Johnny Tremain
Little Island
Madeline's Rescue
Make Way for Ducklings
Millions of Cats
Old Yeller
Perilous Road
Play with Me
Snowy Day
Stone Soup
Time of Wonder
Tree Is Nice
Voyages of Doctor Dolittle
What Do You Say, Dear?
Wheel on the Chimney
White Snow, Bright Snow
Witches of Worm

FILMSTRIP/SOUND

Abraham Lincoln
Across Five Aprils
After the Rain
Alexander and the Wind-Up Mouse

Alexander, Lloyd
All in the Morning Early
Alphabatics
Amazing Bone
Amos Fortune, Free Man
Anansi the Spider
Anatole
And Now Miguel
Andy and the Lion
Annie and the Old One
Anpao
Armstrong, William
Arrow to the Sun
Ashanti to Zulu
Babbitt, Natalie
Bartholomew and the Oobleck
Bear Party
Ben's Trumpet
Big Snow
Biggest Bear
Black Cauldron
Black Pearl
Blueberries for Sal
Bontemps, Arna
Bremen-Town Musicians
Bridge to Terabithia
Brink, Carol Ryrie
Bronze Bow
Byars, Betsy
Caddie Woodlawn
Call It Courage
Carry On, Mr. Bowditch
Castle
Cat Who Went to Heaven
Chair for My Mother
Chanticleer and the Fox
Charlotte's Web
Chúcaro
Cinderella
Cleary, Beverly
Collier, Christopher and James Lincoln
Commodore Perry in the Land of the Shogun
Contest
Cooper, Susan
Courage of Sarah Noble
Cricket in Times Square
Crow Boy
Dark Frigate
Dear Mr. Henshaw
Dicey's Song
Doctor De Soto

Dogsong
Door in the Wall
Dragonwings
Drummer Hoff
Duffy and the Devil
Egypt Game
Emperor and the Kite
Estes, Eleanor
Fables
Family under the Bridge
Finders Keepers
Fine White Dust
Fish in the Air
Fledgling
Fleischman, Sid
Fool of the World and the Flying Ship
Fox Went Out on a Chilly Night
Frederick
Free Fall
Freight Train
Frog and Toad Are Friends
Frog and Toad Together
Frog Went A-Courtin'
From the Mixed-Up Files of Mrs. Basil E. Frankweiler
Funny Little Woman
Gág, Wanda
Gammage Cup
Garden of Abdul Gasazi
Gathering of Days
Gay-Neck
Geisel, Theodor Seuss
George, Jean Craighead
Ginger Pye
Girl Who Loved Wild Horses
Glorious Flight
Goggles!
Golden Goblet
Golem
Graven Images
Great Gilly Hopkins
Green Eyes
Greene, Bette
Grey Lady and the Strawberry Snatcher
Haley, Gail E.
Hamilton, Virginia
Hansel and Gretel
Happy Day
Hatchet
Have You Seen My Duckling?
Headless Cupid
Henry, Marguerite

Hey, Al
Hide and Seek Frog
High King
Highwater, Jamake
Holling, Holling C.
Homesick
Horsecatcher
House of Sixty Fathers
Houses from the Sea
Hundred Dresses
Hundred Penny Box
Hurry Home, Candy
I, Juan de Pareja
If I Ran the Zoo
In the Forest
In the Night Kitchen
Incident at Hawk's Hill
Island of the Blue Dolphins
It Could Always Be Worse
It's Like This, Cat
Jacob Have I Loved
Jennifer, Hecate, Macbeth, William McKinley, and Me,
    Elizabeth
Johnny Tremain
Journey Cake, Ho!
Joyful Noise
Judge
Julie of the Wolves
Jumanji
Just Me
Justin Morgan Had a Horse
King Bidgood's in the Bathtub
King of the Wind
King's Fifth
Knee Knock Rise
Konigsburg, E. L.
L'Engle, Madeleine
Like Jake and Me
Lincoln
Little Bear's Visit
Little House
Little Island
Little Red Riding Hood
Lobel, Arnold
Loner
M. C. Higgins the Great
Madeline
Madeline's Rescue
Make Way for Ducklings
Many Moons
Matchlock Gun

May I Bring a Friend?
McCloskey, Robert
McElligot's Pool
Mice Twice
Millions of Cats
Miracles on Maple Hill
Misty of Chincoteague
Moves Make the Man
Mr. Popper's Penguins
Mr. Rabbit and the Lovely Present
Mrs. Frisby and the Rats of NIMH
Mufaro's Beautiful Daughters
My Brother Sam Is Dead
My Mother Is the Most Beautiful Woman in the World
My Side of the Mountain
Noah's Ark
Noonday Friends
O'Dell, Scott
Old Ramon
Old Yeller
On Market Street
On My Honor
Once a Mouse
One-Eyed Cat
One Fine Day
One Morning in Maine
One Wide River to Cross
Onion John
Owl Moon
Ox-Cart Man
Paddle-to-the-Sea
Paterson, Katherine
Perilous Road
Philip Hall Likes Me, I Reckon Maybe
Planet of Junior Brown
Play with Me
Pocketful of Cricket
Polar Express
Puss in Boots (Marcia Brown, ill.)
Rain Drop Splash
Ramona and Her Father
Ramona Quimby, Age 8
"Randolph Caldecott"
"Reading the Best"
Relatives Came
Rifles for Watie
Ring of Endless Light
Roll of Thunder, Hear My Cry
Rumpelstiltskin
Rylant, Cynthia
Saint George and the Dragon

Sam, Bangs, and Moonshine
Sarah, Plain and Tall
Scorpions
Shadow
Shadow of a Bull
Shen of the Sea
Sign of the Beaver
Sing Down the Moon
Singer, Isaac Bashevis
Slave Dancer
Snowy Day
Song and Dance Man
Song of the Swallows
Sounder
Stone Soup
Story, A Story
Story of Jumping Mouse
Strawberry Girl
Strega Nona
Sugaring Time
Summer of the Swans
Sweet Whispers, Brother Rush
Swimmy
Sylvester and the Magic Pebble
Tales from Silver Lands
Talking Eggs
Ten, Nine, Eight
They Were Strong and Good
Thimble Summer
Thy Friend, Obadiah
Time of Wonder
Tombs of Atuan
Treasure
Tree Is Nice
Truck
Trumpeter of Krakow
Umbrella
Up a Road Slowly
Upon the Head of the Goat
Upstairs Room
Van Allsburg, Chris
Village of Round and Square Houses
Visit to William Blake's Inn
Volcano
Voyages of Doctor Dolittle
Wave
Westing Game
What Do You Say, Dear?
Wheel on the Chimney
Wheel on the School
When I Was Young in the Mountains

When Shlemiel Went to Warsaw
Where the Buffaloes Begin
Where the Wild Things Are
Whipping Boy
White, E. B.
White Snow, Bright Snow
Why Mosquitoes Buzz in People's Ears
Why the Sun and the Moon Live in the Sky
Wilder, Laura Ingalls
Willard, Nancy
Wish Giver
Witch of Blackbird Pond
Witches of Worm
Wrinkle in Time
Yates, Elizabeth
Yep, Laurence
Young Fu of the Upper Yangtze
Zlateh the Goat
Zolotow, Charlotte

KIT

Byars, Betsy
Castle
Cleary, Beverly
dePaola, Tomie
Duffy and the Devil
Marshall, James
McCloskey, Robert
O'Dell, Scott
One Fine Day
Sendak, Maurice
Speare, Elizabeth George
Spier, Peter
Sylvester and the Magic Pebble
Taylor, Mildred D.
Why Mosquitoes Buzz in People's Ears

LARGE PRINT

After the Rain
Bridge to Terabithia
By the Shores of Silver Lake
Caddie Woodlawn
Call It Courage
Charlotte's Web
Cricket in Times Square
Dark Is Rising
Dear Mr. Henshaw

Dicey's Song
Dragonwings
From the Mixed-Up Files of Mrs. Basil E. Frankweiler
Ginger Pye
Great Gilly Hopkins
Grey King
Hatchet
Hero and the Crown
Homesick
Island of the Blue Dolphins
Jacob Have I Loved
Jennifer, Hecate, Macbeth, William McKinley, and Me, Elizabeth
Johnny Tremain
Julie of the Wolves
M. C. Higgins the Great
Moves Make the Man
Mrs. Frisby and the Rats of NIMH
My Brother Sam is Dead
On My Honor
On the Banks of Plum Creek
One-Eyed Cat
Philip Hall Likes Me, I Reckon Maybe
Planet of Junior Brown
Ramona and Her Father
Ramona Quimby, Age 8
Roll of Thunder, Hear My Cry
Sarah, Plain and Tall
Sign of the Beaver
Sing Down the Moon
Slave Dancer
Sounder
Summer of the Swans
Tombs of Atuan
Westing Game
Whipping Boy
Witch of Blackbird Pond
Wrinkle in Time

POSTCARDS

"Caldecott Banner Postcards"

POSTER

Abel's Island
Abraham Lincoln
Across Five Aprils
Blue Willow

Bridge to Terabithia
Byars, Betsy
Caddie Woodlawn
Call It Courage
Chanticleer and the Fox
Charlotte's Web
Cinderella
Cleary, Beverly
Dear Mr. Henshaw
Dicey's Song
Egg Tree
Fables
Fritz, Jean
Frog and Toad Are Friends
Frog Went A-Courtin'
From the Mixed-Up Files of Mrs. Basil E. Frankweiler
Gathering of Days
Goble, Paul
Grey King
Henry, Marguerite
Hero and the Crown
High King
Hitty
In the Night Kitchen
Island of the Blue Dolphins
Jacob Have I Loved
Johnny Tremain
Julie of the Wolves
King Bidgood's in the Bathtub
Lobel, Arnold
Long Winter
M. C. Higgins the Great
Madeline
Madeline's Rescue
Make Way for Ducklings
Many Moons
May I Bring a Friend?
Mei Li
Miss Hickory
Mrs. Frisby and the Rats of NIMH
My Side of the Mountain
Ness, Evaline
Nine Days to Christmas
Old Yeller
One-Eyed Cat
Polar Express
Ramona and Her Father
Ramona Quimby, Age 8
Roll of Thunder, Hear My Cry
Saint George and the Dragon
Sarah, Plain and Tall

Shadow of a Bull
Sign of the Beaver
Slave Dancer
Snowy Day
Song of the Swallows
Sounder
Summer of the Swans
Visit to William Blake's Inn
Westing Game
Where the Wild Things Are
Whipping Boy
Witch of Blackbird Pond
Wrinkle in Time
Yolen, Jane

READ-ALONG

Abel's Island
Abraham Lincoln
Alexander and the Wind-Up Mouse
Alphabatics
Amazing Bone
Anansi the Spider
Andy and the Lion
Angry Moon
Annie and the Old One
Arrow to the Sun
Ashanti to Zulu
Bartholomew and the Oobleck
Bear Party
Big Snow
Biggest Bear
Blueberries for Sal
Bremen-Town Musicians
Chair for My Mother
Chanticleer and the Fox
Cinderella
Crow Boy
Doctor De Soto
Drummer Hoff
Duffy and the Devil
Fables
Fool of the World and the Flying Ship
Fox Went Out on a Chilly Night
Frederick
Frog and Toad Are Friends
Frog and Toad Together
Frog Went A-Courtin'
From the Mixed-Up Files of Mrs. Basil E. Frankweiler
Garden of Abdul Gasazi

Girl Who Loved Wild Horses
Glorious Flight
Goggles!
Hansel and Gretel
Happy Day
Hey, Al
Homesick
If I Ran the Zoo
In the Forest
In the Night Kitchen
It Could Always Be Worse
Jennifer, Hecate, Macbeth, William McKinley, and Me, Elizabeth
Journey Cake, Ho!
Jumanji
Just Me
King Bidgood's in the Bathtub
Like Jake and Me
Little Bear's Visit
Little House
Little Island
Madeline
Madeline's Rescue
Make Way for Ducklings
May I Bring a Friend?
McElligot's Pool
Mice Twice
Millions of Cats
Mr. Rabbit and the Lovely Present
Mufaro's Beautiful Daughters
Noah's Ark
On Market Street
One Fine Day
Owl Moon
Ox-Cart Man
Play with Me
Polar Express
Relatives Came
Rumpelstiltskin
Saint George and the Dragon
Sam, Bangs, and Moonshine
Shadow
Snowy Day
Song and Dance Man
Song of the Swallows
Stone Soup
Story, A Story
Story of Jumping Mouse
Strega Nona
Swimmy
Sylvester and the Magic Pebble

Talking Eggs
Ten, Nine, Eight
They Were Strong and Good
Time of Wonder
Tree Is Nice
Umbrella
Village of Round and Square Houses
Visit to William Blake's Inn
What Do You Say, Dear?
Wheel on the Chimney
When I Was Young in the Mountains
Where the Buffaloes Begin
Where the Wild Things Are
White Snow, Bright Snow
Why Mosquitoes Buzz in People's Ears

SOFTWARE

Caddie Woodlawn
Courage of Sarah Noble
If I Ran the Zoo
Island of the Blue Dolphins
Johnny Tremain
My Side of the Mountain
One Fine Day
Sarah, Plain and Tall
Where the Wild Things Are
Wrinkle in Time

TALKING BOOK

ABC Bunny
Abel's Island
Abraham Lincoln
Abraham Lincoln's World
Across Five Aprils
Adam of the Road
After the Rain
Afternoon of the Elves
Alexander and the Wind-Up Mouse
All in the Morning Early
Always Room for One More
Amazing Bone
America Is Born
America Moves Forward
Amos Fortune, Free Man
Anatole
Anatole and the Cat
And Now Miguel

Andy and the Lion
Animal Family
Annie and the Old One
Anpao
Arrow to the Sun
Baboushka and the Three Kings
Banner in the Sky
Bartholomew and the Oobleck
Bears on Hemlock Mountain
Big Snow
Biggest Bear
Bill Peet
Black Cauldron
Black Pearl
Blue Sword
Blueberries for Sal
Boats on the River
Book of Nursery and Mother Goose Rhymes
Boy with a Pack
Bridge to Terabithia
Bronze Bow
By the Shores of Silver Lake
Caddie Woodlawn
Calico Bush
Call It Courage
Carry On, Mr. Bowditch
Cat Who Went to Heaven
Cathedral
Chair for My Mother
Charlotte's Web
Cinderella
Commodore Perry in the Land of the Shogun
Courage of Sarah Noble
Cow-Tail Switch
Cricket in Times Square
Daniel Boone
Dark Frigate
Dark Is Rising
Day We Saw the Sun Come Up
Dear Mr. Henshaw
Dicey's Song
Dick Whittington and His Cat
Dobry
Doctor De Soto
Dogsong
Door in the Wall
Dragonwings
Egg Tree
Egypt Game
Emperor and the Kite
Enchantress from the Stars

Fables
Family under the Bridge
Fearsome Inn
Finders Keepers
Fly High, Fly Low
Fool of the World and the Flying Ship
Frederick
From the Mixed-Up Files of Mrs. Basil E. Frankweiler
Frontier Living
Funny Little Woman
Gammage Cup
Gathering of Days
George Washington's World
Gillespie and the Guards
Ginger Pye
Goggles!
Golden Fleece
Golden Goblet
Gone-Away Lake
Good Master
Graven Images
Great Gilly Hopkins
Grey King
Hansel and Gretel
Headless Cupid
"Hello the Boat!"
Hero and the Crown
Hershel and the Hanukkah Goblins
Hidden Treasure of Glaston
High King
Hitty
Homesick
Horsecatcher
House of Sixty Fathers
Hundred Penny Box
I, Juan de Pareja
If I Ran the Zoo
In My Mother's House
In the Night Kitchen
Invincible Louisa
Island of the Blue Dolphins
It Could Always Be Worse
It's Like This, Cat
Jacob Have I Loved
Jazz Man
Jennifer, Hecate, Macbeth, William McKinley, and Me, Elizabeth
Johnny Tremain
Joyful Noise
Julie of the Wolves
Jumanji

Justin Morgan Had a Horse
Kildee House
King Bidgood's in the Bathtub
King of the Wind
King's Fifth
Knee Knock Rise
Li Lun
Like Jake and Me
Lincoln
Little Bear's Visit
Little House
Little Town on the Prairie
Loner
Long Winter
M. C. Higgins the Great
Madeline
Madeline's Rescue
Make Way for Ducklings
Matchlock Gun
McElligot's Pool
Mei Li
Men of Athens
Middle Moffat
Miracles on Maple Hill
Miss Hickory
Misty of Chincoteague
Moves Make the Man
Mr. Justice Holmes
Mr. Popper's Penguins
Mrs. Frisby and the Rats of NIMH
Mufaro's Beautiful Daughters
My Brother Sam Is Dead
My Father's Dragon
My Mother Is the Most Beautiful Woman in the World
My Side of the Mountain
Nansen
Nine Days to Christmas
Noonday Friends
Nothing at All
Old Yeller
On My Honor
On the Banks of Plum Creek
Once a Mouse
One-Eyed Cat
One Fine Day
One Morning in Maine
Onion John
Ox-Cart Man
Paddle-to-the-Sea
Pecos Bill
Pedro

Perilous Gard
Philip Hall Likes Me, I Reckon Maybe
Polar Express
Pop Corn and Ma Goodness
Prayer for a Child
Rabbit Hill
Ramona and Her Father
Ramona Quimby, Age 8
Rascal
Rawlings, Marjorie Kinnan
Rifles for Watie
Ring of Endless Light
Road from Home
Roll of Thunder, Hear My Cry
Roller Skates
Rooster Crows
Rufus M.
Rumpelstiltskin
Saint George and the Dragon
Sarah, Plain and Tall
Seabird
Scorpions
Secret of the Andes
Secret River
Seven Simeons
Shadow of a Bull
Shadrach
Shen of the Sea
Sign of the Beaver
Sing Down the Moon
Slave Dancer
Smoky, the Cowhorse
Snow White and the Seven Dwarfs (Wanda Gág, ill.)
Snowy Day
Solitary Blue
Song of the Swallows
Sounder
Story, A Story
Story of Jumping Mouse
Story of Mankind
Strawberry Girl
Strega Nona
String in the Harp
Summer of the Swans
Sweet Whispers, Brother Rush
Swimmy
Sylvester and the Magic Pebble
Tales from Silver Lands
Thanksgiving Story
These Happy Golden Years
Thimble Summer

Thy Friend, Obadiah
Time of Wonder
Timothy Turtle
To Be a Slave
Tom Paine
Tombs of Atuan
Trumpeter of Krakow
Twenty-One Balloons
Umbrella
Up a Road Slowly
Upstairs Room
Village of Round and Square Houses
Visit to William Blake's Inn
Voyages of Doctor Dolittle
Waterless Mountain
Wave
Way to Start a Day
Westing Game
What Do You Say, Dear?
Wheel on the Chimney
Wheel on the School
When I Was Young in the Mountains
When Shlemiel Went to Warsaw
Where the Buffaloes Begin
Where the Wild Things Are
White Snow, Bright Snow
Why Mosquitoes Buzz in People's Ears
Whipping Boy
White Stag
Wilder, Laura Ingalls
Wish Giver
Witch of Blackbird Pond
Witches of Worm
Wrinkle in Time
Young Fu of the Upper Yangtze
Zlateh the Goat

TALKING BOOK/PRINT

Duffy and the Devil
Frog and Toad Are Friends
Frog and Toad Together
Hildilid's Night
Inch by Inch
Journey Cake, Ho!
Many Moons
Mother Goose
One Fine Day

TELEVISION

By the Shores of Silver Lake
Incident at Hawk's Hill
Little Town on the Prairie
Long Winter
On the Banks of Plum Creek
Sarah, Plain and Tall
These Happy Golden Years

VIDEO

Abel's Island
Abraham Lincoln
Across Five Aprils
After the Rain
Alexander and the Wind-Up Mouse
Alexander, Lloyd
All in the Morning Early
Along Came a Dog
Alphabatics
Amazing Bone
Amos Fortune, Free Man
Anansi the Spider
And Now Miguel
Andy and the Lion
Angry Moon
Annie and the Old One
Arrow to the Sun
Banner in the Sky
Bartholomew and the Oobleck
Bears on Hemlock Mountain
Belling the Tiger
Ben's Trumpet
Black Cauldron
Black Pearl
Blue Willow
Blueberries for Sal
Bontemps, Arna
"Book Week"
Bremen-Town Musicians
Bridge to Terabithia
Caddie Woodlawn
"Caldecott at Fifty"
Call It Courage
Castle
Cathedral
Chair for My Mother
Charlotte's Web
"Choosing the Best in Children's Video"

Cooney, Barbara
Courage of Sarah Noble
Cow-Tail Switch
Cricket in Times Square
Crow Boy
Dark is Rising
Daugherty, James
d'Aulaire, Edgar Parin and Ingri
De Angeli, Marguerite
Dear Mr. Henshaw
Dicey's Song
Doctor De Soto
Dogsong
Door in the Wall
Drummer Hoff
Duffy and the Devil
Egypt Game
Estes, Eleanor
Fables
Feelings, Muriel and Tom
Fine White Dust
Fledgling
Fleischman, Sid
Fox Went Out on a Chilly Night
Frederick
Free Fall
Freedman, Russell
Freeman, Don
Fritz, Jean
Frog and Toad Are Friends
Frog and Toad Together
Frog Went A-Courtin'
From the Mixed-Up Files of Mrs. Basil E. Frankweiler
Gág, Wanda
Garden of Abdul Gasazi
George, Jean Craighead
Ginger Pye
Girl Who Loved Wild Horses
Glorious Flight
Goggles!
Goldilocks and the Three Bears
Gray, Elizabeth Janet
Green Eyes
Grey Lady and the Strawberry Snatcher
Great Gilly Hopkins
Hall, Donald
Hansel and Gretel
Hatchet
Hawk, I'm Your Brother
Headless Cupid
Henry, Marguerite

Holling, Holling C.
House of Sixty Fathers
Hundred Dresses
Hundred Penny Box
Hunt, Irene
If I Ran the Zoo
In the Night Kitchen
Incident at Hawk's Hill
Island of the Blue Dolphins
It Could Always Be Worse
It's Like This, Cat
Jacob Have I Loved
James, Will
Jennifer, Hecate, Macbeth, William McKinley, and Me, Elizabeth
Johnny Tremain
Journey Cake, Ho!
Joyful Noise
Judge
Jukes, Mavis
Julie of the Wolves
Jumanji
Justin Morgan Had a Horse
Keats, Ezra Jack
King Bidgood's in the Bathtub
King of the Wind
Krumgold, Joseph
L'Engle, Madeleine
Like Jake and Me
Lincoln
Little House
Lobel, Arnold
Loner
Long Winter
Lowry, Lois
M. C. Higgins the Great
Macaulay, David
Madeline
Madeline's Rescue
Make Way for Ducklings
Marshall, James
Matchlock Gun
May I Bring a Friend?
McCloskey, Robert
McElligot's Pool
Mice Twice
Mighty Hunter
Millions of Cats
Misty of Chincoteague
Mr. Popper's Penguins
Mr. Rabbit and the Lovely Present

INDEX TO WINNING AUTHORS, ILLUSTRATORS, AND BOOKS BY SHORT TITLE

Paulette Bochnig Sharkey is a professional librarian and author in Madison, Wisconsin. She has written and compiled numerous works, including the *Neal-Schuman Index to Sports Figures in Collective Biographies.*

Jim Roginski, co-compiler and editor, is a New York City author and literary agent. He was formerly the Children's Literature Specialist for the Dallas Public Library.

Book Design: Sheldon Winicour

Cover Design: Apicella Design

Typography: C. Roberts Typesetting